THE TRUTH WAS SWEPT
UNDER THE DRUG . . .

We had both been sure that a long rest from work would relieve Barbara's attacks, but her anxiety followed us all the way to Europe. In London she panicked at the West End theater crowds. In Paris she became terrified of heights. Ghosts followed us everywhere. She regaled me with detailed stories of her miseries. And it got worse. Any time she had to leave the safety of a hotel room, Barbara swallowed so much Valium and booze I thought she would turn into Rubber Woman . . .

PRINCE VALIUM

ANTON HOLDEN

STEIN AND DAY/*Publishers*/New York

FIRST STEIN AND DAY PAPERBACK EDITION 1984
Prince Valium was first published in hardcover
by Stein and Day/*Publishers* in 1982.

Copyright © 1982 by Anton Holden
All rights reserved, Stein and Day, Incorporated
Designed by Judith E. Dalzell
Printed in the United States of America
STEIN AND DAY/*Publishers*
Scarborough House
Briarcliff Manor, N.Y. 10510
ISBN 0-8128-8074-9

For Ruth

This story is true. Only some
locations and the names and details
of other people's lives have been
changed to protect their identity.

PRINCE VALIUM

PART I

ONE

I met Barbara in front of a Moviola. It was in New York's public TV station, WNET, where I was one of six editors who cut short documentaries for a local nightly news show. It was a far cry from the hot new movie director I had been some years earlier, but I had been out of work for nearly a year and had already hocked my Nikon so my family could eat. I was so desperate I took the job originally as an assistant editor. It was better than driving a cab. After a few weeks they saw what I could do and made me a full editor. They gave me a cutting room and my own Moviola, a new console model made for 16 mm. At that point in my career I was putting all my creative energy into writing screenplays I hoped to direct. Editing bought me the time to write. But I liked editing. I was good at it. I've been a movie gypsy for a lot of years and I always felt at home sitting at a Moviola.

Oh. What is a Moviola? It's a name that is so familiar to me, I forget that most people have never seen one. "Moviola" is the trademark of a number of different American film editing machines. Moviolas don't edit, of course, I do that. They're basically only projectors that can run forward and backward, slowly and fast, and stop instantly to mark a single frame for cutting. Moviolas are green. The original stand-up models are painted a light institution green. The newer 16 mm "flat-beds" we used are painted a light institution avocado. These are sleek, modern consoles with lit-up switches and electronic counters. The rolls of film and sound track lie flat on a table in front of you and the picture screen is mounted above them at eye level. They make little noise above the slight hum of the motor and the whisper of a cooling fan. Barbara and I spent the richest hours of our lives working together in front of a Moviola.

There was a kind of class warfare at the station between the producers and the editors. It heated up occasionally, like the time Sy, a burly bearded editor, punched out his producer over a delicate decision, but it was usually kept just under the surface. The producers silently suffered the butchery of us proletarian mechanics, while, on our side, the editors openly despised the producers as a bunch of college journalism students who hadn't the faintest notion of the medium they worked with. Editing assignments were given out with little thought as to who would work with whom, so I was intrigued when Jeff, the assignment editor, took me aside to ask, "Would it bother you to, ahh, work with a woman producer?"

"Not at all," I said. "Why?"

"I was looking for an editor for Barbara Gordon's next piece. Some of the guys have problems taking orders from a woman, you know."

I waved his fears away. "Oh, don't worry about that. Strong women don't threaten me. I was raised by some pretty formidable ladies. I'd enjoy it."

He looked relieved.

"Oh thanks. The dailies should be out. You can start right away."

As I picked up the dailies, I heard some more ominous mumblings behind me when the lab crew saw I would be cutting for "*Mzzzzz* Gordon!" She had obviously touched a nerve in some of these he-man technicians, but that made me more intrigued with the thought of meeting and working with her. By this time the new spokespeople of the liberated woman had begun to appear on late-night TV talk shows and I used to fantasize meeting them and having love affairs. I didn't do it out loud, because my wife usually sat next to me. Yes, I was married, but I was primed and ready for Ms. Marvelous.

She was late. I polished my glasses and lit up another pipe. I practically chain-smoked a pipe then. I carried three of them with me in my briefcase so each would have a chance to cool off between smokings. I arranged the rolls in order on the editing table and waited.

Barbara finally appeared, and with her a lot of unfinished business. I watched, fascinated, as her calls went out and calls came in about prior shows, shows in the future, and shows that were only thoughts in Barbara's head. She took care of her business with a furious determination and she seemed to have it all under control. She was in her late thirties, near my age give or take a year. She was tall and slender, but soft in her hips and breasts. She looked a lot like Glenda Jackson, with the same circumflex brows and sharp eyes. Her chin was small and pointed under a full mouth that spoke whatever her eyes saw. Her brown hair hung behind her shoulders from under a bright yellow-orange scarf tied in a babushka. She wore silky black pants and a tight red top thing with long sleeves and a row of buttons that touched each other from her throat to her waist. There must have been at least twenty buttons in the lineup. The top ten were open, showing the beginning curve of her breasts which were clearly outlined under the stretch-knit fabric.

Barbara's assistant, Jill, came in and hiked herself up on the editing table to take notes. Jill was an attractive redhead in her early twenties, an escapee from the Irish penal colony in the West Bronx. She was funny. Nicole, the still photographer for the show, squeezed behind me into the corner. Nicole's long dark hair fell in a mass of curls and she blushed whenever she smiled. She and Jill were both young and attractive, but they didn't interest me in the way that Barbara did. It was the combination of Barbara's looks and the power she brought to her work that got to me. She finished her calls and rolled her chair beside me in front of the Moviola. I introduced myself and we shook hands.

"I'm Barbara Gordon. Are you any better than the cretins they call editors in this asylum?"

She came on even stronger than I imagined. No wonder the local machos were terrified of her.

"I haven't had any complaints yet," I said.

"Good."

"But then, I haven't been here very long."

She ignored that and we went through the transcript she had marked as an outline of her show. I noticed she had the strong good hands of a woman who works. As she spoke, she tucked one leg under the other, which made her silky black pants stretch tightly up against the cleft between her legs. Her patent leather boot stuck out from under her trim behind. I guessed she was about five-ten in bare feet, but she wore boots with 2-inch heels. I loved it! There was no compromise in this woman. She was everything that attracted me.

With four people filling up the tiny room, my assistant Marvin stood in the doorway, pleased that he didn't have to pretend to be busy. Marvin was a beefy alcoholic. I couldn't stand him. I didn't need him for this kind of cutting, but once the union won you the right to have an assistant, you had one. Fortunately, Marvin was easy to get rid of. There was a bar right downstairs. He whispered in my ear, "Listen, it's so crowded in here, maybe it'd be better for you if I stay outside while you screen."

"Good idea, Marv. There's nothing for you to do today, anyway."

"But I'll be downstairs if you need me."

"Sure, Marv."

Barbara finished her outline and it was time to screen the footage. I switched on the Moviola. Its little buttons lit up and its cooling fans breathed just audibly. I got up to switch off the overhead light and turned the table lamp to the wall for a little light to take notes. I like my cutting room dark. The racks of reels, the trim barrels, the editing table and chairs all disappear into the shadows. In this dim glow nothing is real but the moving picture on the screen.

Editing is slow work at first. There were about two hours of footage to screen about the care, or rather the lack of care, for old people in the city. Barbara and her crew had shot a lot of footage in a city-run club for old men and women. It was only a basement apartment, but it was a place for them to go to. They could get out of their tiny rooms, play cards and bingo and board games, and get a hot meal. For many of them it was the one good meal of their day. Barbara took the camera into the living room after lunch. The old men and women danced together, some just able to move. A fat old woman played the piano and sang.

"She used to be in vaudeville," Barbara said. "Her name is Mamie. I promised her she'd be on. We have to use her. If you don't mind, that is."

"Are you kidding? You think I'd let this go by? What a fantastic place for them to have."

"Yes, but they're closing. Funding's gone."

"It can't cost much to keep that place going," I said.

She barely controlled her anger as she replied, "Nixon withheld the entire OEO allocation. Johnson's poverty program. Headstart and that—"

"But a president can't withhold money on his own. How could he do that?"

"A lot of people would like to know. That's why we're doing the piece. These old people's clubs are the first to go. The city has no money for them."

"Where will the people go?"

"No one seems to know," she replied sadly. "No one seems to care."

"It's grotesque the way they treat old people in this country," I said.

Before Barbara could respond, a woman on the Moviola screen spoke. "It makes you think the young are trying to kill off the old people purposely."

Our conversation had blended into the next interview. The on-screen Barbara was interviewing a woman doctor who was saying the same things we were and much more.

"Wait! Wait!" Barbara yelled.

She hit the "Stop" button, halting the film instantly.

"Stop! Back it up!" she said. "This one is important. I definitely want to use this." She looked suddenly guilty.

"Oh, I'm sorry," she said. "I'm not supposed to touch the Moviola, am I? Union rules or something."

"Go right ahead. You won't hurt anything."

"Other editors can't stand that."

"I don't give a shit."

"No, you do it," she said. "You work it faster, anyway. I'm sorry."

I shrugged and reversed the film, then jogged it forward until the doctor said again, "Makes you think the young—"

"That's it!" Barbara shouted. "'Makes you think . . .' Mark that for a cut."

"Okay. I have an idea where it will go, too."

"No, you don't. Here's roll five. Put it up now. You'll see what I mean. It's all MOS."

"MOS" means a scene shot without a sound track. When sound movies first came in, teutonic directors were very fashionable in Hollywood. When Herr Direktor was about to shoot a silent scene, he would shout, "Und now ve shoodt dis scene mitout zoundt!" And that's how it's been ever since in American movies. Silent scenes are marked MOS, short for Mit Out Sound.

Roll five was all MOS shots of old people alone. There were old people in the closet-sized rooms of a single occupancy hotel. Old people on the street. Old people sitting. Walking. Staring. Shopping. Carefully spending the few pennies they had, and portioning them out with an exactness that had no margin for error. There was more than sympathy in the way Barbara had shot the footage. An edge of fear showed when she spoke about the people on the screen, a fear that must haunt a woman alone, making it by herself. Will that be me when I am old? Abandoned? Alone? Living in a smudgy old hotel? Will that be me?

"Fast forward through this chazerei," she said. "You'll look at it later. We don't have to screen it together. You'll know what to do with it."

I turned the speed control to its fastest setting and the old people jumped comically in blurred high speed. The roll ran out and the suddenly white screen blinded us until I switched off the Moviola. Jill and Nicole spoke together.

"It's great, Barb!"

"I loved the part where—"

Barbara ignored them and looked at me for a long moment, searching for my reaction.

"You think there's a good piece there, Anton?"

"Absolutely," I said. "I can't tell you exactly what it's going to look like yet, but we'll find the synapses, the structure will happen. It's all in there."

"Anything you need, more MOS, anything you can think of, just let me know. I like my editors to have more than they need."

"I never heard that around here before. You won't need any more, I don't think. It's all there. It's going to be good."

She thought for a moment and then said, "I think you know what you're doing."

"I do. Don't worry. We're making the same movie."

"Hunh!" was all she replied. Everyone stood up and stretched in the shadowed room. Barbara and I were close. I was taller than she. She looked up at me and our eyes connected somewhere deeply for a fleeting moment before she abruptly turned away and strode out of the editing room. Jill and Nicole hurried after her, trying to keep up.

I had enough work to do alone for the rest of that day and the next. Except I wasn't entirely alone. Barbara was in the film I screened over and over. She was a great interviewer. She controlled her subjects brilliantly without leading questions or cheap shots. You get to know every nuance of a person's behavior by watching them on unedited film this way. I liked the Barbara I saw. And that look she had when our eyes met told me she liked me, too. I thought I might have a pretty good chance with her if she was available.

We were alone when we screened my rough assembly. Barbara

gradually relaxed as she began to sense what her movie would look like. I had put in a few surprises for her, cuts I knew she would react to, sequences juxtaposed in unexpected places. And she liked most of them. She said immediately what she didn't like and why and I usually agreed. There was no argument, just two people working together toward the same goal. The last scene of the rough assembly ran out and the gate flared with bright white light. I slowed the flapping rolls of film with my hand and waited for her reaction.

"How is it that none of the cretins I've worked with before can cut so fast?" she said.

"I take it that means you like what you saw?"

"Oh, it's going to take a lot of work, lots more work. You left out one shot I wanted. Do you remember? It was right after the woman's son who came to the hospital . . . Oh, what was it?"

"How about lunch?" I said.

"Lunch?"

"Yeah, it's two o'clock. We have a natural break here. I'd like to take you to lunch."

"What do you mean, 'lunch'?"

"Just lunch."

"You're married, aren't you?" she asked.

"Yes. What does that have to do with anything?"

"There's no such thing as 'just lunch' with you. It'll be a seduction scene."

She had anticipated my thoughts and caught me completely by surprise. It was reassuring to know I wasn't alone in my fantasy, though. I had to think a moment.

"The thought had crossed my mind," I said. "But really, just lunch. If anything else comes up, terrific."

"No more married men for me. I've had that. More than once."

"I don't remember asking."

"You didn't have to."

"We're going to be in this room together for a while," I said. "There isn't much difference. Anything that could happen at lunch could happen here, right?"

We eyed each other squarely, both of us very much amused with the other. But it was up to her to respond.

"I'm picking up the check," she said. "Does that bother you?"

"No. Why should it?"

"It does a lot of men. But I'm the producer. *I* pick up the check for a business lunch."

"It doesn't bother me, boss lady."

"Wo-man!"

"It doesn't bother me at all, boss woman."

On the west side of Manhattan in the Fifties you can still find cheap restaurants with a different flavor. We chose Greek. I was new at the station and a stranger in the restaurant, but they knew Barbara. She fell in step with the bouzouki music blasting from the Wurlitzer and danced with the owner across the room. She said she had once danced on the docks of Piraeus with the men. And even though she was laughing at herself she had their same sad look, with her head thrown back, her half-closed eyes searching far away for something that would never come. What did come was mousaka, spinach pie, feta cheese salad, and wine.

We never knew the name of the restaurant. There was a Greek letter on the sign that looked like the number 4, followed with roman letters spelling "delphia." No one spoke much English. They used that lingua franca for answering all WASPs: smile wide, say "Yes!", head for the back room, and forget it. Our crowd from the public TV news shows were radical blacks, Indians, hippies with Jewish naturals, and Puerto Rican nacionalistas, but to a Greek illegal alien waiter we were all WASPs. The waiters all grinned and said "Yes!" louder each time we asked the name of the place, so we ended up calling it the "Four-a-delphia," which is where Barbara and I had our first lunch.

She hated being on camera, so I hadn't recognized her when we first met. By now I had connected her name with many shows she had produced for the public TV network. She had been an investigative reporter long before it became a television chiché. She described herself as having been a "First Amendment Freak" for as long as she could remember. She had taken on the FBI, the CIA, the AMA, the senate—the more sacred the cow, the better. She seemed out of place in this rinky-dink local news show. But she was coming up from a low point in her life that was a lot worse than mine.

At the time we met Barbara was literally hatching out of a shell: a steel shell. She told me that she had a disc operation at eighteen and her back was never the same again. She had spent a good part of her life with her back in spasm, trapped in a steel brace that enclosed her body from her chest to her hips. For long periods of time, she could only wear dresses that hung loosely around the brace. It had haunted her for seventeen years, getting worse and worse. The last years she'd be in conference rooms and editing rooms stretched out on the floor to get some relief. Eventually not even that helped. She could no longer work. All her doctors diagnosed hysterical paralysis and refused to do a myelogram to see if there was anything physically wrong. Through some friends she finally got to see Fritz, the international fusion man in Mexico City. He agreed to do a myelogram.

"You get the captain of all headaches from that," she said.

The myelogram revealed that her first schmuck doctor had left in half a disc, and Barbara had been walking around with it in her spine for seventeen years. Fritz didn't know how she had survived this long. He operated immediately, fusing L-4, L-5, and S-1.

The fusion held. Barbara's back was still weak, but getting stronger every day. She had a little spasm now and then, to remind her she was mortal, but she could play tennis or make love any time. It was solid as a rock. It was the basis for her ultimate oath: "I swear by my fusion." She had just bought a whole new wardrobe to fit her new body: hip huggers, tight tops, even a bikini. Her friend Samantha had to convince her that her body was good. Barbara used to avoid looking at her body. The summer just past was the first summer she spent without the brace. This job was the first she was offered. She didn't care where it was as long as she was back at work again. She was starting a new life where everything was possible, a life with no pain. Barbara had been reborn a few months before we met and she was just starting to fly.

"How long have you been married?" she asked.

"About twenty years. Not to the same woman of course, but about that long."

"What? How many wives have you had?"

"Three. I—"

"I don't believe it," she said. "You don't look old enough."

"Oh, I am. I started when I was eighteen. I have three kids, two girls and a boy, but I haven't seen them in years. My first two wives took off for parts unknown when we split."

"Why did you get married so many times?"

"I like being married. I must. But I'm a working-class artist and that's not the most secure way to raise a family. But I always tried. I gave my wives the shirt off my back and then one day they looked up and realized that they were married to a guy with no shirt on his back which made them feel very insecure and they took off. So I was left with no wife and no kids and no shirt. And that's the story of my life."

She laughed. "I was married once, and once was enough for me. I was twenty-three. My mother and father wanted me to. I never could stand him. We broke up after a year. Steve Gordon. His last name was all I got out of that marriage. I've lived alone for twelve years and that's the way I like it. I have no intention of changing." She lost herself in thought for a long moment and then she said, "I never met anyone . . . a man, I mean, who I could talk with and laugh with like we do."

"That's good," I said. "That makes me happy."

"I meant what I said about no more married men."

"You might like me, you know."

"No 'might,'" she said. "I know I would. Too much. That's why I won't do it. You would be no small thing."

"It might not hurt. You'd be surprised."

"Un-unh! No more of that hidden-furtive-touched-with-angst love making and 'I'll see you again on Monday'! Those weekends alone? The showers at night to get rid of my smell before you go back to her bed? And I know you say you haven't slept with her for years, but where did Kim and Buzzer and Abe Jr. come from? No thanks! I have too much experience with that. I just left one, in fact. I haven't been with a man for six months. And not because I don't want to. I haven't found a man good enough."

"Well, I'm not about to get unmarried. I love my wife, really. We have a great marriage. I'm not looking for affairs. I don't believe in that."

"What do you call this?" she said.

"Oh, if something happens by chance, that's different. But you don't go looking for it. Looking for it means you're in trouble. It means you really don't want to be with your wife."

"You know," she said, "I've never understood why a man and a woman can't be just good friends. I enjoy being with you just to talk."

"Well, someday maybe I'll be flying west to L.A. and you'll be flying east to New York and both our planes will be forced down at O'Hare. And we'll meet by chance in the waiting room, and then we'll have dinner together, and then . . . "

"Why O'Hare?"

"Do you know it?"

"Of course," she said. "Been there a hundred times. It's a frightening place. Like being nowhere."

"Exactly! An utter limbo place. Now, if you and I met in a situation like that would you hesitate to go to bed with me?"

"We-ell, maybe not, but we're in New York now. It's different."

Did you ever hear such bullshit in your life? Here were two supposedly intelligent adults, kidding themselves at an incredible rate and coming on with each other like there's no tomorrow. We had more of these lunches and late dinners the rest of that week. We worked until the early hours of the morning and then I walked her home. She lived on Central Park South, near Sixth Avenue. It was only three blocks from the editing room. I lived on West Seventy-first Street, not far away. It wasn't necessary to repeat the conversation we had at the "Four-a-delphia." If she was interested, she would. If she wasn't, she wouldn't. I had told her how I felt, and I enjoyed being with her and working with her anyway.

The cutting went well. Barbara would get brilliant ideas and I would structure them, make them work. Sometimes the positions reversed. I'd get some far-out concept, and she'd show me a cut that had been staring me in the face for days. Altogether a rich collaboration—what it's supposed to be between producer and editor. It led to talk about writing together. She had a screenplay she'd been working on for a year and couldn't pull together. She said Jane Fonda liked the idea and might want to do it. She asked me if I would be interested in working on it with her. I told her I was very interested and I was ready to start writing whenever she was. Such a stimulus was just what I needed at this low point in my career. Except I knew it would not go over very big with my wife. She didn't suffer lightly the presence of another woman in my life. Platonically working on a script with Barbara—would my wife ever believe that? Would *I* ever believe it? Yeah. Would. Did. And I would believe a lot more improbable things than that before this saga was over.

TWO

You may have noticed a certain matter-of-factness concerning infidelity. I wasn't always like that. For most of my life, infidelity would have been unthinkable. I was morbidly shy, emaciated, covered with acne, and I could hardly see. When I was a baby my eyesight was so bad that my mother thought I was nearly blind. She accepted this as fact as a punishment for her sins and she never had me examined for glasses. I could only see hazy images, colors, and light and dark shadows. I lived an isolated kind of life, turned completely inward. I never played with boys, played no sports, nothing. I couldn't touch people casually, not men or women. I was so afraid of contact with other people that even into my teens I was terrified to answer the telephone and I never did if I was alone. I would just let it ring until it stopped.

My only contact was with my relatives, who were mostly women. My family runs to women. A story by herself, my grandmother ruled a matriarchal clan. Except for one tame son, she bred five girls and they bred girls, too, mostly. Their men seemed to come in only two types: They were either weak and good for nothing or, like my father, they seduced helpless women and then abandoned them and their children. Both types frightened the women when they drank too much and never made enough money. Listening to the never-ending conversations in a houseful of women, I naturally grew up with the assumption that the male sex was responsible for all the trouble in women's lives. And yet there was an undeniable attraction there, since the women in my family bred like rabbits. They all seemed to tolerate the presence of men only long enough to breed and get their offspring toddling, after which they had no use for them. I didn't understand this puzzling ambivalence for a long time, but I always felt I had to prove that I wasn't one of those males they seemed to dislike so much. And with no male image in my life that might balance the picture,

15

this unconscious attitude dominated my behavior towards women for most of my life.

I never knew my father. He and my mother only lived together for a few months after I was born. They had never bothered to marry. My mother was a bohemian Greenwich Village poet. One of my earliest memories is standing with her while she tacked sheets of her poetry on the green wooden fence on Waverly Place. Then my father went to Canada to cut trees or something and disappeared, or so my mother always said. I never knew exactly. When you're young you don't ask your mother questions that send her into hysterics. She always wrote "dead" in the blank space after "Father" on my official forms. That's what I wrote at school; there was no reason to doubt her. When I got older she said he had abandoned her, and that sounded reasonable too. But when I got a lot older I realized that an illegal German alien who had jumped ship and carried a murdered man's passport might have some difficulty finding work during the Depression. Also, being partly Jewish, he might have wanted to avoid deportation back to sunny Germany. It didn't matter to me way back then, though. Since there was no man in her life, I got nursed for nearly two years and was rather close to Mummy, sleeping with her and taking Daddy's place somewhat, I suppose, until she met another man.

It was in the forties. World War II was happening then. He was a writer who was also a sailor. She did seem to like traveling men. When he saw how close we were, he told Mummy she shouldn't mother me so much or I'd grow up queer. I was rudely cast from the maternal bed. Mummy never did anything halfway. When she cast me out, it was *out*! Overnight, I went from being kissed and held to never so much as touched by her again for the rest of my life. But kids have their ways of getting back. Also overnight, I got the most horrible asthma you ever heard. They had to rush me to a hospital where I was put in an oxygen tent. They didn't spend much time in bed those nights!

Then, what do you know? My father came back to New York and tried to see me. My mother called the FBI, who were then rounding up German aliens and locking them in prison camps for the duration. She fingered Dad to the Feds. By this time Dad had had some experience with women and the law, and he was a survivor if nothing else. He managed to evade the FBI and a post card eventually came from Mexico saying, "I bet you thought I'd never make it." I had no idea this was going on at the time, of course. I heard it all much later. My mother told the story at family gatherings and her sisters filled in the details.

Because of my appalling eyesight, my first years in school were spent in what they called the Sight Conservation Class which was filled with retarded kids, cerebral palsied, the crazies, and all the castoffs of the old school system. No one thought to examine me until some nurse did in the third grade. My mother took me to the Manhattan Eye and Ear Clinic and, lo and behold, with the right glasses I could suddenly see. I moved into normal classes in school and rapidly advanced, but the pattern of introversion had been fixed for so long that the glasses didn't change it.

I got my first big input of love and affection when I was thirteen. It came with such an intoxicating rush that it shaped the rest of my life. I entered a joke-telling contest at my junior high school. It was held in a huge auditorium with the whole school present. I had never been in front of an audience before. Do you know how that feels to a morbidly shy kid? First, there's only fear. The sweat soaks your shirt when your turn approaches. When you stand up your knees buckle. Your legs don't want to carry you up the three steps to the stage, but you make them do it. You stand on the stage sweating and shaking. You can hear the audience breathe. Somehow you start talking. Your voice creaks. It's a long shaggy dog story. They listen. They give you more confidence. You embellish here and fall into a country accent there to build it higher. They're letting you. They want you to. You can feel it. And you can feel when you're stretching them to the limit. It's like a wire tightening as far as it will go. You guess the moment, and snap the punch line at them. There's a split second of silence and then a roar starts and builds and soon the whole auditorium rocks with laughter. They loved it. They loved me. I won the contest. That was the rest of my life right there. That's show biz, kid. It really does get in your blood. I auditioned for the High School of Performing Arts and they accepted me.

By now, my mother had settled down somewhat with an English poet who was busy writing Welsh plays while they lived on City Island, just off the rugged coast of the Bronx. Impractical? Maybe. Except his father had a lot of money and they got regular income supplements of houses, cars, and money from a doting Grandpa and Grandma who had been (need you ask?) separated for years in that neat English manner. My poet stepfather didn't give me love, but he

17

gave me books: *The Golden Bough*, D.H. Lawrence, Lincoln Steffens, and more like them. I read them all before I was fifteen. He took us to see Maria Tallchief dance "Firebird" once. I never forgot that.

I spent three high school years getting steeped in the "theatah," but something kept rearing its ugly head—something between my legs. And before you could say "Jack Trojan," presto! There was a baby growing inside my teenage girl friend. This was the first woman I had ever slept with and I was in love. After a few conversations with my pregnant angel, I realized that I had a hidden desire to have a wife and family. Amazing. I never knew that before. My girl friend wasn't influencing me, either. I had just discovered love and it was overwhelming. Whatever would make my teenage Venus happy was what I naturally wanted.

I had planned to go to UCLA to study motion pictures after high school. That had been my dream; it would just have to be put off for a while. I had no idea how long "a while" it would be. My mother got ominously silent as she always did when she felt she was being punished for past sins. Her sisters were more sympathetic. All four of them had been through this when they were sixteen and they wanted to spare me. They knew the illegal abortion circuit, they practically had season tickets. They offered to chip in the money for an abortion, but I wouldn't hear of it. What I thought I wanted most of all in life was a wife and children. I was sure I could develop my creative life at the same time.

We got married and at eighteen I was suddenly in the world, with a wife, a baby girl, rent to pay, food to buy, hospital bills, electric bills, phone bills, and. . . . It never occurred to us to go on welfare. We could have used it. My mother and stepfather told me that it was necessary for me to be independent and build my character, therefore any help in my new life was out of the question. They weren't cruel people. They had my best interests at heart. So when any emergency came up, no matter how grave, they refused any help. I was completely on my own without the faintest notion of how to go about making a living and still so shy that I would sometimes walk around the block for half a day trying to get up the courage to go into a strange office for a job interview.

One of my first jobs was in an old film processing laboratory. I worked the graveyard shift for the few extra bucks. As I was leaving at eight A.M., the old Irishman who ran the freight elevator took me aside. There were tears in his drunken eyes as he revealed to me the secret of all life.

"But are ya learning a thrade, lad?" he said. "You can dream a' this an' that, but a man's got to have a thrade. You don't want to end up like me."

I had no intention of ending up like him. For a WASP in the U.S. of WASPerica, it's not too difficult to make a living if you work hard. But the old man was right. At eighteen, without a trade, with no help, it was a little difficult to get ahead of the game for quite a number of years. Each time I'd get economically pulled together, there would be something else. A year after our love child was born, we decided it would be a nice idea for our little girl to have someone to play with as she grew up. My wife didn't want her child to be as lonely as she had been. I brought home dozens of roses the next night. She lay in the buds and petals. They were all over her, in every fold and opening. That little sperm must have been hanging ten on a rose petal when he surfed upstream to become a baby girl.

But there was always that shaggy dog story. I couldn't stop chasing that muse's wagging tail. That was my trade. Everyone I knew wrote books or poetry, wrought plays, painted paintings, or performed. My friends from Performing Arts were going to college now, majoring in some creative skill. I tried to go to school at night, tried to write, tried to make a movie, all of which took time away from making a living. The only thing I was successful at without trying was going broke. The frustration was driving me nuts. Funny things began to happen to our ethereal relationship. Our passionate love slowly turned cold. I don't know whether it was the hard money times or that my wife may have begun to think there might be another man who would be better suited to her. I don't know for sure. I was very naive then and didn't pay much attention to things like that. We split amicably. We both thought we were understanding and fulfilling each other's needs. We thought we knew a lot at twenty-one.

I was lonely at first, but it was okay, I was writing. I gave all my money to my wife and kids but there never seemed to be enough. She got one of those made-up New York "adultery" divorces and after we were divorced I was promptly drafted. I did two years in sunny Germany. At least I didn't have to worry about money in the army. My wife got allotment checks for her and the girls and I got "three hots and a cot." I never ate so well. I went from a 135-pound, six-foot-two skeleton to a hard 175 in a few months.

My wife had written that she had settled in with a much older man for a lover. I thought everything was going to be okay, but when I got out of the army I found that she had disappeared completely. She had received and cashed the allotment checks all right, but she was no longer living at that address and she left no forwarding address. She had no relationship with my family or, for all I knew, her own. She was as alone a person as I was. She simply vanished. There wasn't much I could do. I had two hundred dollars in my pocket. All the money I made in the army had gone to my wife and kids. At the time I got out they weren't giving out any mustering-out pay, G.I. Bill, or any of that stuff. I had to take care of myself and fast.

All the time I was in the army I had dreamed of going to school in San Francisco and writing. I was only a few days out of the army and still packed for travel. I took my few bucks and flew to San Francisco. I got a job and started school, but then I fell in love right away and got married again. Pat was a tiny, short-haired gamine who looked and dressed like a Smith College sophomore, although she was actually six years older than me. She had a son who was the same age as my daughters but neither one of us intended to have any more children. I didn't want to interrupt my career again. We took the precautions available then, but Pat got pregnant in our first year. She said she knew a doctor in New York she was sure would perform an illegal abortion so we packed up the car and drove to New York with our last dollar. It turned out that her doctor was a Catholic in a Catholic hospital. We were penniless and it was too late and that's how I had another child. I loved Pat. What I wanted for me would just have to be put off for a while. I know it sounds familiar, but what else could I do? I was back in New York starting out from the beginning all over, all over again.

It was tough getting started again, but a lot of things came together this time. I was writing out a story idea one night and it suddenly occurred to me that it would make a good short movie. So I made one. I knew next to nothing about movies but I wanted to do it and I was going to make it professional, 35 mm and all. I wrote it, produced it, hired crew, cast and all, directed it, cut it, and paid for it all. I taught myself everything. I remember the first splice I ever made. I stared at that film for a long time before making that first cut, as though once cut it could never be put back together again. The tension was unbearable as I pulled down the blade to separate one frame from the other. Then I spliced the two ends together and ran it through the Moviola. Magic! My first cut. It was an event. It still is, that first cut of any movie. It's virginal somehow, like a surgeon's first incision.

While making that movie I finally learned my trade. It was a synthesis of everything I'd done up to then: acting, directing, play-wrighting, photography, set designing, everything came together in this medium. I felt like I had a toehold on life at last, a thin fingergrip on the mountainside and I could start to climb it. I also learned the primary lesson of the movie business: Never finance your own movie. I put *all* I had into it and went instantly broke. But I was determined to break into the movie business. This is not so easy when you have a family to support and you're just beginning. We were months behind in the rent and the other bills were worse. This went on for a year or so until the strain finally got to Pat. I came back home one night to find a note tacked to the front door of an empty house. She wrote that she had packed everything into the station wagon and she was going away. She didn't bother to tell me where. Now I had no wife, no son, no daughters and no money, but I had learned a trade. Was it all worth it? Yep. Within a year I was writing and directing my first feature. I just wish it didn't have to happen that way.

There didn't seem to be any way I could have both a family and a career. Maybe it was a fantasy. I found Pat working at a private school in a remote corner of New Hampshire. Her only explanation for running out was that if she was going to have to work, she wanted to live alone. After I found her, she filed for a divorce. I didn't contest it as long as I had visitation with my son.

It was a bit difficult getting up to New Hampshire, so I made long visits with my son once a month or so. After I began to go up regularly, a funny relationship developed. Pat and I began sleeping together again. I took her out on the visits, too. It became very much as though I was visiting another of my children, complete with her joking, "Oh, what did you bring for me, Daddy?" every time I went up. The visits were so pleasant that I even tried to persuade her to come back to New York and live together again, but nothing doing. She insisted she was happier living alone. This halfway relationship continued for almost a year, but it all came to a screeching halt when I met Maggie, who was to be my third wife.

I'm still not sure how that marriage ever happened. Another marriage was the last thing I needed or wanted then. I was riding high. I had recently written and directed a half-dozen cheapie exploitation films, one of which caught Lew Wasserman's eye, and I was offered a contract with Universal Pictures to develop low-budget movies which I would produce and direct in New York. Universal wasn't paying me a hell of a lot of money, but it was the big time. I was realizing all my dreams. I was being paid to write whatever I wanted. Marriage was the furthest thing from my mind.

But when you spend your formative years as a skinny, introverted, four-eyed geek covered with acne, there are certain girls you know are unattainable. Then, sometime after thirty, women begin to look at you in a different way. Over the years your acne has disappeared, you are no longer a skinny geek, the "modified aviator style" frames around your thick glasses now give you character, and these goddesses suddenly become available. Want you, even. But that frightened skinny geek is still inside and hasn't developed any defenses for this sort of encounter. About all you can do is say "Yes," and hope you've said it fast enough so you don't lose her.

Margaret was an ash-blonde beauty with perfect features and she was tailored. She had a beautiful voice, a kind of stage American English she had acquired when she had been an actress some years earlier. She was separated from her husband and living alone with their daughter. She was in her thirties and she was gorgeous, but that wouldn't account for my jumping into another marriage so soon. Her daughter influenced me, too. My life had been dominated by having children and taking care of them since I was seventeen. That leaves a kind of nurturing habit that a kid of the same age naturally fits into. Very soon after we began seeing each other regularly, Maggie began to worry about the damage to her daughter's psyche if we kept sleeping together without being married. I didn't understand this, since we weren't living together and we only made love at my place or when her daughter wasn't home, but after a few tear-filled nights I said why not? I was madly in love with her, she was working, her daughter was twelve and taking care of herself to a large extent, Maggie's ex-husband was sending huge support checks, so why not? This marriage couldn't possibly conflict with my career. I happily married Maggie.

I quit Universal after a frustrating year. They weren't buying the screenplays I was writing. I had no idea yet of how to make my way through a major studio and besides, the money people were far away in Hollywood while I was in New York. I should have moved to the coast while I had that momentum, but I had no money, I knew no one out there and now there was Maggie to think of, who, like most New Yorkers, was horrified at the thought of living in Los Angeles. New York is a dependency that is very hard to break, especially if you were born in midtown Manhattan, as I was, and have lived and worked there all your life. I suppose that's another way of saying I didn't have the guts to move. I thought I could do just as well raising independent financing for a movie in New York. I had plenty of work making industrial films and commercials and this left me time to write. But it didn't last long.

Maggie had been working fulltime when we met, but she quit her job a month after we were married. She didn't want to act anymore and it would take time for her to find a new career. She could take her time. We were in good shape. She refused to learn any of what she called "those humiliating office skills," but she was so good-looking, spoke so beautifully, and handled herself so well that she had no trouble getting jobs. There was, however, a problem keeping them. Her jobs never lasted more than a few weeks.

During our first year, Maggie's ex-husband had the first of what was to be a succession of nervous breakdowns, until he was spending more time in mental hospitals than out of them. His support checks dwindled and then permanently stopped. He never resumed them again. This had a strange effect on Margaret. She stopped looking for work altogether. She would read paperback gothics and eat potato chips until three or four in the morning and then sleep until the afternoon. Then her daughter had to go to a private school because the New York schools were so bad. And then we needed more room so we had to move into a larger apartment. And then we had it decorated, since she allowed no one to step into the undecorated place. I did most of the decorating. We had hired a maid to help clean the big apartment and do the ironing when Maggie was out working or looking for work; but now that she was home all the time, the maid was somehow still a necessity.

Shopping became the most exciting experience in Maggie's life. She might spend weeks shopping for a single item. She searched through all her decorating magazines, examined her friends' homes

23

for ideas, and went to the best stores in New York. It wasn't the buying she liked, it was the shopping. Buying was like having the orgasm. She liked to build up to it gradually, teasing and courting herself for weeks. She would get flushed with excitement telling me about her shopping experiences. The Anticipation. The Search. The Disappointments. The Find. The Bargaining. And then, The Buy! She was Emma Bovary with a Bloomingdale's charge card.

I wasn't suicidal. By that age I knew very well what I wanted out of life, but Margaret could manipulate me with ridiculous ease. I resisted her expenditures time and again but she never gave up. She worked on me for weeks and months until she got what she wanted. Everything I resisted eventually became an emergency. Each little thing became a drama, a proof that I loved her with a new material purchase. And I had a need to prove that I really loved her. She eventually got everything she wanted. I couldn't believe what was happening. Just when I had finally connected in my career, I found myself with another huge household to support. I couldn't work fast enough to keep the money coming in. Any time that I wanted to write in order to develop my career had to be put aside. I had thought this marriage would be different, but it didn't seem possible for me to have both a career and a family. My life slowly started to fall away around me.

Maggie was a knockout to look at but she always had been passive sexually. It got worse. After a year of marriage she could only relax enough when her daughter was out of the house visiting her father. That often worked out to a grand total of three times a month, but I wasn't counting then. I still thought I loved her. I bought gradually cheaper scotch in larger and larger bottles, but it wasn't enough to relieve the pressure. Something had to happen. It did. Women. I discovered infidelity.

I was amazed at how easy it was. The first time was almost an accident. Her name was Nadine and she was the production secretary in a movie company I was working for. She was tiny, elfin, with no breasts at all, not even a swelling. She showed off her legs, though, with a mini-mini-skirt. The slightest movement and the two curves of her little behind appeared and . . . Ah well! She knew I was married. We flirted and teased and joked. Everyone else was out on location, and there wasn't much to do. I said "How about lunch?" She said "Where?" and I listened to "How about your place?" coming out of my mouth. She said "Sure." I was flabbergasted for a moment. I was only playing, I think. I had no idea she would take me seriously, but I certainly wasn't going to turn her down. We went to her place and munched on lunch and other things. We met the next day, and the next, and so on. She lived on Sixty-ninth Street, just around the corner. It was even on the way home. If a day was too busy for "lunch," we made a stop there in the evening before I went back to my wife and Nadine went out with her boyfriend.

And then there was Kim, then Marianne, then Ellie . . . Manhattan seemed to hold an inexhaustible supply of women in their twenties who liked making love with married men. I always told them I loved Margaret. I never pretended I didn't sleep with her. They told me all about the boyfriends they loved and planned to marry, too. The cheating seemed to go both ways. I had no desire to jeopardize my marriage. I never wanted to lie to Maggie about working late, so I didn't go out on dates where I would have to account for the missing time. I did my love making during long lunches or in the time between leaving the office and coming home. Two sexy people can make a lot of love in those hours. It's a nice aspect of living and working in midtown Manhattan.

Was that "love"? You bet! I was wanted for myself alone. I never had to promise anything except that moment we would be alone together. After a lifetime of thinking I had to knock myself out to get a woman to love me, it was a revelation that I could get that love without some sort of price tag. Women opened themselves freely to me and gave me warmth, touching, and satisfaction—for only a moment, yes, but that moment is all anyone needs. Infidelity kept me sane, I think. It certainly kept our marriage together. Maybe it doesn't seem like much of a marriage to hold together, but it was all I had. My other marriages had ended in such shambles, I wanted this one to work. I wanted it so badly that I refused to see the reality of our relationship.

Maggie and I lived in this limbo until the recession. The movie business in New York was hit hard. I was broke again and getting broker. I had been self-employed for so long there wasn't even unemployment. I got occasional one-day jobs but we sank relentlessly into debt. Margaret hadn't worked in years. I had asked her repeatedly, but she wouldn't do it. She got so depressed that she went out and bought a new set of three chests of drawers to console herself. She paid down the little cash we had left and signed for the rest. That's when I had to hock my camera for food money. When I got the assistant editor's job it wasn't enough to maintain the status quo, but I was able to pay the maid, who still came in to do the cleaning and ironing.

I don't think Maggie and I were made for each other. There had been good times and loving, but only for a little while in the beginning. By the last year of our marriage we were two silent people, living silently in the same house together. But I kept deceiving myself. Any time I thought about our relationship or spoke about Maggie to anyone, I would describe a perfect marriage to an incredibly beautiful, hard-working, creative woman, my wife. And I believed it. Doesn't everybody?

At the time of this story I found myself at the age my father was when he had sired me. No matter how many times I had tried to prove I was not that archetypal good-for-nothing male, I had ended up exactly like him. I was forever broke, and a lecherous, frustrated artist who seduced women and abandoned his children. The cycle was complete. It seemed like it would go on forever. Then I met Barbara.

THREE

After Barbara's show was cut and broadcast, I hadn't heard another word from her. I was surprised because I thought she had been serious about writing together. I often wandered through the newsroom past her office trying to accidentally meet, but she was never there. More than a month went by with no sign of her. Oh well. If she had been interested she would have made herself available long before this. She obviously wasn't interested. When I had put her completely out of my mind, I saw her name on the leaders of a stack of freshly developed film: "Chateau D'Vie—Prod. B. Gordon." I stopped by the assignment editor's desk.

"Oh, Jeff, hi," I said. "How's it going today?"

"Huh?"

He was surprised at my casual friendliness. The production staff had little to do with the editors outside of the cutting room.

"Listen, Jeff, I'll be finished with Harper's LNG story by Thursday definitely. I don't know whether you have any plans for Barbara's next piece, but I'd appreciate it if you'd assign it to me. I know she's had problems working with other editors, but I enjoyed it, so if you could . . ."

"I'll see what I can do," he said.

I didn't know that Barbara had already made the same request. She said later that she had told Jeff she would quit if he didn't assign me to her story, but he never let on, the little shit. She was out right now shooting a second story and I had been assigned to work on that one, too. We would be working together for more than a month.

We screened the dailies on Friday morning. Everyone connected with the shoot squeezed into the editing room: the cameraman, the lighting man, the sound girl, Nicole, Jill, and the ubiquitous Marvin. I told Marvin I didn't need him yet and he left. Barbara arrived last and we waited through her phone calls and unfinished business. She was wearing a tight black jump suit with nothing underneath.

"Chateau D'Vie" was a film story about two New York entrepreneurs who had turned a failing Catskill resort into a singles-only country club. Barbara had filmed the opening sales weekend. The huge main room, "The Rotunda Room," was packed with hundreds of single men and women looking the place over. Salesmen escorted small groups on tours of the club. They served cheese, crackers, and sangria, and were promising eventual classes in yoga, poetry, and assertiveness along with tennis, swimming, and golf. They even supplied a wing of rooms for two for an additional charge per night. These entrepreneurs had guessed right. There was a need. The hungry eyes of the singles showed it. They knew they were being exploited, but they were still searching and hoping. There might be a better chance in this setup; and it was different, anyway. They sized each other up acutely, weighing the membership fee against the possible mates taking the tour with them. They joked about their singleness, but in their eyes was a desperation deeper than the one they talked about on camera. Barbara had caught it on film. All that was needed was to pull it out and splice it in the right places.

"You think there's a good piece there?" she asked.

"Oh, yeah."

"It's nothing important, I know. But I had to take it."

"Why do you put it down?" I said. "It's a light piece, but it's going to be fun. There are some great moments. Look at this."

I backed up the film and stopped at a single frame where a woman glanced furtively at a possible man.

"For a title background—"

"No, no! Back up further!" she said. "I have another idea."

The tiny room was filled with her crew all talking and laughing with us as the film played, but Barbara and I were alone, working together again. And there was something new this time, a closeness, an acceptance of touching as though it had happened before. I leaned back and stretched my arm out over the back of her chair, letting it rest on her shoulder. It was deliberate and she knew it. She leaned back slightly and rested some of her weight on my arm.

"Wait! Wait! Stop!" she shouted.

Her hand touched mine to stop the Moviola. She left it there as I ran the film back to a particularly juicy shot so we could savor it again. I

28

marked it with a yellow grease pencil to be pulled later. We went on this way to the end of the dailies. The last sequence was a ride home in a chartered bus. They were mostly women. A few were drowsing but most stared out of the windows, unaware of the camera. They seemed to be thinking of a time long gone or some time to come. Barbara jumped up, threw her arms around the cameraman, and kissed him.

"Beautiful, Mario! Just beautiful!"

He leaned close up to the Moviola screen, examining his work.

"I was worried the bus footage might be too dark," he said. "There wasn't enough light for a reading so I had to shoot wide open and hope."

"What do you think, Anton?" she asked. "Will it be all right on system?"

"Just those highlights on the faces, perfect," I said. "I was wondering how we would end, but this is it. This is going to be the ending."

Those lovely sad shots played all the way to the runout. The film flared. No more images. The life on the screen was gone. The editing room was quiet and dark. It seemed for a moment like three o'clock in the morning, and then the normal sounds of the building drifted through the walls. We came back to reality. It was time for lunch. The people in the room pulled themselves together and left, one by one.

Barbara and I were alone. Standing close together, we went over her notes spread out on the table. There was a lot to do. The piece had to be on the air in two weeks. She already had Jeff's approval for any overtime we needed. My hand rested lightly on her hip. She wore nothing underneath the jump suit. I could feel the woman under the black knit fabric fitting snugly to her body. Her shoulder fit comfortably into the hollow of my shoulder and chest. Our small movements led gently to a kiss. Her lips were soft and full. We kissed for a long moment. The door was open, the hall quiet. Everyone had left for lunch. We kissed for minutes more, then pulled slowly apart, watching each other's eyes. My pulse was racing and I could hardly catch my breath. Judging by her kiss, I guessed that Barbara had changed her mind about having an affair with this married man. She took a long deep breath.

"Oooh," she sighed. "I think we'd better go to lunch."

"Yeah, I think you're right."

We elbowed into the crowded elevator and leaned against the back wall. Our hands were hidden from the people getting on and off. We touched and squeezed hands all the way down. She stayed close to me as we left the building and turned west on Fifty-eighth Street. There was a restaurant a few doors down.

My hand rested lightly on her hip. We kept a little daylight between us. I was anticipating a delightful love affair but for now we were still producer and editor. She squeezed my arm tightly to her side. I could feel her heart pounding, too. She was as excited about it as I was. I was not at all prepared for what followed. It seemed as though Barbara tripped, but it wasn't like that exactly. As I grabbed for her, her body felt as though there was no life in it. She recovered in a moment and I helped her steady herself.

"Are you all right?" I asked.

She waved my anxious look away and spoke through her rapid breathing, "Don't worry. It happens to me sometimes. I just have to sit. C'mon. Take me inside."

We walked the few steps into the restaurant and pushed through the crowd to an open table. She sat heavily on the banquette as though exhausted. "Oh, thanks," she said. "Don't worry. It's something I get. Anxiety. Free-floating anxiety. If you're going to work with me, you'll have to get used to it. All my editors know."

The waitress was surprised to see us already seated, but Barbara immediately ordered a drink and so did I. She took out a brown plastic vial and swallowed two yellow tablets. I watched her in silence, not knowing what to say. Our drinks came.

"It's just Valium,"* she said.

Now I'm not a medicine lover. I hate the stuff, in fact. I don't even take aspirin, so I didn't have any of the contemporary drug expertise. Barbara obviously took my dumb silence as disapproval, because she rattled off all kinds of explanations I hadn't asked for.

"Oh, it's harmless," she said. "Valium is only a mild muscle relaxant. My back . . . before I had my fusion—thank you, Fritz!—my back went into spasm regularly. I started taking Valium to relieve the back spasm. Then last summer, after my fusion, I began getting vertigo. It would hit me any time without warning. And than I got really bad anxiety attacks. That one just now was nothing. My psychiatrist prescribed Valium for my anxiety, too. So I've been taking it for about ten years. But it's harmless."

* Valium is a registered trademark of Hoffman-LaRoche Inc.

I held up my glass and laughed, "I prescribe scotch for my anxiety. It's harmless, too."

"That's not funny! It's not the same. This is different. This is a real attack. Nobody knows what causes it."

At another time I might have argued that point, but as long as it didn't get in the way of what looked like a very exciting love affair, who was I to moralize with my scotch? I kept my mouth shut, opening it every now and then to sip scotch, eat lunch, and make conversation.

We finished lunch quickly and went back to the editing room. No one was there. I closed and latched the door behind us. Nothing more had to be said after that first kiss. I moved my hands over her body and her hands searched mine as we kissed again. I opened her front zipper. It slid smoothly down, almost by itself. She shrugged the jump suit open. The stretchy fabric parted over her small, high breasts. She had nothing on underneath. I stroked her breast and then slipped my hand down her bare skin over the soft, full curve of her stomach. I reached down further, my fingers parting her rough pubic hair. Her thighs relaxed open. She was wet and flowing. I softly touched her tiny hard bud. She groaned and her body shook. She slid her hand down, following the hard length of my cock. I could feel her open my pants and lift it out. She stared at it, looking concerned.

"Your . . . " she hesitated, "why doesn't it . . . ?"

I didn't know what she was talking about for a moment. Then I understood.

"I'm not circumcised," I said. "It pulls back. See?"

She still didn't understand. I took her hand and circled her fingers tightly around the end. Then I guided her hand to slide back the foreskin. She was fascinated as the familiar swelling head emerged from her clenched fingers.

"I've never seen that before," she said. "Doesn't it hurt you?"

"Un-unh," I murmured. "That's the original design."

She touched the swollen dark skin and shivered. The doorknob rattled and someone kicked on the door. We froze.

"Yeah?" I called.

"It's me."

Marvin.

"Just a minute, Marv."

I levered my protesting cock into one pants leg. We both zipped ourselves closed. As I went to the door, I gestured to her lap. Even on

31

the black fabric, the spreading wet circle between her thighs was obvious. She moved her legs together and reached for a clipboard to cover it up. I started the Moviola as though we had been screening and just locked the door for privacy. Barbara acted preoccupied with the action on the screen. Marvin lurched carefully into the room and sat up on the editing table. It sagged under his weight, but didn't crack.

"Got anything for me yet?" he said.

He couldn't speak clearly. He had been gone for five hours by this time, but he was practiced in covering up his smashed state.

"We're still screening," I said. "Nothing to do yet."

"Oh."

He sat there, staring straight ahead, sinking into his fat. He didn't say a word or move. I tried to make light conversation about the movie on the screen, but Barbara couldn't stand it for very long. She bolted out of her chair.

"I have to go," she said. "See you later."

"When?"

"You know what we want. You can work without me."

"Sure."

And she was gone, leaving me with Marvin, about the last person I wanted to be alone with. I had a guilty feeling. Could he smell the overpowering sex that I smelled in the stuffy room? If he did, he didn't show it. I started pulling takes. I cut the film at the tail of the shot I wanted and ran the Moviola backward at high speed, guiding the festoons of picture and track into the trim barrel at my side. Flat-bed Moviolas do this faster than any other machine. That's why I love them. When I got to the head of the shot I split it again and wrote its sequence number on it with a white grease pencil. I slipped the two head ends of film on a pin in the rod suspended over the trim barrel. The rest of the shot was piled loosely in the barrel below. I spliced the ends of the rolls together again and switched to the fast speed to search for another take. Marvin slid off the table and swayed slightly.

"I'll do that," he said.

"Most of the takes aren't marked, Marv. I just have notes."

I showed him a yellow pad covered with Barbara's indecipherable handwriting.

"Oh," he said.

He yawned long and loud. I wasn't sure he was going to make it through the day. It was his job as assistant, but I desperately needed something to do with my hands. Nice, relaxing mechanical work. He watched the scenes go by and snorted a sarcastic "Humph!" now and then. By the end of the day I had a rough assembly ready to screen. Marvin had nodded off in the stuffy room. He blinked himself awake and checked his watch. He had made two hours overtime in his sleep.

"Well, if you don't need me any more . . . " he said. "Want to stop for a drink?"

"No thanks. I still have to screen this tonight."

"See you tomorrow."

He wandered out. I called Barbara's office. She was still there. We were alone when we screened the film, but we sat carefully out of touching range. And we only talked about the film. We didn't say a word about what had gone on earlier. After dinner and drinks, we never made it back to the cutting room.

Barbara's apartment was on the sixteenth floor of a building on Central Park South. It was in the back and faced downtown. A soft orange glow separated the skyscrapers that disappeared into the distant haze. From up here the traffic noise blended into a steady hum with only an isolated horn or a hurrying siren. I used to stare at the glittering windows of Central Park South nearly every night when I walked Alfie, our dog, to the Sheep Meadow in the park to do his stuff. The lights from Times Square silhouetted the Essex House and the St. Moritz and the Plaza Hotel and all the towers in between. I had always loved looking up at that skyline, and here I was in it, looking out, a drink in my hands, touching shoulders with my lady.

The small apartment was cluttered with books, records, paintings, and stacks and stacks of papers and file folders—the accumulated research of many shows. It wasn't spotlessly clean, but it wasn't dirty, either. It looked as though she got in and out of it very carefully each day so as to disturb as little as possible. Books were stacked up every which way on the shelves. I touched her copy of *The Bell Jar* and everything moved. A faded book fell from between two Vonneguts, I caught it in mid-air, holding upright the title on its spine. I didn't have to open it, the memory tumbled out.

"'The poems to come are for you and for me and are not for mostpeople,'" I recited the introduction I knew so well, "'—it's no use trying to pretend that mostpeople and ourselves are alike. Mostpeople have less in common with ourselves than the squarerootofminusone . . . ,'"

"How do you know that?" she said. "Cummings is my favorite poet."

"I was raised on that stuff, but it was a long, long time ago."

As I put e. e. back, I noticed a familiar Picasso on the wall, an etching of an artist and his nude model. I looked closer. It wasn't a reproduction. It was real.

"Abe gave me that," she said. "He had class when he gave gifts. Which is about all the class he had."

She gestured to a small lithograph of an abstract blue bird on a white background by another modern French heavyweight whose name I forget now. It was no reproduction, either.

"The bluebird is my favorite," she said. "The Goldsteins gave me that. They sent it from Paris for good luck with my back operation."

She finished the grand tour at the bedroom.

"Welcome to the Boutique," she said.

"The Boutique" was a pile of a week or so's clothes thrown on one side of the bed. She picked them up with both arms and dropped them on a chair already piled high with clothes.

"In case you hadn't noticed," she said, "I'm not a housewife. I wasn't meant to be and I don't give a damn!"

"That's not why I'm here," I said.

There was only the faintest trace of perfume on her skin, not enough to mask the smell of an aroused woman that is like no perfume made. Her scent was strong in the soft hollows behind her ears and on her neck. It rose from her breasts as I opened her jump suit and kissed her there. We undressed and she fell softly back on the bed. I followed her down, inhaling her scent deeply as I kissed her long naked body. I tasted the fine sweet sweat in the fold between her breast and ribs. The scent was stronger yet in the pale hollows joining her belly and thighs, and I followed it to the source. She was flowing already. The hard pink bud stood out from its folds as though still waiting since earlier that afternoon. I kissed her softly and took its tiny length in my lips and tongue. She gasped, and then gave up all thought. It wasn't long before she pulled herself away and then pushed me over on my back. She straddled me and inched herself down. Her hips moved slowly and evenly. She arched her back, proudly showing off her breasts. I reached up and gently held them. She sat upright and the slow rhythm of her hips changed, shoving faster now. The same rhythm went on deep inside. I hadn't felt the pull of those muscles in a long time. She moved faster and faster and then her body shook violently. It was irresistible. I joined her willingly and she trembled again when she felt me come. She slowly collapsed on top of me. We stayed that way for a long while before she roused herself and rolled over on her back. I sipped the remains of a drink that was mostly water. She lit up a cigarette.

"Do you always make love with your glasses on?" she said.

"I forgot. But I'm almost blind without them. I like to see."

She looked at me steadily now and said, "Is it like this with you all the time?"

"Hmmm?"

"I haven't come that easily in . . . maybe never."

"You should. You're a very sexy lady."

"Does it happen with all the women you know?"

"Of course not," I said. "It takes a woman who can respond like you. A lot of women can't."

"Don't bullshit me."

"I'm not. You're a natural woman."

"And you're a natural bullshitter. But I love it."

That wasn't recycled Don Juan, that line about Barbara being a sexy and responsive woman. It was true. And with the last unemployed year and no money to move around, it had been a long time since I'd been with such a loving woman. I wasn't going to miss a moment with her. My fingers traced the long, gentle curves of her body. We were in no hurry. We stroked and kissed each other, still moist with that silvery mix of man and woman. She was fascinated with my soft penis, playing with it like a new toy.

"I never saw a natural one before," she said. "Look! He has a turtle neck sweater on . . . and then he pulls the sweater over his head like this and hides inside. And nooow it's . . . down again around his neck. And now he comes aaall the way out!"

She stretched the "sweater" all the way down this time. The strain made the head start to swell again. It felt good. She may not have seen Nature's own before, but she sure taught herself fast. She caressed the swelling head tenderly with her lips and tongue. My kind of girl.

After she had her way with me, I kissed my way down her delicious body. She relaxed her legs apart as my lips approached her patch of curly hair. She spread the pink folds and with a nudge of her hips, she offered it to me. A hot, clear liquid had washed her clean and was still flowing. I went down on her. As I slowly kissed her, I looked up over her taut belly. Her head was thrown back. I could only see her mouth, strained open in a grimace of pleasure. She had been so sexually high that she rapidly reached the edge and came with a groaning shudder. I didn't stop, but softened the kiss so it wouldn't be too much. She came to the edge again and floated over. She came over and over, each time closer together until everything blended into an unbroken sexual flight. She stayed out there a long time and then she began to shake her head. She pulled on my ears.

"I can't . . . " she gasped. "I can't. . . . No more . . . Please!"

She lifted my face. Her inner lips were pulsing intensely now. I blew softly on the hot skin. She made nervous grabbing motions in the air and her eyes were wild. I was ready again. I turned her over on all fours and got on my knees behind her. And there it was. Her fusion scar neatly traced the vertebrae in the curve of her lower back. It seemed so exposed, so vulnerable. I touched it gingerly.

"Your fusion . . . I'm afraid I'll hurt you."

"No, no! It's perfect. Like a rock. Put it in my cunt. Give me that fucking prick!"

She grabbed it and stuck it in, hunching herself backwards. I still wasn't sure of her back. She gasped excitedly.

"You can't hurt me! Slam into me!"

I shoved in hard.

"Again!" she shouted. "Harder. HARDER! Fuck me, dammit!"

I smacked against her again and again, fucking her as hard as I could.

"Yes, yes!" she yelled. "More! Bang into me!"

I forgot any fear I had of hurting her. I couldn't stop now. With every shove, my body loudly smacked into hers. The strokes were shorter and deeper. I pulled her hips closer to me. My fingers sank into her thighs as I clutched her tightly against me. I felt her deep tissues swell and tighten as I pushed in again and again. Her hoarse breathing became a growl. Then her swollen flesh opened and she came with a deafening howl. I let go, and it seemed like my whole body jetted into hers. Her slippery body kept convulsing in my hands and then she screamed.

"I can't see! I can't see!"

She panicked and tried to rise, but her body was so drained that she collapsed under me. We both rolled down and over. She waved her hands in front of her face and in a few minutes she could see them again. She relaxed and stared at me for a long while. I spoke first.

"Are you all right?"

"Huh!"

"Do you think anyone heard?" I said.

"Heard what?"

"Your yelling."

She looked at me with a blank stare.

"You screamed," I said. "Roared, more like it."

"No, I didn't. I'd know if I did."

"It was kinda loud. Your voice is even hoarse now, don't you notice it?"

"You're crazy," she said.

She rolled over and rested her head on my thigh. I didn't worry about it. On rare occasions I had seen other women black out momentarily like that with the unaccustomed rush of blood down to the pelvis. And Barbara had restrained her movements for so long by her fear of putting her back into spasm that she had probably never allowed herself to have this intense a physical reaction to anything. I heard her talking in a low voice. Her head was still on my thigh.

"What do you think, Sam?"

"Huh?" I said.

"This is private. Just between me and Sam. Right, Sam?"

I looked down. She held my numb penis in her fingers and nodded its head yes and no in answer to her questions.

"You going to make him come back, Sam?" she asked.

Sam nodded yes.

"You know what I'll do for you next time, if you bring him back?"

Sam nodded no.

"Well . . . " she began. She whispered conspiratorially behind her cupped hand.

" . . . would you like that?" she asked.

Sam nodded yes, wildly.

She talked a while longer to her Sam, whispering behind her hand. I was too numb to feel anything. It was strictly between the two of them. She kissed him goodbye and rolled under the covers.

"Now you'd better get dressed and go home," she said. "It's almost two o'clock. Your wife will wonder where you are. And take a shower! You've got to get rid of my smell or she'll really kill you. Good night."

She pulled up the covers. I showered and dressed and then climbed across the bed on my hands and knees and kissed Barbara goodnight. She was already fast asleep.

As I walked into the street, my legs wobbled beneath me. They would never hold me up all the way home. I hailed a cab. Margaret was still awake when I got in. She was lying in our fake antique four-poster bed, reading another gothic novel and eating potato chips. She didn't lift her eyes from the book as I undressed again and slipped into bed beside her. I was asleep in a moment.

FOUR

Barbara and I made love every chance we could. I completely ignored the precautions I used to take. I still went back home each night, but I had always worked late hours so I assumed Maggie didn't notice anything unusual. One night after an evening with Barbara, the bedroom was dark and Margaret was asleep when I came back. I undressed quietly and slipped into bed. As I closed my eyes I heard her perfect diction from the pillow beside mine.

"Are you sleeping with another woman?"

She had never asked me that during the times I'd been seeing any of the other women. I didn't know what to say. I hadn't bothered to prepare a lie. It had never been necessary before. Her question came completely out of the blue, or from some blue in her senses, somehow reading my thoughts. When I didn't respond immediately, she pulled herself upright against the headboard and switched on the light. Now there was real curiosity in her voice.

"Are you sleeping with someone else?" she asked.

"Yes," I said.

There was a long silence. She was taken completely by surprise. Maybe she expected me to deny it. She certainly wasn't prepared for the answer she got. Neither was I. It surprised me just as much. The one word, "yes," came out so easily that more tumbled out after it.

"Yes, I am," I said. "And I intend to continue. And I'm not going to discuss it with you. I'll move out as soon as I can get enough money to rent a room somewhere."

"When will that be?" she asked.

"I have no idea. As soon as I can. Good night."

She didn't say anything, which was amazing. It was the only time since I had known her that she didn't cry or scream when she was frustrated. I could sense wheels spinning in her head, but she couldn't find anything to say. I don't wonder. It was the first time anything like that had ever been as much as mentioned and I imagine Margaret was in shock. She had not been prepared for that simple "Yes." I rolled over and closed my eyes. I had never consciously thought of leaving her until that moment when I automatically answered "Yes." But having said it, I knew I had unconsciously wanted it for years.

Meeting Barbara had snapped something inside me. There had been many other women and I had never had this reaction before. With Barbara it was different. My past relationships had always come into conflict with my creative self. I started out each relationship considering the woman independent and somewhere along the way it always changed. Barbara would not be that way. She was the first truly independent woman I had ever met. I wanted her.

As I lay there, I felt as though layers of a thick, gray substance were starting to lift from me: worries, tensions, money. Heavy layers of fear and desperation were floating off me and away. I was facing freedom for the first time in a chain of dependent relationships. There was an end to it. I had a grasp on my life. I had willed an independent action for the first time in my life. And all because of a woman named Barbara Gordon. It was marvelous lying there on that bed. I was so peaceful and calm, eyes closed, dreaming of Barbara. It must have galled Margaret that I could reject her so casually.

"Well," she said, "you don't expect that I'll have you sleeping in my *bed*, do you?"

I got out of bed and pulled a blanket from the closet.

"We've got this damn huge apartment, full of all this damn furniture," I said, "I might as well make use of it."

I went into the dining room, stretched out on one of our three couches, and went to sleep.

Sleeping on the couch couldn't last forever, but for a little while I came home late each night, quietly got my dinner, and just as quietly bedded down alone on the dining room couch. There was no money to move yet. It didn't bother me to sleep at home and Barbara didn't question it. She had plenty of practice with married men. She seemed content with the arrangement.

In the weeks that followed, I noticed that Barbara was subtly wooing me in an area in which I was completely vulnerable. I recall walking her home one Friday night when she made a great point of waving her paycheck inches from my nose and complaining about how much tax they took out because she was single. She made a good salary as a producer. Then she insisted that I help her figure out her possible taxes for the year, since she had no head for math. It didn't occur to me that she must have had a high-priced CPA to do her figuring for her. (She did.) In the course of this session, she neatly outlined her yearly income and all her assets which were something of a surprise. Her father had sold his business to a conglomerate the year before and had divided the stock between himself, Barbara, and her younger brother. The stock split once, went right back up to its old value and split again. With the money Barbara had made and saved by herself, she had almost a million dollars. I couldn't know exactly, but it seemed that much to me. Her money was being slowly invested in safe municipal bonds. I had been dirt poor for most of my life and now it seemed that the woman of my dreams was attracted by my lack of money. It gave her security, I suppose. It was something she could offer me outside herself. We were a strange Romeo and Juliet.

The "Chateau D'Vie" film was cut and ready for air. I was alone in the editing room for a last fine cut, trimming it down to time. The phone rang. It was Barbara. She started out relating a conversation she had had the night before with Nicole.

" . . . and then Nicole said to me, 'Why don't you ask Anton to stay at your place? He isn't going to have any money for a while. If you really like him that much, why don't you ask him to move in?' It never occurred to me before, but when I thought about it, I said to myself, yeah, why not? . . . Well?"

I couldn't speak. I was totally unprepared for such an offer.

"Well?" she asked again.

"Ahhh, gee . . . "

You dream of eloquence at great moments, but unless you've had a chance to rehearse it, what usually comes out is, "Ahhh, gee . . . " I went on, trying to think and respond at the same time.

"Ahhh . . . I don't know what to say . . . . Oh it's not that I don't want to, but . . . this is so unexpected. I have to think a minute. I don't want you to get the idea that I would be just trading dependencies, or something. I . . . I want to break that chain in my life."

I was too surprised to articulate my fears. I had lived with a woman almost every day of my adult life. Security? Habit? Odd how in this society one must defend behavior that has been considered normal and healthy for all the time humans have been on earth. It feels right to live with a woman. And Barbara was the one woman I could conceive of who would not become dependent on me. I felt myself being drawn inexorably toward Ms. Marvelous on the other end of the phone. I put on the bravest front I could.

"But... but, but if I did," I said, "I'll pay my share. I was planning to get my own, so I'm prepared."

"No, you won't," she said. "You don't have a penny. I pay the rent whether you live there or not. And the phone and electric. It's no difference to me. Then you can have all the time you need to write or whatever."

"I just .... It's a fantastic offer, Barbara, don't get me wrong. It's just a little too much to think of at once. Let me think about it for a while. And I'll see you later. Okay?"

"Sure. 'Bye now."

What was there to think about? My career had been down so long it was a fantasy to any outside observer. I had come to realize that the one thing I was undeniably accomplished at was making love. Well, why not let it support me for a while? In my thoughts about Barbara I had a clear awareness of a possible future that I could make happen if I became her lover, her escort, her—What's the word? Like Prince Phillip or Prince Albert—Consort. That's it. Barbara was a dynamite lady and a lot more important in the world than I was, or ever might be. And it's not that I would stop working. I needed my own walking around money and I knew I would have to pay Margaret alimony. I couldn't and wouldn't ask Barbara for that.

And for the rest? It made me dizzy to think of it. I had an immediate future through her and her contacts. Collaborating with Barbara on my writing and hers, there was a real chance of moving rapidly in my career. I might never have to worry about money again. She was beginning to show some of her famous temperament, but I could handle that. I had been raised by nervous women. I felt right at home with her. Her craziness was not destructive toward me. It was generous. Barbara was offering me everything I could imagine in exchange for a very good time. I would have to be a good boy, no more fooling around, but I wouldn't need another woman with the way Barbara made love.

While all these thoughts were going around in my head, the "Chateau D'Vie" was going through the Moviola in front of me. How different those lonely singles looked to me now. Their moments on film remained the same. Time hadn't happened to them as it had happened to me. There was a hollowness about those seekers for love. And I realized I was very much like them. I had married each wife with the unconscious belief that it was somehow a miracle that a woman would love me. I had sacrificed my career for them because I felt that I was unworthy of being loved and had to constantly prove myself. Watching those sad singles pass by on the Moviola screen, I realized that no matter how many times I had tried and failed, I had something better than they did. I was worthy of being loved.

Late that night, I walked Barbara home. We strolled along Central Park South, past the uniformed doormen, the hansom cabs, the limousines, the couples in evening clothes, and finally into the polished stone doorway of her building. The elevator man touched the bill of his cap as we passed.

"Evening, Ms. Gordon," he said.

"Evening Arnold," she said.

"Evening, sir," he said to me.

"Evening," I said.

It was unbelieveable. I had a choice. Twelve blocks north: misery, frustration, no money, no career, a dependent woman. Twelve blocks south: happiness. It wasn't a plan or a wish or a dream that would take years of work. It was right here. All I had to do was say yes to this terrific woman who was holding on to my arm.

I said "Yes."

FIVE

Maggie was in a daze as she watched me pack a suitcase with the few clothes I was taking with me. She must have been in shock. This was only days from her first news of my infidelity, and she couldn't quite grasp what was happening. I'm sure she thought that it would be a much longer time before I could afford to move out and that I might change my mind by then. Even if I had we could never have gone back to our old life, but she had nothing else to turn to except such vain hopes. In the years we were together she had never developed an independent life. She had no career, not even a job. Being abandoned is no fun. It had happened to me a couple of times and I knew the desolation she must have been feeling. It would be nice if two people could break up when it was the right time for both of them, but I doubt if it ever happens that way. I felt sorry for Maggie, but I couldn't procrastinate. I picked up the suitcase, my typewriter, my Nikon, and the Braun coffee grinder and walked out.

"You'll need keys," Barbara said.

We stood outside her door for a long time as she rummaged through the bottom of her handbag trying to find a complete set. Top lock, bottom lock, outside door for late night, and mailbox. One by one she sieved them up from the tobacco shreds, papers, and Valium tablets that filled the bottom of her bag. I laughed when she dropped the last key into my hand. " . . . and with this key, I thee wed," I said.

"What does *that* mean?"

"Lovers don't exchange rings or vows anymore, just keys."

"I'm not marrying you or anyone," she insisted. "That's not what this is going to be."

"Just a funny thought."

"It's not funny."

"No, it isn't," I said. "These keys mean more to me than any marriage ever did. Thank you, Barbara."

I kissed her until her tight lips softened and her body began to move. And then, using her keys for the first time, I fumbled with the unfamiliar old locks and opened the door. We hurried inside and made love.

Over the next weeks, Barbara introduced me to her family. Not her father and mother—they were tucked away in a Fort Lauderdale condominium. Her real family was a close-knit group of couples who had known each other for ten to fifteen years. It was they who nursed her through her back attacks, carried her, took her to hospitals, and brought food to her at home when she was recovering. She had never learned to drive so they gave her lifts to their various beach houses where she was a regular guest. They had a poker game that had been going on since the early days when they were all poor and shared an old house on Fire Island. The game would begin each Saturday night and go on till dawn, efficiently using up Barbara's weekends through her years of married lovers. And the "family" held her together through the inevitable breakup with each married man. They had long since given up trying to find a match for her. Then I appeared with Barbara happily holding onto my arm. Intellectually, creatively, sexually, we seemed a perfect match.

I had lived two lives for so long; eight hours working full time for whatever family, then, as soon as I finished, my real work, writing, in the few hours I could scrape together. This kind of life left little time for socializing. I had few long-term friends outside of the people I worked with. So I gained a family, too. Everyone who loved Barbara loved me. They had never seen her look so well. I couldn't count how many fingers pinched her blooming cheeks. Then they would move on and pinch mine. Both at once.

"Barbara, he's a prince!" all the women exclaimed.

"Lemme see this prince!"

Paul Isaacs' Brooklyn accent blasted through the cutting room door before he did. Then I saw his shiny bald head and tough little frame. He shook hands and bearhugged the breath out of me. Barbara stood proudly behind him.

"This woman is absolutely nuts about you. I never thought I'd see her act this way with any man. How the hell do you do it?"

Paul was a member of another part of Barbara's wide "family."

These were men with whom she had worked and with whom she had casual affairs over the years. Like Paul, they tended to be radical political writers or TV journalists, all very much to the Left. There was a sprinkling of actors and politicians, too. Many of them would pop into town and leave not-so-discreet messages on her service. She would accept their invitations to late dinners and then bring me along to show me off. She was very proud of me. I think she was also letting them know that she wouldn't be available any longer and that she wanted to remain good friends. She never mentioned that aspect of their friendship to me, but it's easy to tell when someone is with a former lover. Even ten years later, the switches inside them click automatically. And you can tell the man who thought he was going to get laid after dinner and who finds himself sitting across the table from his date's new lover. It became a familiar ritual until they all got her message.

I asked what her psychiatrist thought of all this. Her closest friends couldn't help noticing the change in her. What did he think about her living with a man after so many years of living alone?

"Oh, he doesn't even know about you," she said. "I might've mentioned you when we started to work together again, but since then I've missed all my appointments. I haven't seen him in months. Just been too busy."

"Well, is everything okay?" I asked.

"Okay? I wasn't even whole before I met you. And now . . . I never knew what it could be like to want to share the planet with someone. . . . A man. I haven't had an anxiety attack since you moved in. All my doctor did lately was write out my Valium prescription and I certainly don't need any now."

I realized I hadn't seen that brown plastic bottle in her hands since our new life started. And I saw her twenty-four hours a day. We'd sleep together, make love first thing in the morning, have breakfast, walk to the studio, work on a show, have dinner, make love, and sleep together again. As my grandmother would say, "an excellent suffi-ciency" of loving, living, and creating together.

Let me tell you what it's like living with a perfect modern woman. I caught a three-day flu, the kind that really knocks you back. Barbara insisted that I stay home so that she could take care of me. She called her best friend, Samantha, for a recipe for real chicken soup. She put the chicken in at eight o'clock in the morning and then left. She had to be in her office for a lot of important meetings. She apologized all over the place that she couldn't stay with me, but she wouldn't let me touch the soup. She cabbed home between meetings to spoon the fat and add vegetables. I dozed through it all. She came in at cocktail time. She still had a meeting to go to, an important dinner. I was in bed. The fever was getting worse. Barbara served out a big bowl of soup and a glass of iced Polish vodka. Then another bowl of soup and another vodka. As I finished the second bowl of soup and the second vodka, I slowly slid down under the covers, all that warmth and goodness suffusing me. I felt Barbara's fingers brush along my leg, sliding the covers off. Her Sam was stiff and hot with a fever all his own. Like a modern Florence Nightingale, she unselfishly nursed him, kissing him deeply and lovingly. He responded mightily to her medical care and I collapsed into heaven. She took the bowl out of my hands, kissed my half-closed eyes. and went off to her dinner. I did sleep the sleep of angels that night.

I was lying in bed with Barbara late Saturday night. We were doing the Crostic puzzle. Neither of us had ever been able to do it alone, but together we polished it off in no time. The phone rang. Barbara answered it and handed it to me. Maggie's familiar voice emanated from the phone in an oddly conversational tone.

"I assume you're not coming back then?" she asked.

"I thought you understood that."

"She's really got her claws into you, hasn't she?"

"I wouldn't put it that way," I said.

"You've always been weak, you know that."

"Oh."

"Well, since you're not coming back, I have everything of yours packed and I want it out tomorrow night."

"What do you mean, tomorrow night?" I said. "There's no time—"

"I mean tomorrow night!"

"But my stuff has been there for weeks. Why does it suddenly bother you?"

"It bothers me," she said. "And if you don't come tomorrow night, I'm throwing it out on the street."

"You can't do that!"

"Everything's packed and waiting. Goodbye."

It turned out that it really wasn't "everything." Anything of value to me, anything worth money, anything for my business was stashed in some mysterious "other place" awaiting the settlement. These boxes were full of clothes, books, things that smelled of me. They were stacked at the door as I stepped into the apartment. And then I remembered. It was Sunday. Lisa was visiting her father. Maggie and I were alone in the apartment. And somehow, in no more than twenty minutes, we had traveled from the front door to the bedroom and I was lying in our old four-poster bed making love to this now strange, but also disturbingly familiar, naked woman.

As I held Maggie in my arms and made love to her, I couldn't imagine how I had ever fallen for this woman. Her lingering scent of *Jungle Gardenia* was as oppressive as it always had been. Her skin didn't feel right. It was soft where Barbara's was firm. All those potato chips had swollen her hips and thighs. Not a hair, not a false eyelash was out of place. And she was passive, as always. Everything was the same as it always had been except that her old fantasy image was gone. I saw her as she really was, perhaps for the first time.

After it was over we rested side by side on the sheets. We were still naked but we didn't touch any more. She smoked a cigarette. Why on earth had I made love to her? I suppose there's the inevitable male ego: the sex athlete leaping from one bed to another only minutes apart and satisfying both women. There was that titillation of strangeness and familiarity, a different skin, a different touch. And I felt sympathy for her, too. Or maybe it was guilt because I had left her and she wasn't getting much. Couldn't be getting much if she had to do this. Could she? Hmmm. It certainly wasn't because she was good in bed. She seemed to sense my indifference as she puffed on her cigarette.

"No good, huh?" she said.

"We-ell, you can't use those words exactly," I said. "Relationships change. There's a vulnerability and . . . and trust that people have . . ."

"I'll bet she sucks your cock, too."

She had never used such words since I had known her.

"Well, yes, as a matter of fact," I said.

You know, I regretted saying that even as the impulse zapped through my nerves and the words formed in my mouth. But it was too late.

"Don't you know that's a sign of a repressed homosexual?" she said.

"The last thing she is is homosexual," I said.

Margaret shook her head with deep understanding and sympathy. She touched a gentle fingertip to my arm.

"I meant . . ." she paused, meaningfully, "but then, how would *you* know?"

"Oh, Maggie!" I sighed. "I'm happy. For the first time in my life."

She shook her head sadly. "Poor Anton," she said.

I don't know how she had expected me to react to her nickel and dime psychology, but she had gotten nowhere with it and the act was fading fast. Maggie lay on her back, looking straight ahead. Her jaw tightened. Her eyes narrowed. The scene had passed the stage of titillation and the above-mentioned genital felt suddenly exposed in its nakedness. It seemed to have a brain and thoughts of its own. It seemed to be talking to me. "Be smart," it said. "Get dressed. Move out. Take the clothes and books. *Pay* the ten dollars!"

I sat up on the bed with my feet on the floor, my back to her. Not too fast now. I didn't want her to get the impression that I was afraid of her. That would only set her off again and I didn't want to be around for the next one. I wondered how long I had been there. Barbara must be getting worried. I reached over to pick up my watch from the night table and I suddenly became totally disorientated. I didn't know where I was. I stared at the night table for a long moment trying to get my bearings. My watch lay next to a familiar brown plastic cylinder, but I had never seen it *there*. That's what was confusing me. I looked closer. It was the same bottle, even the same pharmacy typewriting: "Take two before retiring." It was a brown plastic bottle of yellow Valium tablets. Barbara didn't need Valium now that I was living with her, but since I'd left Maggie, she was taking it regularly. I started to laugh inside. Through my body flowed the active ingredient of Valium. I was Prince Valium!

SIX

I brought the boxes and clothes over that night. They sat in the living room for a week or so while Barbara threw out a lot of her old clothes and emptied a closet for me. I filled it with my clothes and went through all my boxes as I put them away. I had accumulated many boxes of photographs and negatives, dating from my first camera, which I got when I was fifteen. I hadn't looked at these pictures in a long while. I've always had a camera around me. Most of my first jobs were in photographic darkrooms and I could make all the prints I wanted at night. There were photographs of my children in the first years of their lives. This was all I had of them now. There were shots of my wives and other women who I only knew when photographing them. I noticed that every photograph of Maggie was missing. She must have gone carefully through each box, removing every single negative and print. I held them out to Barbara as I went through them all, tiny contact prints, 8x10s, 16x20s, and larger. Barbara became strangely silent, watching my life flip by, but whatever she thought she kept to herself. She got up and walked out of the room without a word.

And then there were my boxes of manuscripts. Even with the little time I had to write, there was quite an accumulation of bad or unfinished stories, plays, and screenplays. There was a box of legal proceedings, mostly about my son, Robin. I had carried this stash and added to it through all my life. It was, in a way, the only proof that I had existed on this earth. It filled a dozen cardboard boxes of various sizes which I fit into the back of the closet like a three dimensional Chinese puzzle. I was officially moved in.

Barbara offered me a corner of the bedroom for my work and left it up to me to figure out how to use it. There was a door to the tiny kitchen that had always been in the way. I took it off its hinges, filled in the doorknob hole, painted it white and rested it on a file cabinet on one side and a pair of steel legs on the other. That was my desk, with the typewriter in the middle. The manuscripts I was going to work on went into the file cabinet. I put up bookshelves all through the apartment for Barbara's books as well as my own.

"In all the years I've lived here," she said, "I never thought to do that with that *verdreght* door. And the men I've known wouldn't have thought to do it, either. Except Ben. Ben is good like that. You'll see when we go to their house."

"It's nothing spectacular," I said. "I grew up in a house full of women. The only way they could fix something was with advanced bobby pin technology, and if that didn't work, they'd have to call—"

"Call the man!" Barbara said. "I know the feeling. It proves what I've always thought. Men are much more interested in nest building than women are. I don't have any nest building instincts at all."

I took her in my arms.

"And that's why I love you," I said.

There was a knock on the door. I turned to get it.

"It's awfully late," I said. "Who could that be? Do your neighbors usually . . . ?"

Barbara grabbed my arm and held me back. She shook her head and whispered.

"It might be *her*! Don't open it!"

It took me a while to realize which "her" she meant. I tiptoed to the door and carefully looked out the peephole. Sure enough, Margaret was standing there staring at me. Staring at the door, actually. It was a tiny peephole. She couldn't see me. I made sure not to let any light through as I closed it. I never imagined she would show up here. How had Barbara suspected? Is there a wavelength that men can't hear? I went into the bedroom. Barbara was trembling. She swallowed two Valium.

"How did she get into the building?" she said. "The doorman didn't call."

"Oh, she's good at that," I whispered. "She probably told the doorman she's your best friend and wanted to surprise you."

Margaret knocked again, louder this time. I was angry now, but Barbara held my arm.

"Don't open the door. Please!" she whispered. "She doesn't know whether we're in or not."

Margaret waited outside the door for a long time. I watched her

52

through the peephole as she examined the length of the hall. She went into the two fire stairs. Perhaps she was looking for a service entrance. She came out again and sat in front of me, leaning her back against the other side of the door. I waited until she finally gave up and left. I gave her time to get home and then another half hour. Then I telephoned.

"What are you doing?" Barbara said.

"I have to at least call and yell at her. I can't let her get away with that shit. She'll do it again. You don't know her."

"Be careful."

Margaret answered the phone.

"Hello?"

"Hi, it's me," I said.

"Well, I'm glad I finally—"

"I just got back," I interrupted. "The doorman told me there had been a woman waiting at this apartment for a long time. From his description I figured it must have been you. I can't allow you to—"

"It's important," she said. "It's an emergency."

"I don't care what it is!" I shouted. "There's a telephone and they still deliver the mail! You can reach me any time you want, but you are never, never to do that again! Is that clear?"

"You have to take the dog," she said.

"What?"

I wasn't sure I heard right.

"Alfie. You have to take Alfie."

"This is your emergency? This is why you came over here?"

"That dog is driving me crazy!" She said.

"What's he doing?"

"He wants to go out all the time and I can't take him out."

"That's simple enough," I said. "You're not working. You have plenty of time."

"Every time he looks up at me with those eyes, I can't stand it. You have to take him."

"First of all, I don't have to do anything just because you want me to. Second, I can't take him. They don't allow pets in this building."

"Just temporarily," she begged, "until—"

"Third, I work long hours as I always have and there isn't any time. I'm certainly not going to ask Barbara to take care of your dog."

"He's not my dog!"

"He's not mine either," I said. "Maybe it's a little less convenient for

53

you now that I'm not there, but you'll have to adjust sometime, so now seems like an ideal—"

"I can't!" she yelled. "Don't ask me again!"

I yelled louder, "Well, I'm not going to take him, so you'll have to figure something out for yourself!"

She slammed the phone down.

"What was that all about?" Barbara said.

"You won't believe it," I said, "She wants me to take the dog."

"I can't stand to have a dog around, but I suppose if you have to I could manage somehow."

"Don't worry. You know I wouldn't do that to you. It's all taken care of."

That was not the end of Alfie, our shared love object. Barbara, Jill, and I were in the editing room screening film for Barbara's next piece. The phone rang. Barbara grabbed it.

"McGovern Headquarters!" she answered.

Jill and I laughed. Barbara silently handed the phone over to me. It was Margaret. Barbara and Jill discreetly left the editing room to talk outside in the hall.

"What is it?" I said.

"I have to see you."

She sounded urgent.

"You can talk to me over the telephone," I said. "What is it?"

"No, it's important. I have to see you."

"Look, I haven't cashed my check yet today. I don't have any money. It's not due till Friday anyway."

"Oh, you think that's all I'm interested in, money?"

"Well, why did you call?"

"This has nothing to do with money."

"And you can't tell me over the phone?"

"No, I can't!"

"I'll meet you downstairs," I said. "Ten minutes?"

"I'll be there."

Barbara and Jill were still talking in the hall. I told Barbara I had to see my wife for lunch and then go to the bank so I'd be a little while. I assured her there was no problem. Jill was the only other person in the hall, so we kissed a long moment before I split.

I took Margaret to a nearby delicatessen. The lunch crowds were filling the place so we had to share a table with two other people. I ordered two briskets and a Doctor Brown's Cel-Ray. And then something with alcohol in it for me. She was quiet until my drink came. I sipped it.

"What are you going to do about the dog?" she said flatly.

"Is that why you had to meet me?"

"I can't stand it anymore," she said. "He's driving me crazy!"

"To tell you the truth, I really haven't thought much about it. I tried a couple of people I thought might want him, but they said no. I told you that already."

"What are you going to do about it?"

"I don't see that it's any of my business," I said. "If you won't take care of him then find another home for him. And if you can't find a home for him, then take him to the ASPCA. What am I supposed to do?"

"Nobody will take him," she said.

"Are you sure you've tried?"

"Yes, I've tried! Nobody wants him."

"Then why should I take him if nobody else wants him? I can make choices just like you do. I don't want him either."

The sandwiches arrived. I picked mine up and held it for a moment before biting into it. "I'm working too much," I said. "I don't have the time. There's no room in my life now for any dog or pets or—"

"No room, huh!" She stood up and yelled, "No room for *anybody*? You just toss them out when you're done!"

The noisy deli went silent for a moment and then slowly came back to life. Maggie stood there looking down at me, shaking with rage. The two people at our table looked studiously the other way and continued eating. I knew Maggie was hurt, but that was no reason to give in to her. All I could do was try to quiet her down.

"I can't have you coming here and making trouble," I said, "I can't afford to lose this job."

"Oh, don't worry. You won't lose your precious job. I won't hurt you. That would only make her love you more. I'll hurt *her*. That way I can hurt you both."

She turned and walked out. I paid and went to the bank to cash my check. All the time I stood in line at the bank, something was bothering me. I couldn't put my finger on it. Why had she come to see me? She could have telephoned. Why did she leave without money? And why did I keep worrying about it?

The cutting room was empty when I got back. The chair had fallen over somehow. As I picked it up, Sy poked his head in the doorway. He grinned through his beard.

"Hey, man, your wife was just here. She was having a fight with Barbara but we quieted her down. Marvin took her home."

Guilt rushed through me immediately. That's what I had been unconsciously afraid of, but I couldn't bring myself to believe that she'd actually do it. I should have known better.

"Where's Barbara?" I asked.

He shrugged. "Try the newsroom."

Barbara was stretched out on a couch in the newsroom. The station staff crowded around her but they couldn't do much. I pushed through to her. She was shaking and having difficulty breathing.

"Are you hurt, Babe?" I said.

"No. Anxiety attack."

"I'm so sorry. I should have been with you."

"Help me home."

She pulled herself up. Then she screamed and froze in position, a foot above the couch. Twenty pairs of hands reached for her. She was in pain.

"Ohh no!" she groaned. "Fritz! I didn't . . . "

"What's wrong, Babe?"

"It's okay! Just a spa—asm!"

She carefully lifted herself to an upright position, supporting herself every inch of the way, swallowing her pain. She stood stiff as a plaster mannequin, not moving any part of her body as though she was afraid it would break. She moved one leg cautiously and then the other, still keeping her upper body rigid.

"Easy, Babe," I said. "Easy. Maybe you'd—"

"No. Home. Got some Valium. I'll feel better."

I helped her walk out past the crowd of her friends. They watched helplessly, their hands ready to grab for her if she fell.

Barbara's steel back brace was still at the back of the closet under a pile of clothes. I helped her strap it on. She still couldn't move. She downed a few Valium.

"It's my fault," she said painfully. "Fritz told me the fusion would be worthless if I didn't exercise those muscles. But I never do. It's my fault."

She had to wear the brace to bed for a week. It was the only way she could sleep. But worse than the pain was her humiliation at being a trapped and helpless invalid in front of me. She hated having me see her like that. At night in bed, I automatically reached out to hold her and instead touched the canvas-covered steel bands that encased her body. I shivered instinctively. It was an ugly, inhuman thing where Barbara's responsive body should have been. Seeing it made me very nervous. I knew Maggie had no idea what the consequences of her temper would be but I hated her for having done this.

Maggie's looks had been her primary security and my leaving so suddenly must have been a powerful shock to her pride. She had nothing to replace it with. From her point of view, Barbara had everything: money, career, and now her man, and Maggie had lost everything. She was trying to get to me by terrifying Barbara. I wasn't sure what I was going to do about this, if there was anything I could do. All I knew was that I had better make damn sure that these two women never met again.

SEVEN

After a week in bed, Barbara's spasm relaxed enough for her to be able to take the back brace off for short intervals. Another week and she was able to move freely again. As part of our relationship from now on, I was going to make sure that she exercised regularly. Her two closest friends, Ben and Lian, invited us for dinner out in Sag Harbor, an artists' and vacation community out on the south fork of Long Island. They lived there all year round. Ben, who was now a real estate agent, was an ex-lover of Barbara's. Barbara had been talking about renting a summer place on Long Island and we took this opportunity to visit and look for a house at the same time.

I rented a car, and as we made the long drive Barbara briefed me on the intricate politics that she had evolved to maintain a relationship with two couples who were her closest friends but couldn't stand each other. Somehow, Barbara had managed through many years to stay very close to each couple without the other knowing.

"Now when you meet Ben and Lian," Barbara said, "you are never to mention Dale and Samantha. It's as though they don't exist. Okay?"

"Whatever you say, Babe."

"Ben the bourgeois," she mused. "You wouldn't believe the change in him if you had known him when we were lovers. He used to be the free spirit in our crowd. He was an artist, a painter. He lived in a loft in Soho before anyone did that. He even sold some of his paintings through a gallery. But then he married Lian and they had their twins and now he's a real estate agent in Sag Harbor and he doesn't have time to paint any more. He thinks he's going to make a killing in real estate some day and then he'll retire and do nothing but paint, but it never seems to happen."

"I know the whole story," I said sympathetically.

"We all shared a summer house in Fire Island. It was real primitive.

No electricity. No running water, only a well in the back. No television. We didn't even have a radio. We played poker all night long under kerosene lamps. I loved the ocean. I loved to watch the waves battering the beach endlessly. Ben got this special salt water soap from Abercrombie and Fitch. We washed in the ocean with it. We didn't have a bathtub or shower in the house. Steve came out once. He was completely out of place."

"Steve, your husband?" I said.

"The cretin I married. He came out dressed for some yachting weekend or something. He couldn't relax with us."

"But you were still going with Ben then, right?"

"Oh, sure. Steve had known me from high school and he wanted desperately to marry me. He kept coming to the Village every weekend to see me. I made Ben take his clothes out of the closet every time Steve came up."

"So Ben knew about him?" I asked.

"Oh yeah. He didn't like it at all. He wanted me to choose between him and Steve."

"And you chose Steve."

"Yeah," she said. "And Lian knows all about that. About me and Ben. We're all good friends."

"Why did you choose Steve to marry? Ben seems like he would have been an ideal guy for you."

"It was to please my parents," she said. "They liked Steve. They wanted me to get married."

"You, the arch rebel, did what they wanted you to?"

"You don't understand what it is to be raised by a Jewish family."

"I suppose not."

"Then only later you realize how bad it is," she went on. "I was miserable from the beginning. Everything went wrong. He started to drink a lot and then one night when he was drunk, he came after me with a kitchen knife. He really was going to kill me. Just went out of his head."

"I don't blame you for getting out."

"My work was more important to me than being a housewife. Abe had just given me an opportunity to write for his television show. I was just a researcher. He asked me one day what I thought of the show and I told him. Imagine me, fresh out of college, telling a big producer how to run a network television show. But he listened, or something, cause he came around a week later and asked me out to lunch."

"Oh, so you knew Abe before you broke up with Steve?"

"Yeah, but . . . we weren't sleeping together or anything like that then. That was only after I split up with Steve and moved back to the city. That relationship with Abe lasted for five years. Every year he promised to get a divorce but there was always something. One kid would be graduating and going to college so it wouldn't be a good time, and then each year it was something else. He kept putting it off until I couldn't take it anymore. But it lasted longer than any relationship I ever had. And then there was Abe Ostreicher and Abe—I always did have a thing for married men named Abe."

"But my name's Anton."

"Oh, you're my pussycat. None of them were good lovers. Except Ben. He was good. He was fantastic. I think there's a real correlation between a successful man and his sex."

"What do you mean?" I asked.

"Well, that a successful man is successful because he can't fuck well."

I laughed. She went right on.

"You laugh, but believe me, I know! I've known a lot of very successful men and they've all been lousy in bed. There's got to be a relationship between a drive for success being overcompensation for being a lousy lover. See, Ben was a fantastic lover and he was always poor."

"Where does that leave me?" I said. "I have every intention of being successful."

She thought about that for a moment.

"I don't know," she said. "You're not like any man I ever knew before. For one thing, I never could talk like this with any man I ever knew. Does it bother you for me to talk about having sex with other men?"

"No, not at all. As long as you don't mind me talking about other women."

"That's where we turn off," she said. "See that little sign? Make a right. Then we have to follow the dirt road all the way. But go slowly. Their house is set way back from the road. You'll go right by it. Now remember, you're never to mention Dale and Samantha's names while we're here."

"Got it."

It's always a shock to a city person like me to step out of a car and suddenly see the stars overhead. Not just the big bright ones you can

61

see in the city on clear nights, but a sky full of them. A thick, soft blanket of stars pulled up from horizon to horizon when the beach goes to sleep. Their house was an old cottage on the edge of a secluded bay. The bay was sheltered with a long curving arm of deserted marshland. The water was motionless under the moonlight. We didn't stay to look very long because it was April and it was fucking cold out.

A pair of ten-year-old twin boys let us in. The house took us in its arms as we walked through the door. It was all white and wicker with the exposed two-by-fours shelving books and plants. There was a fire blazing in the fireplace. Ben and Lian were in the kitchen making dinner. They came out to welcome us. Ben was my size with black hair like a gypsy. He was past fifty and healthy. Lian was a dark-haired French beauty who was pushing fifty with no disguises. When she smiled, her facial lines made her sexier than ever. There was much kissing and hugging, with Ben (and me, too) managing a free feel.

"Oh, he's sexy, too," Lian said. "Where did you find this gorgeous man, Barbara?"

"I got a ghost for ya' Barbara," said Ben. "DHP!"

"DHP?" Barbara replied.

"Yep. D. H. P."

"These games bore me," Lian said.

She went back in the kitchen, leaving Barbara and Ben to play their old game.

"It's a hard one," Ben said as he poked at the fire.

"I don't understand," I said.

"Didn't you ever play Ghost?" said Barbara.

"Nope."

"It's a game Ben and I used to play for hours on Fire Island. I give you three letters from the middle of a word and you have to guess the rest of the word. Like, ummm . . . NGU."

I thought for a moment.

"Unguent?"

"That's right. I was thinking of penguin but unguent's good. When you get a good one it's tough. Ben! DHP? There is no such word."

"Oh, yes there is," he said.

"I give up. Tell me!"

"No. You have to work on it more."

He enjoyed teasing her. His eyes were so dark they twinkled as he laughed.

After dinner, Barbara and I went to sleep in Ben's studio. It was an uninsulated room that had been added to the house, but we were warm under an electric blanket. The room smelled of linseed oil and paint. There were dusty canvases stacked against the walls. There was one on an easel, but it looked like it had been untouched for a long time. Another frustrated artist. I was so glad I didn't have to live that way anymore, thanks to Barbara.

Next morning, Ben drove us around to show Barbara some houses he had listed for summer rental. He showed us one in Amagansett that was right on the edge of the dune, facing the Atlantic Ocean. The house wasn't anything special, except when you walked out on the huge deck and watched the surf pound on the beach a hundred yards from your feet. The beach was empty. And the ocean was empty too, stretching blue-black to the horizon and beyond. Barbara and I walked along the beach, our bare feet just out of reach of the pounding waves. The ocean was on our left, the dunes covered with beach plum towered high on our right, and the deserted beach stretched to the horizon in front of us.

"What do you think of it?" Barbara asked.

"I think eight thousand dollars for a summer rental is a lot of money."

"What do you think about getting it for the summer? Just for us. Houses on the ocean go fast. We can't wait long."

"Wait a minute," I said. "I couldn't possibly afford it, to split it or anything. I couldn't rent a doghouse out here."

"Okay, right now I'm making a fiat," she said. "And my fiat is that there will be no more talk of money. You want a beach house? We'll get one. And it won't cost me that much. All my friends are in the business, sort of. My accountant laid it all out to me last year how I could entertain and write a lot of it off. I've got a lot of summers to pay back. Ben and Lian and Dale and Samantha and David and Roxanne and Billy and Jessica and Al and . . . and there's a room for you to write. You could write all summer with no one to bother you. I'd come out on weekends. Well? What do you think?"

"It's fantastic. I was thinking about my son just then. I have enough money now to go to court in Arizona. Good things happen so easily around you, maybe even . . . If I could get a visit with him this summer, this beach house would be a perfect place. If that would be all right with you. I know you don't like kids that much."

"Of course," she said, and then she paused for a moment. "How old is your son now?"

"Let me think. It's been so long. Thirteen or fourteen. Thirteen."

"You miss him."

"Oh, after the first five years you get used to it."

She took my arm and stared out at the ocean.

"There's plenty of room for him. Any time you want."

The life I had fantasized with Barbara was beginning to happen. I felt loved and warm and cared for.

"Okay," I said. "You're on. Let's get the house."

Ben's voice boomed behind us, louder than the surf.

"Barbara! Did you figure it out yet?"

Ben and Lian walked arm in arm toward us. Their twin boys splashed in the waves, not feeling the cold.

"Don't bother Aunt Barbara, boys!" Lian called.

"Figure out what?" Barbara yelled back.

"The ghost! DHP!" he said.

"Oh no! I really give up, Ben. Tell me. What is it?"

"Jodhpur," he said.

"Ohhh," she groaned. "You have the most unbelievable ghosts, Ben. Got any more?"

"Just wait," he said, grinning devilishly.

Barbara made arrangements with Ben to rent the house. And the next weekend we had dinner with the other family in that feud. Samantha and Dale Wensley lived in Great Neck, also on Long Island, but a lot closer to New York City. Samantha was Barbara's closest woman friend and she wanted me to meet them.

"Now don't forget," Barbara said as we drove out, "you mustn't mention Ben and Lian when we're there."

"I know, I remember."

"I just don't want you to let it slip."

"I won't. What is that all about, anyway?"

"Oh, Ben and Dale had some silly argument a long time ago. I love them both dearly but they can't be in the same room together. Samantha and Lian have never met. Lian doesn't know anything about it. I mean, she knows their names and she knows they're my dearest friends and she's always trying to get us together, but I always make some excuse. So you'll just never talk about them."

"Sure," I said. "That must have been some argument."

"No, not really. They're stubborn. Sam was going out with Dale and Ben at the same time. I saw Sam and Ben having lunch in the Down Under Café in Rockefeller Center. Sam never knew I caught her cheating on Dale. She wasn't married to him yet, but she was talking about it. She couldn't make up her mind between Ben and Dale so one night they all met in the Carnegie Coffee Shop to decide who would get her."

"Sounds like *Pylon*," I said. "Robert Stack throwing sugar-cube dice for Dorothy Malone."

"They wish it was so romantic. They're a couple of Portnoys."

"They're both your close friends, how do you manage to keep them apart? Do you always split your life between them?"

"It's hard sometimes, but I love them both and I want to stay friends. Dale is a big screenwriter. Ever since he won his Oscar he spends most of his time in Hollywood. That way he and Sam don't have to deal with the fact that they don't live together anymore. For some reason they still keep up a front. And what a front! Sam has the biggest tits in the world."

Samantha may very well have had the biggest tits in the world and she wore a black dress with a plunging neckline to show them off. She had her long hair in a pony tail. Dale had just come in from the Coast. He had curly blondish hair and he was wearing a safari jacket. He had good grass. He nodded quietly on the end of the couch while Samantha questioned me endlessly.

"I couldn't wait to meet you. You don't understand, Barbara. You being so in love is a terrible blow to us married women. All those years that you were unhappy with men reassured us. We envied you your career, but seeing how unhappy you were we could always kid ourselves that a woman couldn't have both a career and a happy love life. Your misery was a security blanket for us to hide under. Now that you have this prince here, I don't know what we're going to do. I suppose we'll all have to go back to work."

Barbara sat next to Sam and put her arms around her.

"Sam is my dearest friend," Barbara said. "When I finally broke up with Abe after five years of waiting for his kids to grow up so he could

65

leave his wife, I was so depressed I tried to take every pill in this house. Samantha nursed me out of that depression. She came over every morning and night to feed me and take care of me. I was a wreck. I also had a back attack at the same time. I was paralyzed for weeks. Samantha and Dale used to carry me from place to place. Sam massaged my back every night so I could sleep. That's where I got the recipe for chicken soup. She made it for me every day. I don't know what I would have done without her. She lived right around the corner then at the Carnegie Apartments. You know, right above Carnegie Hall?"

"I know it very well," I said. "My wife used to live there."

"Oh, really?" said Sam. "What did she look like?"

"Ugly!" Barbara blurted out. "She's an awful creature!"

I described my wife and Sam's eyes lit up.

"Oh, I *knew* Maggie," Sam said. "You're wrong, Barbara. I don't know what she's like to live with but she is a beautiful woman."

"Oh, no she's not!" Barbara shouted, and with that she let loose a stream of invective about Maggie that I had never heard before. I had seen Barbara angry, but never like this. This was a level of rage that was beyond anger. I didn't know she was still so mad at Margaret. Her anger disappeared again as suddenly as it came. Maybe it was Dale's dope that had released it. There was a long moment of silence while we all came back to normal. Samantha spoke first.

"Really, Barbara, she was quite attractive."

Barbara turned on Sam with a fury that made Sam instinctively back away.

"Don't you ever mention her in front of me again! You hear me?"

"Sure, Barbara, sure," Sam said.

Though they claimed to be the closest of friends, there was a hostility between Barbara and Samantha just below the surface that didn't seem to have any logical explanation. Later that night when we were in bed, Barbara revealed a jealousy I had never seen in her toward another woman.

"Couldn't keep your eyes off her big tits, could you?"

"It's kind of hard not to, the way she dresses."

"Don't worry," Barbara said. "I understand. Every man wants to get his hands on them at least once."

"Babe, I was nursed till I was nearly two years old so I've had my fill. They're no big deal to me."

"Oh, yeah!"

"Samantha is the exact opposite of the type of woman who attracts me."

"I don't believe you. What is your type?"

"You're my type."

"Ohhh," she groaned, "I don't need bullshit."

"No. I mean that. The only thing about you that's not my type is that I am usually attracted to women with very short hair."

"Oh, really? You never told me that."

"There's something about it. Maybe it takes care of any latent homosexuality I have, but I don't think it's that. There's something extremely sensual about the back of a woman's neck."

"Why didn't you ever tell me that before?" she said.

"No reason. I like you exactly the way you are. I like you to be yourself."

When Barbara came home the following evening she whipped the scarf from her head revealing a new hair cut. She had only a cap of very short, ragged hair.

"Do you like it?" she said.

"I like it very much."

I mussed her hair and nuzzled her neck.

"It's very sexy, but I'm not sure I like the responsibility of you changing yourself to suit me."

"Well, I was going to do it first for you, but when I thought about it, I really liked the idea. I never did it before because most men like a woman to have long hair."

She tousled her new cut with both hands.

"But now that it's cut, I love it! I feel like I've lost ten pounds and it's off my face forever. I don't have to do anything but wash it. I never want to tease and fuss with hair again. You really like it?"

"Yep. Very much."

"You don't secretly like Sam's long hair better?"

"Nope."

"Good."

Barbara kept that short, ragged cut for as long as we lived together.

EIGHT

The newsroom was filled with the laughter of the staff just before quitting for lunch. I sat on Barbara's desk, joking with Jill and Nicole while I waited for her to get back from a meeting. Margaret appeared in the doorway.

"I've been searching this building all over for you," she said.

Everyone in the newsroom looked up. They froze when they remembered Maggie's last visit. She stood silently, holding Alfie's leash out for me to take, almost as though it was her own. I had to get her out of there before Barbara came in and there was a repeat of their last meeting. I quickly crossed the newsroom and took her by the arm.

"You're getting out of here, now!" I said.

She wouldn't leave. She struggled with me so I pulled her into an empty office.

"What do you want here?" I said.

"I'm not leaving unless you take care of the dog."

She opened the suitcase and showed me what she had brought. It was full of cans of dog food and Alfie's water dish. I had to smile in spite of myself. All the world was a stage to Maggie. She lived key moments of her life with broad, theatrical gestures.

"Here's all his food and his dish and . . . "

Now that she had my attention, she chattered on as though there was nothing unusual about her visit. I picked up the suitcase and led her out of the office.

"What are you doing?" she said.

"I'm going home with you."

"Well, I'm glad you're finally—"

"Shut up!" I said. "Don't talk to me. Don't say another word."

I took her down in the elevator and out of the building. I looked straight ahead as we walked the ten blocks home. I had to do something. But what? Nothing I said made any difference to her. So, what's new? She never listened to you before, schmuck! Why should she change now? The dog was only an excuse. She was going to pull these games whenever she pleased. And if I didn't do something to stop her, she was only going to get worse. She had hurt Barbara once and put her in a back brace for weeks. She would do it again any time she was angry enough. I couldn't allow her to jeopardize this relationship. I had to stop her. There was only one thing I could think of that she might understand. Something that I had never done before in my life.

Margaret opened the door to let me in. Alfie was pacing nervously. He was a red-haired Irish terrier whose ears refused to flop down as a good terrier's should. I dropped the suitcase to the floor. Maggie put her hand to her forehead to indicate her great anguish.

"He's been just *too* much for me to manage."

"Now you listen to me," I said quietly. "I told you the first time you prowled outside the apartment, you were never to come near that woman again. And then last week you came up to the editing room and got into a fight with her—"

"Oh, I didn't do anything," she said. "She's exaggerating."

I slapped her face.

"Oh!"

She was more surprised than anything. I had never touched her in all the years of our marriage. She stared at me in disbelief.

"What do you think this is," I said, "some kind of play you're acting in? These are other people's lives."

"Ohhh, don't you give me—"

I slapped her harder. Her head flew back from that one. She recovered quickly and held her head up high.

"How *dare* you!" she gasped.

"You won't listen to me," I said. "Apparently I have to make you listen so that you will understand that I am dead serious. Now shut up!"

"You can't—"

"Shut up and listen!" I yelled.

I slammed her back against the wall. She staggered. I grabbed her hair and yanked her face to mine. I slapped her mouth again and again, talking in between the slaps.

"I don't want to ever . . . ever . . . ever see you in that studio . . . or anywhere around that woman again. . . . "

She lifted her hands but I hit them and her face and neck and arms. I

70

hit her coldly and mechanically. I felt no anger. I didn't like what I was doing, but I had to do something. Alfie watched nervously, unsure what he should do.

"And if you ever do . . . what you're getting now . . . is nothing to what you'll get . . . when I get my hands on you . . . . Is . . . that . . . clear?"

She sobbed hysterically. I pushed her up against the wall, yelling inches from her reddened face.

"Is that clear?!"

She cried so loud I could hardly hear myself.

"Answer me, dammit! Is that clear?"

I reached back to hit her again. Her hands flew up to protect.

"I can hear you!" she said. "Don't hit me!"

"Now, if you insist that I take this dog, I will take him. But I will not take him home. I will take him to . . . "

She turned her face away. I gripped her chin and forced her to face me.

"Listen to me, dammit!" I yelled. "If you insist, I will take this dog to the ASPCA. They'll hold him for three days, and if no one claims him, they'll kill him. No fucking euthemism, they'll kill him! Now, which do you want?"

She started sobbing again.

"I assume then you want me to take him? Do you understand what I'm saying to you?"

She sobbed louder.

"Do you understand?"

She wouldn't answer. I shook her and slapped her again. She stopped crying instantly. All pain gone, she snarled at me.

"Yes, I understand! You don't have to hit me again."

"And you are never to threaten that woman again. Is that clear?"

"Ohhh!" She was triumphant. "Did I upset your sweet, marvelous—"

I slapped her again.

"I mean it," I said. "I'm not going through this one more time."

I let her go and she collapsed on the floor. Alfie sniffed at her anxiously. He looked up at me, not sure who the enemy was. I shouted down at her.

"And if you want to do something useful for the first time in your life, then get off your ass . . . "

I kicked her ass hard and she slid a little on the highly polished floor.

" . . . and get . . . "

I kicked her again.

" . . . a goddamn . . . "

And again.

" . . . fucking . . . "

And again.

" . . . job!"

By the last kick she had slid across the room. She lay there sobbing in a silken heap. I put the leash on Alfie and took him in a taxi to the ASPCA. He jumped nervously all over the seat. He wasn't used to riding in cars. I stroked him and scratched his stuckup ears. He quieted down, resting his muzzle on my leg. I scratched his wiry back the way he liked.

"I'm sorry Alfie, but nobody's going to spoil this. No more."

There was no pleasure in hitting Maggie. Most people learn early how to stake out their territory and fight for it. I was learning for the first time who I was and what was mine. I had staked out that bit of territory with Barbara in the middle and I was learning what it took to defend it. I had always capitulated to women in the interest of being loved. Now I was fighting back. Maggie had been so accustomed to getting her way with me, that she fought down to the wire. There had never been such violence in my life before, but if this is what it took, so be it.

I carried Alfie into the antiseptic white tile waiting room. Dog yelps and whines echoed from somewhere far away. I filled out the form. The steel counter was strangely warm under my fingers. I slid the form across and the man silently gave me a receipt. I handed Alfie over the counter. He looked lost and scared. I turned away and walked out of the damned place.

I was alone in the editing room. I was still shaken from the experience with Maggie as I finished trimming and cleaning Barbara's film. It was going on the air that night. I dropped it off at the studio. Barbara saw me and came over. She looked worried. I kissed her lightly.

"Hi, Babe," I said. "How'd the meeting go?"

"Are you all right? Jill told me your wife was here again. What happened?"

"Don't worry, Babe. She won't bother you again."

And she never did. I was fired at the end of the week. Out of curiosity, I asked the production manager if it was because of Margaret's visits to the studio. He wouldn't give me a straight answer, but this did provide me with something to say to her lawyer when we all met to discuss alimony.

"Two hundred fifty dollars a week?" I said. "I'm on unemployment!"

"That's not my fault," she said.

"Oh, yes it is," I said. "I got laid off because of your rampages through the studio. Do you wonder that they fired me?"

"You can get it from *her*!" she yelled at me. Then she yelled at her lawyer, "Make him! Make him get it from that homewrecker! That cunt he lives with!"

"I'm afraid we can't do that," her lawyer said, "but . . ."

He opened a file folder and slipped some papers out while he spoke.

" . . . but we have records from your production company for nineteen sixty-nine and seventy, showing receipt of a great deal of money."

My books. She had them all.

"That's true," I said, "but that money wasn't my income. I subcontracted a lot of commercials and other films. Most of that money was paid out to crews and equipment rentals, studios, cast, lab costs . . . I got a producer's fee and fees for work as a director and sometimes an editor. That's assuming I brought it in under budget. Very little of that money went to me."

"How do you intend to prove that?" he said.

"That's no problem. I have all the cancelled checks."

"What checks?" he said. "Can you show them to me?"

"Well . . . I, ahh . . . I left them back at . . . "

At that moment I must have looked like a silent movie straight man just before he gets hit in the face with a cream pie, because that's what I felt like, innocent and dumb, even as the pie was whizzing through the air.

"She's got them, I suppose," I said. "With all my other stuff."

"Really?" her lawyer said. "Well, I wouldn't know about that."

"She can't do that!" I said.

"Do you want to sue her?" he said.

"But they're mine!"

He shook with barely stifled laughter as the pie hit home.

"That was your first mistake," he laughed. "The way I see it, we have evidence of your income being somewhere around seventy thousand dollars a year. Unless you can prove otherwise."

I turned to my lawyer. "Can she do this?"

"Oh, yeah," he said blithely, "she can claim anything she wants about your income when you were together."

"Will a judge believe her?" I said.

"Of course. It's up to you to prove that she's wrong."

"But—Well, let's sue then," I said. "I need those checks to prove it."

"Suing her will cost you more than she's asking. If you succeed. And it seems iffy to me."

This is *my* lawyer talking. He took me aside.

"Look, there's nothing you can do," he said. "I suggest you pay."

"Two hundred fifty dollars a week?" I said. "That's insane! I believe she should have money to readjust for a year or so. That's fair. When we separated I sent her almost all the money I made. I have the cancelled checks to prove that. But not alimony for the rest of her life. We had no children. We were only married a few years. Can a woman do this in this day and age?"

"She'll settle for less," he said.

"For what? Two hundred? A hundred fifty? Unemployment is *ninety-five* dollars a week."

"Borrow it for the time being," he said.

"I can't borrow a dime. My credit is shot. I have no money and there's nothing I can see coming in in the near future. Don't you understand the position I'm in?"

"There's nothing more I can do," he shrugged.

There wasn't anything more I could do, either. I sent her whatever I could, whenever I had it, but it was never enough.

NINE

I'll always remember that summer at the beach in '73. Sun, sand, and ocean, all the time to enjoy it, and all paid for. I obeyed Barbara's fiat and I didn't think about money. I was transported into another world. We just worked hard and played hard. I had put in enough time at NET to qualify for unemployment and for the first time in twenty-odd years, I didn't have to worry about the rent. The elusive "time to write" materialized. I dusted off the last screenplay I had been writing. What a confused jumble it was. It looked different to me now. Every idea fell into place. I knew exactly what to do with it. I schlepped my typewriter and a typing table out to the house and wrote for weeks on end. There was so much stuff stored up in me, I didn't know what a writer's block was. I couldn't get it on paper fast enough.

On weekends we'd fill the three bedrooms and all the living room couches with friends. Barbara wanted to pay back all her visits as the lone woman semi-invalid guest they had all cared for all those tired weekends without her married men. Other weekends we had Jill and Nicole and people who worked with us at NET. It was never too crowded. They'd spill out on to the vast, empty beach as soon as the sun was up. We fed and hosted our guests happily from breakfasts to the late evenings when we'd collect in the tiny kitchen stoned, drunk, and laughing, washing the last of the weekend's dishes before leaving for New York.

How can I describe how great the beaches of eastern Long Island are? If you've been there, you know. If you haven't seen them you'll never believe it. Just imagine the greatest ocean beach in the world, empty, sloping sharply up to a twenty-foot dune, crested with beach grass and tangled bayberry bushes. Behind the dune put an isolated house. You like 1842 landed gentry? You got it. You like Bauhaus? You got that too. Migrant workers from South Carolina digging in a potato field fifty yards from the ocean turn you on? Eastern Long

Island has them too. People tend to think of it as part of New York City, but it's two counties and a hundred miles away from Brighton Beach.

Barbara had just taken up tennis and she loved it. I had wanted to play for some time. I hadn't played much of anything when I was young and when I was older there never seemed to be time or money for such things. Now, all I had to do was mention it and we signed up at a local tennis club, paid for from Barbara's checkbook. She was a bit awkward on the tennis court. Her back muscles were weak and she favored them, but she played hard. And she always played to win, even if she was only showing me the basics. Tennis suited her warring spirit.

She was like that with her poker games. Barbara could go on till six in the morning. Even if her back muscles stiffened and became painful, she'd deal yet another hand while the rest of the couples fell asleep on their cards. I joined the poker game a few nights, but I couldn't get that life-or-death interest in games that Barbara had.

We had a big color TV set in our rustic beach cottage and Barbara got the treat of her life when we watched the harbingers of Watergate. Walter Cronkite was only talking about a couple of Cuban refugees, but Barbara immediately shouted,

"It's *him*! *He's* behind it. I know it."

When Barbara said *him* she said it like a curse uttered with all the repugnance reserved for Beelzebub. She meant only one being, her personal devil incarnate, Richard Milhous Nixon. We brought home each afternoon paper, thinking to save its historic headline, then the very next day that would be supplanted by another historic headline, which would be surpassed the next week by an even more historic headline until it was obvious this was going to run longer and deeper than anyone (besides Barbara) dared imagine. We threw out all our "historic" front page headlines and watched, fascinated, the daily descent into the ninth circle of Watergate.

We planned to move into the beach house for Barbara's August vacation, but until then we divided our time between Amagansett and the city. Barbara had little to do at the station but attend staff meetings to plan out the next season so we were able to make do with four- and sometimes five-day weekends during June and July. Not so bad. We got a car to make the two-hour drive to happiness and Barbara immediately developed a very personal relationship with it.

"I love this car so much. Gooood Bernie," she cooed, stroking his dashboard affectionately. "You'll get us out to the house one more time, won't you?"

Bernie didn't talk much, but he ran. Bernie was a dented ten-year-old Ford station wagon Barbara had located through a friend in the poker game. She named it Bernie in his honor. She didn't drive and wanted no part of it, so Bernie was my responsibility. A car is a pain in the ass in midtown Manhattan, but it is handy for Long Island summer weekends. I insisted that I buy it and pay for the garage and the insurance and whatever else was needed to keep it running. It was my way of sharing our summer expenses. I couldn't get too involved with Barbara's anthropomorphization, but Bernie was a living presence to her and she felt very safe and warm driving in him—it.

"People don't keep old cars nowadays," I mused. "There used to be a certain cachet to an old station wagon. Can't you remember all those New Yorker stories that began with, 'The battered station wagon waited for him in the Westport parking lot. Harold dreaded the sight of it . . . ' Or, Hemingway with his big villa in Cuba driving an old 'Bueeck' with the wood falling off the sides. I mean, there's a romance to it that seems to have disappeared."

"Daddy always had a new car," she said. "No matter how strapped he was, one thing he had to have was a new Cadillac every year. And they always made fun of me because of it."

"Who?"

"The kids in the neighborhood. Everybody at school used to laugh at me when they saw it. Well, you know . . . "

Yes, I did know. I didn't say anything. I look like such a WASP, Americans relax their native anti-semitism in my presence and freely utter words like "jewmobile."

"It got so I dreaded to go for a ride in it," she went on, "I hated it so much. Bernie suits me just fine."

She stroked the dash again.

"Do you remember the way Mrs. Smith stared at this car when we drove up?" I said. "She must have thought she had rented her beach house to the Joad family come to Amagansett, until you whipped out your checkbook for all four payments in advance."

We both laughed. Then she got serious again.

"You have to promise me something," she said.

"Sure."

"Well, you know about my money and all, I don't want us to have any secrets. But my friends. I've never told my friends. Oh, they know Daddy gave me some stocks, but they think it's like what they have, you know, twenty, thirty thousand. They don't have any idea how much. But they work so hard for their money and to get their beach houses, and you know, they wouldn't understand."

"They all seem so nice to me," I said. "I'm sure it wouldn't mean anything to them."

"Money does funny things to people. You don't know. They'd all resent me if they knew I didn't work for every penny like they have to. I know it. But regardless, this is how I've set it up and this is what I want you to do."

Those things you know and don't know at the same time. I remember the first time I came in contact with it. I was cleaning up the living room. Barbara and I had an easy understanding about house-work; whoever wanted to clean up did it. I was vacuuming behind the couch and found this big crumpled paper shopping bag. It looked like garbage, but Barbara kept all her research for shows in bags like this. It might be valuable, you never know. I checked inside. The first thing I saw was a folder with that intricate engraving used for money or stocks. It was a municipal bond for some mid-American city's water department. I had never seen one before. I knew it was valuable and I thought maybe she had misplaced it, but the bag was stuffed with similar bonds. I counted almost fifty thousand dollars worth that had been sitting in this bag behind the couch all the time I'd been in the house. My stomach fell. Barbara used the same broker in Fort Lauder-dale her father did. I thought he took care of all her money with the stock transfer receipts and dividend checks Barbara received regularly. I hid the bonds in the safest place I could find, way at the back of the bedroom closet. When Barbara came home that night, I held the shopping bag out to her.

"Barbara."

"Hmmm?"

"I found this behind the couch."

"Oh yeah."

She seemed distant, uninterested in the bonds I held out to her.

"Well, ah, ever since I've been here," I said, "There have been two robberies in the building."

"Oh, I suppose I should do something about them, shouldn't I?" she replied.

"I think this is in the neighborhood of urgent. I mean, anybody can take these anywhere and cash them when the coupons are due. They're just like cash."

I didn't know whether they were in the category of negotiable bonds, but I didn't want to find out.

"Don't you have a safe deposit box?" I asked.

"Oh, yeah. There's one at Banker's Trust," she replied, excited now. "Jim and I, we—we got one to hide the Schiavone tapes from the CIA while we were cutting the spy show. We figured that would be the only safe place . . ."

"No, I mean for you, personally."

"I never had anything to put in."

"Would you do me a great favor?" I said. "Tomorrow? Before you go to work? Go to your bank and get a safe deposit box. They're very cheap."

"Yeah, okay. You're right. There's more, too."

She opened the drawers of a bureau in the living room. Green bonds, brown ones, blue ones popped out of the stuffed drawer. I couldn't believe it. We sorted them out. They were new. The first coupons wouldn't come due till September. She had never counted them before. She had had almost a hundred fifty thousand dollars worth of bonds laying around the house.

She was grinning when she came home from work the next night.

"Well, I took a safe deposit box today like you told me to, and—" She started to laugh.

"What's the matter?" I said.

"As long as I was going to the bank, I figured I'd drop my laundry off, too, so I stuffed it all in the shopping bag. After I signed for the box, the man asked me if there was anything I wanted to put in it now, and I said yes, and started pulling bonds out of this shopping bag full of laundry. I piled them on his desk and when he realized how much there was he got so scared he got a guard over to watch. I piled all the laundry on his desk, too, so I could check the bottom of the bag and make sure I didn't take any to Manny mixed in with my underwear. I think he thought I was very strange, but I took care of it."

"Good, that's a load off my mind."

She handed me a key.

"Here," she said.

"What is it?"

"It's for the box."

"What am I going to do with it? I can't open the box."

"I had an extra one made," she said. "I'm always losing my keys and if I lose this one, I'm up shit creek."

She was always losing her keys. She carried them loose in the bottom of her bag buried in the Valium and tobacco shreds. I went to Bloomingdale's that week and bought her a gold key ring built around an elephant's head. Inside the box with it, I put a card on which I had written, "So you won't ever forget. From your friend Sam." I gave it to her that night. She read the card, then hugged and kissed me. She never forgot her keys again.

An old client of mine offered me a well-paying freelance job. I put my screenplay aside for the few weeks it would take. Barbara was pissed that this work took me away from writing.

"That's why I rented the house," she said. "Why are you working? You don't need the money. I have plenty for both of us. You just have to ask me. I wish you would get to your writing."

"There is an institution in New York City called Alimony Jail, for one thing. It's like the debtors' prisons they used to have in England."

"I know about it. I was going to do a story on it."

"There are certain expenses I can't and will not ask you for. There is a lawyer for my divorce. There is alimony for my wife. I don't believe in permanent alimony, but she does need money to get on her feet. I'm certainly not going to ask you for that. There's a lawyer in Arizona for my son. There is back support for my son. There are current support payments to my son. You're loving and kind and generous and I love you for it, but I can't ask you for money, and certainly not for that."

"Hunh! Well, I still think you don't have to work *that* much."

How strange. In her own way, Barbara had the same unreal idea of money that all my wives had. It was never something you had to work for. They couldn't understand that you had to give something to get it. Money to them was something that was just out there somewhere, waiting to be dispensed by some great father in the sky.

It was never my plan to be dependent on Barbara, even though I know that would have pleased her. I had been supporting myself and my varied families ever since I could remember. I had taken care of myself for too long to change now. Living with Barbara, I could afford to work for a month and write for a month. This was luxury enough for me. I'm a twenty-four-hour writer. I can't write in those few hours after a full working day. The work I do is complicated and creative and comes from the same well as my writing. When I finish a day's movie work, that well is dry. I like to work for long spells and then write for long spells. This also keeps the unemployment up to date. It's the nearest you can get to being a state-supported artist in this country. Barbara's disappointment notwithstanding, I was always writing and accumulating a body of work. It was slow, but I didn't need immediate gratification. I could be patient and write at my own pace.

Now that I had some money coming in, I tried to take care of the many loose ends of my life. I wanted to reach some kind of settlement with Maggie, but she was making it impossible. She had come up with a new demand. She wanted 15 percent of all the income I would ever make until I died, and a 15-percent interest in any creative work I would produce in any form. Preposterous? That's what I thought. But my lawyer said she could do it and keep it in court for years. He told me he was sure she'd settle out of court for seven and a half percent. This was a second lawyer. He was doing a great job.

My dream of having my son visit at the beach house ended up just that, a dream. I had flown to Arizona and reopened the lawsuit. I had three decrees awarding me visitation, but none of them seemed to matter in this new state. I flew back to New York without having had even a glimpse of Robin. True to form, his mother had refused an out-of-court settlement. Pat was going to make a battle out of it. But this was going to be the last one. Now I could carry the lawsuit wherever she moved, as long as she wanted. Living with Barbara made that a reality. Life was opening up for me in every way now.

I had dreamed that Barbara was going to get me contacts and help my career, but she didn't have to. She gave me something far more valuable. I had been so desperate in the last years that at the point where a client asked how much money I wanted, I crawled and hoped I wasn't asking too much. And he would of course think I wasn't worth much. Now I wasn't so desperate. I asked for what I was worth and I got it. I changed into a "consultant" overnight and doubled the fee for my brain. That's what living with Barbara did for me. She gave me breathing space. I could write and work and live without that day-to-day and minute-to-minute money pressure that had haunted me since I was seventeen. With that pressure removed, I grew rapidly. Living with Barbara I had a new sense of myself, and all my work showed it. I was issuing fully formed out of my Athena's head.

I had many good times in my life which I had shared with many loving ladies (my wives definitely included), but that summer I experienced a carefree kind of happiness that I had never known before. The fantasy life I had dreamed of with Barbara came true and the reality was even better. Only one thing interfered with our perfect happiness that summer: Barbara's anxiety attacks returned with a vengeance.

TEN

Barbara had had anxiety attacks before, but as we grew closer and our love deepened, her attacks happened more often and they seemed to get worse and worse. They seemed to plague her in inverse proportion to our happiness. This was a paradox that would haunt our relationship to the end. I became aware of the seriousness of this early in June when our life was at its happiest. I was alone at home writing one morning when I heard a clicking, a sort of scratching sound as though someone was fumbling with the lock. I opened the door and Barbara fell into my arms.

"Babe . . . "

She was shaking. Her skin was white. I helped her take the few steps to the couch and she fell on it, gasping for breath.

"Babe, what is it?"

"Water, quick!"

I hurried for some water. The elevator man stood in the doorway, looking concerned.

"It's all right, Louie," I said. "I'll take care of her."

I closed the door as I passed with the water and sat beside Barbara. She had pulled a plastic vial of Valium from her purse and took a few, while gripping the glass of water with her shaking hands. She still gasped as she tried to speak.

"I didn't think I'd make it," she said.

"Just lie down and take it easy. What happened?"

She lay down on the couch and I began to gently massage her back as she spoke.

"I'm not sure. I was walking up to . . . I couldn't get a cab in front. I walked up to Seventh Avenue. Just as I stepped off the curb I got dizzy. Everything went black. The next thing I knew a policeman was helping me up. He said I was lying unconscious in the middle of

Seventh Avenue. He helped me back to the front door and then Louie got me here."

"Your slacks are smudged, see? Look at this bruise on your leg. You really took a fall."

"Oh why? Why?" she cried. "It's like when I got vertigo, but this is so much worse."

"An attack now and then doesn't mean—"

"It's been happening a lot. I didn't tell you and it hasn't been so bad. But lately for some reason, they've been getting worse. I don't understand why I'm having anxiety attacks now when I'm so happy. I thought they would never come back again, living with you!"

"Take it easy now," I said.

I massaged all the way up her back from the cleft of her behind to where her neck joined her skull. I could feel her slowly relax under my fingers.

"What does your doctor say about it?" I said.

"There's nothing he can do."

"What do you mean?"

"Anxiety attacks are a strange disease. They have no known cause."

My skeptical eyebrow raised itself voluntarily. I had not heard of such an extraterrestrial disease before. I assumed this was her doctor's way of trying to tell Barbara her anxiety was emotional, but there was an almost deliberate childishness to her response that bothered me. It was as though she purposely didn't want to understand what he was trying to tell her. She was too intelligent a woman not to understand that. Her breathing became more regular as I massaged her. Some color was coming back to her face. She tried to get up.

"It's late. I have to go to work."

"Stay, rest a while longer," I said. "You looked pretty wiped out when you came in."

"No! I've got a meeting with the station manager and I'm late already. I can't stand to talk to that worm."

"Well, don't go in. Even Ms. Marvelous takes a sick day."

Barbara suddenly exploded with a rage she had apparently kept bottled up for days.

"Oh, I can't. They don't realize. It's all going down the drain. It's Nixon's revenge on the media. And he's starting with Public Broadcasting. The whole Corporation for Public Broadcasting is a front for censorship. They take *one dollar* of federal funding and it's *gornisht*

84

helfen! There won't be an independent documentary on anything more controversial than the politics of the sixteenth century. It's going to be all arts and crafts from now on. I can see it coming. I couldn't stand the bullshit at the production staff meeting yesterday, and I said, 'You better start polishing your tap shoes, gang, because it's all over!' Quentin was *livid*! He wants the money to get a bigger office for himself. He doesn't care about broadcasting. I have to meet him in ten minutes. He wanted to see me alone this morning. Probably thinks he can shut me up. Ha! I have to go now. I feel better."

"Are you sure?"

She nodded and got to her feet.

"Let me help you down and I'll get you into a cab."

"No. No, you don't have to. Stay here and write. I'm fine."

Barbara was still a little shaky, but her anxiety seemed to have disappeared with the release of her pent-up hostility toward the station manager. We kissed goodbye and she left.

This was the first I saw of the crippling anxiety attacks that were to plague Barbara for the rest of our relationship. Those attacks, her helplessness, the fainting in the street, the drugs, were all new to me and I didn't like it. The people I had lived with before Barbara were as healthy as I was. My stepfather had been a Christian Scientist and while I couldn't make it with Big Mama Eddy, my mother had a similar secular attitude long before she met him. We didn't go to doctors except on rare occasions. My mother had all her children at home. I remember going to the doctor with her for an examination when she was pregnant with my half-brother. When she told the doctor she was going to have the baby at home he said she was crazy and refused to have anything to do with it. He washed his hands of her in his stainless steel basin. She shrugged and said she would call him when it was time and he could do whatever he liked. This was in New York City in the fifties, remember. No one did that in America outside of some remote hill folks.

When my mother's time came, the women gathered. The house was full of them: her mother, her sisters, her nieces, her friends. I can't remember anyone calling them. They just seemed to know when it was time. And they all seemed to know what to do. Her mother took charge (having had six of her own). They went through the preparations as though they had done it all their lives. And then, sure as shit, the doctor came too. My mother had a way with guilt.

She had four healthy children this way. Having all been nursed, we had great disease resistance. There were no patent medicines in the house, no aspirin or stuff like that, certainly no tranquilizers. We simply had no use for them. We didn't express pain. We didn't complain. We rarely got sick. Oh sure, we're human. I had had asthma attacks for twelve years and they were pretty bad, but I never took "medication." I got an attack the first winter I was married and, at eighteen years old, I decided I'd had enough of it. It was getting in the way of living. Also, since I had just exchanged Mother for Wife, I didn't need asthma any more. I knew something about breathing from the voice classes in Performing Arts. When the attacks came, I would stop what I was doing, concentrate, and control my breathing with my diaphragm muscles. The spasms went away. The attacks diminished over a period of two or three years and they never came back. I haven't had one since.

With this background, I was skeptical of Barbara's anxiety attacks from the beginning. Oh, I could see her symptoms. I didn't think she was lying, but she treated her attacks as an illness caused by unknown forces outside herself. She pictured herself as a helpless victim, but the fact that Barbara had these attacks for the three years we lived together and in all that time she never had one of the big fainting ones in my presence was evidence to me that she had some degree of unconscious control over them. They always happened when I wasn't present and then she stumbled back to the apartment, but the worst was past by then. I would help her to lie down, loosen her clothes, undress her, massage her, quiet her, talk to her, and get whatever I could for her, but I never cared for the role. My family was no training ground for the nursing of invalids.

What bothered me most was that Barbara's anxiety attacks conflicted with the image of the independent, stand-up lady that she represented to me. I once made a sardonic crack that her attacks reminded me of a Victorian maiden afflicted with "the vapors" no matter what the twentieth century euphemism might be. Barbara was shocked. She took her attacks with deadly seriousness. I quickly learned to shut my mouth when I felt my customary *galgenhumor* bubbling up. Never was heard a skeptical word in our home on the Central Park range. Certainly not from me. Barbara's attacks were a small price to pay for a relationship and a life that was still better than anything I had ever known.

But then Barbara's anxiety attacks went away as mysteriously as they came. She had been offered a job producing half-hour documentaries for a new show at CBS. It was only the local station, but her predictions about Public Television were happening already. Controversial programs disappeared right and left from the next season's calendar. There was suddenly no funding for them. The only outlet for serious documentaries seemed to be in commercial television. It looked like the right move for her. The only problem was that she'd have to start developing new stories right away and that took care of our August vacation. Barbara threw herself into her new job.

I would have thought that she'd have more conflict, more tension and therefore more anxiety, but it was the other way around. As soon as Barbara started at CBS, her anxiety went away. The only difference in her life was that now we hardly saw each other except on the weekends and sometimes not even then. Barbara worked till all hours. She got home late every night, popped two Valium as sleeping pills, and was unconscious immediately. It was almost as though our being together was somehow associated with her anxiety, but I couldn't imagine how that could be. We were perfectly happy living together. We had no conflicts. We had achieved our ideal relationship of two single people with no other responsibility except our separate careers and our love for each other. That was an ideal relationship that most modern couples wanted, wasn't it?

A funny thing happened to me that summer. Her name was Cathy.

ELEVEN

I had written some narration and I was doing the post-production for the American version of a series of BBC programs. Cathy was one of the receptionists at the editing studio. She couldn't have been more than twenty. That would be about my daughters' age, I realized with some surprise. She kept her wispy, blondish hair combed behind her head. Her large, inquisitive eyes peered out from behind stylish thin frame glasses and soaked up everything around her. She was a street kid from Bushwick Avenue, but she had a gentle way of talking that softened her original Brooklyn accent.

I passed her each morning while she filled the coffee machine. She had to lean over slightly to reach into the alcove where the machine was kept. She looked so cute that after I got to know her, I had to give her a "Good Morning" hug from behind. She didn't mind. She seemed to like it. She stayed hugged, not moving, absorbing the contact of my arms around her. As the days followed, the hugs were longer and squeezier, lifting her off the ground some mornings. She was so cute. That's all I meant by it: just saying "Hello" and "Good Morning." She did feel good in my arms, but I had no intention of cheating on Barbara and it stopped there.

She came in one morning dressed for a date after work. She wore a tight-waisted adaptation of a man's gray pinstriped suit complete with a gray derby. Her hair fell softly beneath the derby. Wearing men's clothing is a devastating sexual combination that can make a woman twenty times more feminine. When Cathy saw me staring at her, she tipped her derby and winked.

"Haddaya like my new lid?" she asked.

"Like it? You wipe me out, kiddo."

I put my arms around her tiny tailored waist.

"Your place or mine?" I asked, nuzzling her neck.

"Mmmmmm," she purred. "Except I don't think my boyfriend would like that."

"Well, we just won't tell him then, will we?"

She grinned. I hugged her especially long that morning.

You don't physically cut videotape like you do film. Each scene has to be rerecorded in sequence. Nowadays most of this work is done on ¾-inch cassettes or 1-inch tape, but then the basic machine was the Quad VTR, an electronic elephant covered with dials and VU meters. Huge reels of 2-inch videotape were mounted on the front of each of three of these machines. I sat with my editor in front of a computer terminal that ran the whole system and concentrated on the monitor as we made each tedious videotape edit. The high-pitched whine of three machines going at once was rather soothing in the darkened room. I felt a presence and Cathy appeared close at my side. She was fascinated with what I was doing. She asked me to explain it all to her. I can never resist that, so I gave her a long description of why and how I made each edit that was going through the monitor. She was so close to me that my arm naturally rose and rested on her hip as I talked. And that seemed so natural that I circled her waist with both arms and closed my hands over the subtle rise of her stomach. She asked me some more questions and her hair brushed my face each time she turned. I love to talk about my work. She liked to listen.

She sat in front of me one afternoon while we silently watched the monitor. I began to gently massage her shoulders. She relaxed under my fingers and stretched like a cat. I worked my way from her shoulders up her neck muscles to her head and then down her back between her shoulder blades. Her eyes got heavy and her head fell slightly forward. She seemed to float as I steadily kneaded the tension out of her strong young muscles. She woke with a start and stood up, looking around her as though she had forgotten where she was. She turned to look at me for a long moment. Then she left the studio and went back to her desk without a word.

I spent most of my lunch hours in the VTR room, going over my notes and timings for the afternoon session. Or sometimes Danny, my editor, would put up the show we had completed and I would eat my lunch while screening the morning's work on the monitor. On one of these lunch hours Cathy came in with her lunch to join me in silently watching my show in the darkened room. Somehow she ended up sitting on my lap. I had both my arms around her and she put her hands on mine as though to keep them there. And, of course, I couldn't help but react to those exquisitely shaped handfuls that squirmed on my lap as she turned to whisper a question about the show. But that's all that was on my mind.

I was wrapping up the last day of editing when Cathy called from the reception desk.

"I heard you were leaving," she said.

"Yeah. This is my last day."

"Danny was going to take you out for lunch on your last day. The company pays."

"Well, I don't have time this week. I'll have to take a raincheck."

"Ohh . . . " She was disappointed.

"To tell you the truth," I said, "Danny bores the shit out of me. After three weeks in the same room with him, I prefer not to have lunch with him. I don't care who pays."

"That's too bad. He told me I could go with you. I wanted to see you before you left."

Hmmm.

"Will you be coming back with another job soon?" she asked.

"Ahhh, no. Not right away. Not that I know of."

"I'll miss you."

Was she serious?

"Yeah, well, I'm going to miss you, too," I said. "Really, I'd like that . . . to have lunch with you . . . . It would be fun."

My thinking got tangled up here. All of what passes for my good intentions flew out the window. I went for it.

"But I'm not thinking about food," I said. "What I really want is to have you for lunch. At your place."

That should have made her stop and think. She didn't do either.

"Okay," she immediately replied, "but today's not good for me. How about next week? Tuesday. I can get Marilyn to cover for me on Tuesdays."

I automatically checked my appointment book. Tuesday was free.

"Ahh, yeah," I said. "Tuesday's fine for me."

I did not ask if her boyfriend would mind.

"But I'll meet you outside," she said. "I don't want anybody around here to know. They'll never let me alone if they find out. Promise?"

"Of course. I'm not that kind of guy. Don't worry."

"Then we can go to my apartment."

"Great. See you then."

It was so easy, just like when I was married. I was looking forward to my upcoming infidelity but I was troubled, too. I thought a lot about it when Barbara and I went out to the beach house that weekend. I thought I was in love with Barbara and here I was coolly cheating on her. Why? Let's not forget Cathy. She was a very appealing little girl. She put out signals and I responded. How could I say no? Well, technically I suppose I had asked her. I know I didn't have to ask her but how could I not? *Why* should I not? I'll tell you why not, you fool, because you don't want to threaten your relationship with Barbara. It has all the promise of a long-term arrangement that will be very good for you. You don't want to wreck it by getting caught at an afternoon's roll in the hay. But I wasn't intending to get caught. Doing it was what bothered me and yet I knew very well that I was going to see Cathy for a long lunch next Tuesday. But why had I asked her?

My mother always used to say, "There's only one way to keep a man at home: drain him dry!" It was true that with Barbara working so much we hardly saw each other during the week and rarely made love except on the weekend. But it wasn't that. Something else was happening inside me and I couldn't figure it out. Was I unconsciously feeling a rivalry between me and Barbara's work? Was I afraid that her work load and her Valium were ways of getting away from me? Was I feeling a rejection from her in all that and was this a way of asserting my ego? Or were these only fancy ways of saying "A stiff cock has no conscience"? Take your pick. It was probably all of the above. The only thing I knew for sure was that I couldn't wait to get back to New York and see that cute little kid from Bushwick Avenue.

I had no doubt that Cathy would be there on Tuesday. She was waiting outside the studio all perky and happy as I arrived. She was as excited as if she was going on a picnic. We hurried away before anyone came out. I was peaking on an adrenalin high as I walked down the street arm in arm with her. Then I remembered we were only a few blocks from CBS. We walked right past the Four-a-delphia restaurant.

Barbara was likely to bump into us on her lunch. New York can be a very small town.

"I better not hold you so close," I said. "Someone from your office might see us."

"You're right. I wasn't thinking," she said breathlessly. "Thanks. I never did this before."

Now if Barbara ran into us at least we wouldn't look like high school sweethearts. I scanned the sidewalk for blocks ahead and turned away from passing taxis as we walked. My nerve endings were tinglingly alert all the way to Cathy's apartment. I only relaxed when she locked her door behind us. The first thing I noticed in the small apartment was the *Cosmopolitan* magazines all around, the cover girls unbuttoned to below the waist in standard *Cosmo* style. We put our arms around each other and kissed, for the first time ever. The tips of eyeglasses clicked together.

"Can I get ya' sump'n?" she asked, gesturing to a coffee table. She had laid out a neat smorgasbord of dope: grass, hash, and some white powder.

"Or there's wine and beer in the ice box," she added.

I could just see the article in one of those *Cosmos*, "Prepare a seductive lunch for your Matinee Man," or something.

"None of that stuff, thanks," I said, "but I will have some wine."

She poured two frosty glasses of white wine for us. We clinked and sipped and kissed again.

"I don't have a lotta time," she said, slipping easily out of her clothes. Ummmm! A young girl's body. She was just maturing, still losing her baby fat. She had little girl breasts, pointed way out. They would be full and large one day soon, but today she was like a bud about to flower. Her glasses on the end of her nose made her look even more naked. I quickly undressed.

"Wow! What a hunk a' man!" she said.

Now, where had she got that expression from? *Cosmo* again? She was too young to remember when that was a Hollywood code word to get around the Hayes office. Maybe that's what the girls in Brooklyn called it now. It was so corny, though, that it was cute coming out of her mouth. She grasped my "hunk a' man" and led me to bed. She pulled back the spread to reveal black satin sheets! She slid her peach-ice-cream body over the slippery black sheets and waited for me. She had prepared a whole seduction scenario. She looked the living porno dream of the innocent nymphet who is totally experienced at the same time. She took her glasses off.

There are many kinds of love making. This was straight and simple. Your basic fuck. That's what she wanted, and that's what a man is for, basically, to satisfy the woman. She has the egg, after all, and that's why there are two sexes. She bounced out of bed and went to the bathroom. She was there for only a moment. She came right back and nestled in my arms, but I couldn't sit still. She was so cute. I caressed her arms and shoulders and kissed her now with more affection than desire. I couldn't keep from touching her naked body. I wanted to feel and caress every part of her, like a mother touches a new baby, examining every bone and muscle. I had seen many mothers with new babies. That's what I felt like. Cathy lay back, her eyes half closed, soaking it all up. When I held her breasts and played with them, they seemed very small in my big hands. My affection gradually gave way to desire. I pressed my mouth together with hers and she answered with her tongue.

I kissed her face and her eyes and all over her body, making my way down to her belly. I kissed around her closed thighs and then gently pushed her legs open. I bent down and encountered one of those alien vaginal sprays. What a horror! I couldn't tell Cathy that, though. She was so eager to please. I wouldn't hurt her feelings for the world. She was only trying to make herself as appealing and sexy as she could. She was learning from TV commercials and *Cosmo* crap. I shouldn't complain. That's probably one reason why we were in bed so easily. *Cosmo,* I mean. *Cosmo* said it was all right. But because they had advertisers to please, *Cosmo* also suggested she use a "feminine deodorant." What's so feminine about it? I never wanted to make love to a plastic rose bush. I doubt if many men have.

My first shock quickly wore off. That was a minor irritant compared to this young woman in front of me. Her lips were so firm and full they stood out like a partly open mouth there in the hollow between her legs. No amount of FDS could keep me from kissing those lips. I bent down and she started at the first touch of my mouth. This may have been new for her, but she went right with it, moving her hips with a barely perceptible roll that magnified the tiny rhythm of my kiss. The phony FDS smell soon washed away in the clean, warm fluids of her woman's soft skin. I could have spent the rest of my life with my head cradled between her thighs. Her body shook and heaved. She came very fast. After a moment I went on kissing her, lightly now, only barely touching, then gradually increasing the sensation.

"Oooooh, it's like purple clouds," she said softly.

She totally charmed me with that innocent remark. After she had floated over a few "purple clouds" it was too much for her. She wasn't used to such feelings. I hunkered up to the pillow and held her in my arms. She was radiant, her pink cheeks glowed. She lay quietly in my arms for a long time. Neither of us said a word. Her alarm clock said eleven-thirty. That was earlier than I had picked her up. I checked my watch.

"It's two-thirty," I said. "Your clock stopped."

"No, I have it set for Los Angeles time," she said. "That's where my boyfriend is. I like to know what time it is where he is. I think about him a lot. We're gonna get married after he comes back."

"Don't you have to go to work soon?"

"Here," she said, gently pushing me back on the satin pillow, "lean back and rest a minute. I have time. I don't have to go yet."

We were quiet for a bit. She rested her head on my stomach, looking down and gently playing with me. Then she turned and looked up, her eyes wide and innocent.

"I dunno how to do it," she said. "I want to do it for you, too. Could you show me how?"

Wow! How easily she moved a part of my insides that had never been moved before. I don't think she knew. I slipped my fingers through her hair, framing her soft face.

"There's nothing to learn," I assured her. "You just give love to your lover. If you love a man, when he feels good, you'll know."

"Show me where it feels good."

I showed her. I suppose *Cosmo* never had an illustrated article on "The Ten Best Ways to Suck Off Your Lover," or "Dr. Brothers' Fellatio Do's and Dont's," because it all starts with the man. A man should never have to ask a woman. A woman can only let herself go if she feels emotionally safe and not exploited. Only the man can create that emotional safety. He should be strong enough to be vulnerable enough to make love to her first. And why not? If you're a man and you love a woman, you kiss her, don't you? You kiss her lips, her eyes, behind her ears, her neck. And here is this woman you adore lying

95

naked before you; you kiss her shoulders, kiss her breasts, and you kiss the nipples especially, because she responds strongly there. And then you kiss those long, undulating indentations down along the rise of her womb, and then there it is, in front of you. How can you stop kissing her? How can you *not* kiss her there? It's the focus of her womanhood at that moment. A soft touch: she trembles. A brushing kiss: her whole body moves. How can you withhold such obvious pleasure from a woman you love? I never could. That was for me the most natural kiss, almost from the first time I ever made love with a woman.

Now, when it was the other way around, a lot of women didn't seem to feel the way I do. At least not any of the women I married. They never had any moral objection to laying back and accepting that pleasure from me, but the other way around? Well, that was different. Maybe once a year each she would fearfully approach, toy with it, tentatively touch it with her tongue, and end up with her hair full of "gooey guck." Or even worse, she would bring me to that moment of complete vulnerability, and as it happened would suddenly leap in horror, tumbling off the bed, and run. Her muffled retching, "Agh! Agh! Agh!" faded away, then echoed louder from the bathroom sink. She turned both taps on full blast and then washed enough to prepare for open heart surgery with her teeth. It does spoil the mood of a rather poignant moment. When I was younger I thought that was the nature of things. But when I got older and fooled around I found with my lovers that it turned women on ferociously to give love to me, just as it turned me on with them. I began to wonder why I always married the other ones. Maybe I was finally learning something.

But then there was always something new to learn, like what was happening to me now? Cathy was making me groan in a delicious agony, but it wasn't what I wanted. She was moving something deep inside me, beyond my brain, more than my senses. I had to be inside her, to join with her. I lifted her flushed face from me. She was lost in a sexual world. She looked up with dazed eyes, not quite sure where she was.

"I want you," I said.

She didn't question. She followed my movements as I turned her over on her hands and knees. I pulled her thighs up to me and went deep inside. I hit bottom and fucked wildly. My movements were all instinctive. I had no control over myself. Cathy lifted her head. As she spoke, her words were shaken by the pounding of my body on hers.

"Holy Mary, mother a' God!" she prayed. "Don't stop now!"

I thought a lot about that afternoon I spent with wide-eyed little Cathy. I wanted to see her again. It wasn't serious. Just sex. I wanted to see her pretty young body again. There was no reason I shouldn't. At least till her boyfriend got back. She liked a lot of loving and so did I. I didn't see much of Barbara lately. She was very worried about her new job. She worked late every night. She got home at 1:00 or 2:00 A.M., took two Valium, and zonked out in a moment.

I called Cathy early one evening. She didn't hesitate a moment. She asked me to come right up. I suppose her boyfriend hadn't come back yet. We made love with the same intensity as before. No: more, I think. We knew each other now. She was very comfortable with me. She let herself go utterly the moment we touched. And she didn't use that awful FDS this time. Had she read my mind? Hmmm. She leaned back on the black satin pillows.

"That was enough lovin' to set me up for the next two months. Thanks."

"Anytime," I said.

She put on her glasses and took a book from the shelf next to her bed.

"What's your sign?"

"Gemini."

"I shoulda known. So'm I."

She leafed through the horoscope book for the proper chapter, leaning forward to get more light on the page. She unconsciously stroked her upper lip with her tongue as she began to read silently. Her legs relaxed open and innocently parted. Droplets of milky dew glistened in the blondish hair.

"I went to parochial school. Sacred Heart. The sisters didn't like for us to read this. Do you believe in astrology?"

"Well, yes and well, no."

"Waddaya mean, yes and no?"

I launched into a long dissertation on the possible material bases for astrological personality traits as long as you extrapolate the information from the birth date to the moment of conception. It's more reasonable that the forces that surround us could influence that profound delicacy of the egg at the moment of conception. I added to that all the seasonal phenomena that can influence a fetus and my list went on and on. There's no stopping me once I get on a train of thought. *Voco, ergo sum*, that's me. I speak, therefore I am. Cathy listened, fascinated.

I found the mix of paternal and sexual very exciting. This particular dynamic of male and female was new to me. My wives and Barbara were approximately the same age as I was, except for Pat, who was six years older. I'd been with much older women and younger women, but not with a woman who could have been my daughter. This was a different kind of relationship. I finally finished my speech and took a long sip of wine.

"You oughta be a writer," she said.

"I am."

"You are? You're a *writer?*"

If I had ridden down Ninth Avenue in a flaming chariot and swept Cathy up beside me to join the setting sun, she couldn't have been more in awe.

"It must be exciting to be a writer," she said.

"I don't know about that part of it. Selling would be exciting, I think. I haven't sold anything in a while, but I do write."

"What do you write about? Tell me."

I described what I was doing as best I could. Cathy pushed her glasses back up her nose and stared at me with a new intensity. She had listened attentively before, but now, now that she thought the words might be written down some time, she clutched each word to her mind, squeezing out every drop of intellectual nourishment that might be inside. She was already on her way from Bushwick Avenue and I (the writer I) was one of the gods in her new pantheon. I could get used to that. Now, if there was a way to have Cathy's adoration and the ease of living that came with Barbara . . .

It was 8:00 P.M. on Cathy's Los Angeles clock. Barbara would be coming home soon. I started to put my clothes on.

"It's eight o'clock in L.A.," I said. "I wonder what they're doing there."

She read more into my remark than I think I intended.

"Men fool around," she said coolly. "Why not women?"

"Why not, indeed. The woman's movement is the greatest thing that ever happened for men."

Cathy eyed me curiously.

"Who is Ms. Gordon?"

"Where did you hear her name?" I asked innocently.

"Every time I called from the studio to confirm your appointments, the answering service gave her name."

"We live together."

"How long?"

"A little while," I said. "Six months or so. Something like that."

"Are you in love with her?"

I hesitated only a moment.

"Yes, sure. Of course I am."

"It's late."

"That's okay. She won't be back yet."

"I think you should go."

We kissed.

"Goodbye."

"Goodbye now."

I thought about Cathy a lot. I wanted to see her again, but she had scared me a little that time. It was the way she asked about Barbara. That had been on her mind a long time before she so innocently asked, "Who is Ms. Gordon?" There was nothing innocent about it. Cathy was young, but she was a woman. I had come back to her. I was attracted to her and she knew it. She had a hold on me, however slight. She was testing it out, just a little. Women must be born with those instincts, because her instincts were absolutely correct. Ultimately, I would not be able to say no to her.

I thought maybe I might meet Cathy accidentally. Then it would be okay to see her. I contrived to walk past her house whenever it was possible. She lived near Ninth Avenue, not that far out of the way while shopping on a Saturday afternoon. I always checked in the local laundromat, stopped at the drugstore, but I never ran into her. I copied down the street number of her building and then looked up "C. Sullivan" in the phone book. When I wrote her number in my address book, I disguised it as someone else's. I must have had the feeling I would give something away if I had to explain who Cathy was.

I didn't want to call Cathy, but I found myself involuntarily stopping in front of phone booths. I'd put in a dime and dial her number, but I always hung up before touching the last number. It was too dangerous. She liked me a lot. If I called to see her once more, she'd know how much I liked her. She'd begin to realize how great a hold

99

she had on me. And I would never be able to say no to her. I couldn't let anything jeopardize my relationship with Barbara. It wasn't worth the risk. Was it because I loved Barbara so much, or was I afraid of losing the wonderful new life that came with the relationship? I don't know, but the next time I needed to edit videotape I used a different studio. I couldn't chance it.

When I lived with Margaret, I didn't have this ambivalence about any of the other women. I could take them or leave them alone if there was a possible conflict. I had lived my life pretty much going from woman to woman. There was rarely a gap of more than a few weeks in between. There always seemed to be a new woman available to replace the old one and sometimes they overlapped, as Barbara and Margaret did. Then, I used the sexual attraction to the new woman as a catalyst to effect a needed break. Cathy moved in me a sexuality over which I had no control and it was scary. Was this a warning? Was that part of me trying to persuade me to break up with Barbara before it was too late? If it was a warning, I didn't listen.

PART II

TWELVE

It's nice to be rich. The gap between wanting and having is so small. And if you're rich enough, there's no gap at all. Wanting is having. You want a beach house? You have a beach house. Just like that. Our weekends in Amagansett had been so happy that Barbara now wanted to buy a beach house of her own for us. She insisted on being on the ocean, no compromise. There are not many ocean houses up for sale. We looked around a bit and found an agent who thought he had something in Quogue that we might like. We signed up with him and he drove us out toward the beach. His voice floated from the front seat of his car, reciting,

> TO ONE WHO HAS BEEN LONG IN CITY PENT,
> 'TIS VERY SWEET TO LOOK INTO THE FAIR
> AND OPEN FACE OF HEAVEN—TO BREATHE A PRAYER
> FULL IN THE SMILE OF THE BLUE FIRMAMENT . . .

He had heard it from one of his clients and was so charmed he had memorized it. For use with intellectual-looking types like us, I supposed to myself.

We could see the house from the road. It was a little old beach cottage, perched high on top of a dune wild with beach plum and bayberry. There was an unbroken view of the ocean and the endless beach. It was old, the windows were small, and it needed a lot of work. But with 75 feet of ocean frontage, 300 feet deep, it was a steal. All her friends came to look. They showed her how much could be done with it. She knew all they had done with their houses which had started in much worse condition. The house was already leased for the next summer by a renter who had been coming there for years. This wasn't any problem, because Barbara planned to rent it out every summer just as her friends did. We probably wouldn't get that much use out of it in the summer anyway, because that's always a busy time for us. In movies and television vacations usually come in the winter. The rental would pay the mortgage with a little to spare. How could she go wrong? It was near her friends' houses where she had been a guest for so long. The little Long Island beach town of Quogue felt familiar and safe. She wanted it.

But there was a little matter of paying for it. Barbara had plenty of money for the down payment but she had no credit. She had forgotten to pay her only Master Charge years before and the bank wouldn't give her a mortgage. She referred them to her broker at Merril Lynch. The mortgage was delivered the following week. She signed the papers. We had a beach house.

In our first month together Barbara didn't want me to answer her phone. I had to let the service get it. Her parents called at least once a week and she was afraid they would get upset if they found out that she was living with a man. Al and Lilly called to say hello and how are you and also to maintain the important family quarrels and tensions. Some people seem to need a certain amount of bickering to justify their existence. Or maybe it means love to them and they don't feel loved enough without regularly taking up the cudgels of their homey quarrel. I never felt the need for it. And, though she joined in lustily, Barbara didn't seem to like it either. She dreaded the inevitable arguments, but the moment she started talking to Lilly, she'd immediately get hooked into the old family games.

She told her parents about me over the summer, and, to her surprise, they didn't get upset at all. Once they had been reassured that I was at least white (Lilly had asked her radical daughter point-blank), they had come to accept the presence of this unknown man in their daughter's life. Now that I was no longer a secret, Barbara made no secret of her love for me. She told them she had at last found a man she wanted to live with. She enjoyed telling Al and Lilly of her great pleasure in all the things we did together: the theater, restaurants, films, our work. The next time they called she told them all about our new dream house on the beach. I thought she would be ecstatic. I couldn't believe the kvetching I heard from her.

"Oh, I don't know, Daddy," she complained, "I'm not sure why I bought it. It's really dark and small and cramped. They all tell me work can be done on it, but that'll just cost more money and I could barely afford this. I had to scrape up every penny for it. It's going to be tough. I'll have to work night and day to make the mortgage payment. I can't take any time off now. I'm really tired, too. I'm so exhausted. I wanted a really nice house, but I couldn't afford it. This little shack will have to do. . . . ''

She went on that way, portraying herself like the little sewing machine girl with the moneylender twisting his moustache and the wolves howling at the door. It made no sense and when she hung up I asked her about it.

"What are you doing to him?" I said.

"What do you mean?"

"Why are you putting your father through all that?"

"Through what?" she said.

"Making yourself out to be so unhappy and miserable and poor and having such a rough time with money. If the house will be such a burden you shouldn't have bought it. But that's not so at all. I know that. You paid the down payment out of your own savings. You didn't even touch your father's money. The rental covers the mortgage and the taxes and there's some left over."

"I may not be able to rent it!" she said. "Then what?"

"Are you kidding? It's rented already, by the same man who's rented it for five years. The lease is in your safe deposit box. You can't not find a summer renter for a Long Island beach house. You told me that. And when we fix it up, you'll be able to practically double the rental. You have six couples of your friends who all told you it was a great deal. You're not in any financial trouble at all. You could have bought it for cash and you wouldn't have felt it."

"Oh, I wouldn't do that."

"Of course. You don't have to. That's what Al gave you, that security. His whole life has been for one purpose, to provide. He knows nothing else. He didn't even wait to die for you to inherit. He gave you the money while he's alive and kicking. That takes a certain kind of class, and a lot of love. All he wants now is to sit back, enjoy his restaurants, get fat, and know that he provided and his children are well and secure all because of him. So that even if it wasn't so, you should tell him that, even if you have to lie to him."

"I don't have to lie," she said quietly, "Al's a good man."

"You never once told him he has given you the means for some very great happiness. You only got the house because of all the stock. You never even said, 'Thank you.' What is that to do to such a man?"

She didn't answer. She walked slowly over to the window and stared out at the city for a long time.

"It's what Lilly used to do," she said. "It's just a habit, nothing more. I don't really feel that way."

"Well, that's Lilly's life. What do you want to do?"

She didn't have to think. She crossed the room, picked up the phone and dialled. She lit up a cigarette while she waited.

"Daddy . . . I just called to tell you, I apologize for . . . No, no, everything's okay. But I wanted to tell you about my beach house. It's only because of you that I could get the house . . . No, I mean it. You made it all happen with the stock you gave me . . . And this is a very good deal. Right now I get five thousand for a summer rental and when it's fixed up, I can get ten easy . . . Oh yeah! That's what they rent for, out there in Quogue . . . Quogue, Daddy . . . Q-u-o-g-u-e. It's near Southampton. *That* Southampton, riiight! . . . It's too good for the goyim, Daddy. You know my friend Lian? She's been getting that much for years now. It's a terrific deal . . . Oh, I know I don't have to rent it. I want to. Anton and I always have to work in the summertime. And in the fall, September and October, those are the best months on the beach. So that way it pays for itself. You always taught me to make a smart deal, didn't you! . . . Well, isn't that a smart deal? . . . Daddy, no, please. . . . Don't . . . I wanted to say think you for making it possible. I never could have done it without the money you gave me. . . . You made me so happy, Daddy. Thank you. . . ."

She held the phone to her ear, listening for a long while. Then she placed it gently back in the cradle. She spoke softly,

"He kept trying to stop me. . . . He kept saying, 'You don't have to tell me that. Please, you don't have to tell me that.' And then he cried. I never heard him cry before."

I took her in my arms. It was hard to keep from crying myself.

"Nobody ever thanked him before," I said.

Barbara soon began to dread her parents' weekly phone calls because Lilly reacted to her daughter's happiness like any normal mother would. She began to bring up the touchy subject of marriage. I sympathized with Barbara's weekly litany of agony, "Mother, we're not going to be married. We don't want to be married. Anton and I don't have to be *married* to be happy!"

When Barbara and I met neither of us thought about marriage. She certainly never did, although she talked a lot about the virtues of

106

staying single. But somewhere along the way her militant singleness began to soften. You had only to know Barbara slightly to realize that her professional life was one of constant conflict. Most of her personal life had been, too. I was the only man she had lived with since her short, unhappy marriage. She found to her surprise that there didn't have to be arguments, or competition, or hidden hostilities suddenly exploding over dumb little things. Our apartment was a quiet refuge from the turmoil of the world around us. She liked living this way.

One of the reasons our life was so harmonious was that I shrugged off eccentricities in Barbara that she told me her middle-class men never tolerated. I was raised as a long-haired bohemian. I went through adolescent rebellion like everybody else, but my rebellion was to cut my hair, shave my beard, and wear a white button-down shirt and a jacket and tie from morning till night. (I met and married Pat during that long period. She may have been misled by my temporary Ivy League appearance. Never thought of that before.) I have been surrounded all my life by mad poets, gay dancers, writers, actors, wigged-out musicians, painters, and artistic crazies of all descriptions. I'm straight compared to the people we knew. Creative eccentricities were not a novelty to us. They were almost a stamp of authenticity on your credentials as an artist. I felt right at home with Barbara and it seemed to me she had earned an imprimatur for her odd quirks by her good deeds for mankind on the television screen.

I had a two-week job in London for Time-Life. My consulting was a combination of a little editing, a little writing, and a little evaluation of the American version of some new BBC shows they had acquired. I had hoped that Barbara would be able to sneak a short vacation and come with me, but at the last minute she had to help produce a local special on the energy crisis. I got back just before Christmas. She looked white and drawn when I saw her at the airport. She was greatly relieved when she spotted me. She ran to me and threw her arms around me. She held on to me for a long time. This was unusual for Barbara. I knew she was exhausted from overwork, but I think she missed me more than she expected. It was the first time we had been separated, the first time she had slept alone since I moved in.

I bought a Christmas tree for us, a little Scotch pine. I set it up on the living room table and put some tiny lights on it, some tinsel and a few decorations. I didn't tell Barbara. I wanted to surprise her. I turned out the lights in the living room and switched on the tree. The colored lights and the tinsel shone brightly in the darkened room. I was cooking dinner for us when she came in. She was surprised, all right. She looked positively frightened of the glittering little tree. She stared at it and skirted around it, now and then reaching out to touch it and then drawing back. I watched her from the kitchen door.

"Is there anything wrong?" I said.

"No. It's strange to me. I never had one."

"You never had a Christmas tree? I thought everybody did these days."

"Al and Lilly weren't orthodox or anything like that. We just never had one. I didn't think about it much. It was something that other people did. And then when I lived alone I was always going with a married man and he had to be home with wifey-poo and the kiddies for Christmas. I mean you knew you didn't even *ask* him about Christmas. My friends always had me as a guest over Christmas. I never had a reason to have a tree. I'm not religious or anything."

"You don't have to be religious. It's for the end of year angst. I've spent some Christmases alone, too. No matter what you believe or don't believe, it's no fun. We always had a nice sort of Christmas when I was young. Even my strange family came together then."

I walked over to her and held her in my arms, my one hand still in a big potholder mitten.

"You and I are our family," I said.

"I'm so glad I have you. You're like nothing in my life before."

"And so this little tree is our celebration of that," I said. "It doesn't have to mean anything outside of you and me, Babe. It celebrates us."

I kissed her, but she was still fascinated by the tree. While I held her in my arms, she reached out and touched the tree for the first time. She toyed with a strand of shimmering tinsel, winding it cautiously around her finger.

THIRTEEN

The dune had been badly eroded when we bought the beach house. It dropped off sheer about 20 feet from the front door. I set out three jagged rows of snow fencing the length of the beach front right after we bought it. All through the winter the sand drifted in and added nearly 10 inches to the dune when we saw it again in the spring. It would be necessary to build a long ramp and a stairway over the dune so we could walk over it without disturbing the precious gathering sand. I had designed a structure during long winter nights at Central Park South, and when we went out to the beach house in March I was ready to build.

I found a lumber yard on the old Montauk Highway and out back, I found Josh Griffing. His family had lived in the Hamptons for five generations. He knew how to build on the beachfront, although he wouldn't have lived in a house there on a bet. He looked at my sketches and corrected all that I didn't know about building on the dunes. He showed me the right size lumber and how to foot the cedar posts when they were buried in the sand. He even showed me the right nails.

I began building on a gusty weekend in March. I clambered over the high, wind-hollowed face of the dune, stretching a line level and hanging a plumb bob. Barbara was fascinated. She was 10 feet below me, planting dune grass and the squat, gray-green Dusty Miller. Before she owned the beach house, Barbara was indifferent about plants. But out here, she had immediately taken on the job of replanting the dune with a dedication I had not seen in her outside of her work. It was a daily ritual at the beach. She always dressed in the same maroon woolen shirt, her orange-yellow babushka, and old Tretorn tennis shoes. She had her own tools for planting: a crumpled cardboard box, an old coffee can, and a trowel. She prowled the lee side of the dune and dug up healthy clumps of grass until she filled her box.

Then she got down on her knees in the new sand that faced the ocean. She patiently separated the large clumps of dune grass into hundreds of individual shoots. She dug a hole with her trowel and then pressed a single shoot into it. She watered it from her coffee can and raised a dam around the shoot to catch the rain. Then she planted another and another, inching her way across the face of the dune. She could do this for hours on end until her back stiffened.

I had the posts and beams up by the end of the first day. The beams were suspended 16 feet above the hollow dune where Barbara patiently planted. As she watched the structure rise above her, there was an excitement in her eyes like something magical was happening. I suppose it's not much different for a female bird watching a nest being built for her by a male. I had practiced building this thing so many times in my mind that I had it up and complete in a three-day weekend. It was a good job. Solid.

We settled easily into the pace of the beach. The blues were running. Early each morning we watched the local fishermen drive up and down the beach trailering a double-ended dory. When they spotted the tell-tale swarms of gulls screeching and diving at a running school of fish, they would quickly slide the dory into the surf and row out, dragging a long seining net, exactly as the Indians had done long before Henry Hudson. If this beach were in Portugal or Indonesia and the fishermen were darker and they had painted bright curlicues and eyes on their boats, they would be considered quaint. These were guys who worked at the local filling station trying to make a few extra bucks on their days off. No less quaint.

Barbara went in for a level of domesticity at the beach house that I had never seen in the apartment. She cleaned until it was spotless and planted grass all day long. It was as though this cottage had been created for just the two of us. She had no unhappy memories to scar it. Other men had been in the apartment with her, but not in this beach house. It was new and it was for us. She was no longer a maiden lady guest. She had her own house and her own man whom she didn't have to share with his wife.

Barbara gave Al a rave review of my construction in her next phone call home. She pleaded with Al and Lilly to make a special trip to see the beach house the next time they were in New York. I guessed they turned her down because she looked sad when she hung up the phone.

"From the way you described the ramp," I said, "they must have thought it was bigger than the house."

"Lilly couldn't care less, but Al is thrilled about it. 'A piece of the rock. You got yourself a piece of the rock, baby.' That's what he said. He's so proud. See, with all of his dealings, he never owned land."

I smiled. She was so happy. It's nice to make someone so happy doing something you like doing anyway.

"By the way . . . " she continued, "he did mention. . . . There's something that Al wanted me to talk to you about."

I looked up. She was concerned.

"What's that, love?"

"He wants you to sign a paper . . . for us to . . . to make an agreement . . . "

I waited.

"That if we were to get married . . . "

There was a long pause. I broke the silence.

"Oh? Are we getting married? When did you start considering that?"

"Oh well, Al and Lilly are always after me, you know. I . . . I told them one time, just to get rid of . . . just to stop them one day, I said we couldn't get married anyway because your wife was making trouble with the divorce. So they took that to mean that once you got a divorce we'd get married. And I didn't say that exactly, but it was easier to let them think that, than . . . you know."

I kissed her and said softly, "The two of us living together was all we planned when I moved in. I met you single and loved you single. I couldn't love you more. You do just what you want about marriage."

This was a development I was unaware of. She had obviously been talking about marriage and for the first time she hadn't told her parents No. Some part of her was beginning to think about marriage. With that one thought, a window opened in front of me that looked out to a rather marvelous future. To be married to Barbara? To actually be a legitimate part of her world of people who don't have to worry about making the rent?

From time to time, I had wondered about being married to Barbara, but I knew marriage was the last thing she wanted and I had always put such thoughts out of my head, until now. Those idle wonderings all came back and they made an interesting picture. I was happy living with Barbara. Marriage wouldn't change our relationship. I

111

had no fears of it. I wouldn't have married so many times if I did. I was very experienced at marriage. I knew what it took to keep a marriage going. I could be very happy married to Barbara. To a proverbial poor kid like me, Barbara's pile of money was definitely an attraction. Marrying it, along with her would assure a very appealing possible future. With that security, I could be whatever I wanted. I would be able to leave the world for long periods like Flaubert and Albee and do nothing else but write until it came out right.

There might even be some stirrings in her about having a child. She seemed so happy with me, she might even overcome that ambivalence. And that would be fine. With her money it wouldn't interrupt either of our careers. It would be the last chance for her. I wondered if she had ever thought about that. With her ambivalence . . . Hell, if she really couldn't handle it and things soured, we could always get a divorce . . . . But no, she would never want the responsibility of taking care of a kid alone. I know! *I'd* take the kid and then she'd pay me alimony and child support. What a switch! I loved it! Barbara's anxious voice slipped through my fantasy.

"So . . . they want you to sign an agreement that . . . "

Oh, that again. I had forgotten.

"An agreement that," she hesitated. "Well, if we were ever to get married, that if anything happens to me, that you have no claim on my money."

One does not have ready answers for news flashes like that. All I could mumble was,

"Ahhh . . . yeah. I . . . I don't quite know what to say. I'm still absorbing the idea that you might want to get married. But, ahhh . . . whatever you want. Whatever you think best. I mean, what can I say."

She sensed my hurt and tried to undo the damage.

"But I don't want to do it! Please understand. Al wants it to go back to the Berkowitz Fortune to keep it intact."

"Yeah. I got the message."

For a moment there, without knowing what she was doing, Barbara had transported me aloft with her into the fantasy world of rich people and a moment later she dropped me back into the second-class section. I was very tired from that sudden trip.

"Whatever you want, Barbara. It's your life, it's your money. It's your family. You have to do what you think is best. Whatever you decide, don't worry about me. I'll still love you."

"You don't understand. It's the last thing I want to do!"

"Well, then, don't do it if it makes you so unhappy. You're thirty-eight years old. You can do whatever the fuck you want. You're a grownup! You don't have a bedtime anymore. You can go to sleepaway camp any time you want, and even fuck the counselor if you want and no one will punish you because you're grown up. You're a big girl. I can understand Al. And I could understand you, if this is what you want. But you want to do what Al wants and have no guilt for your decision. You can't have both."

"You don't understand. I love you but I also have a responsibility to the Berkowitz . . . to Al."

I wished she wouldn't defend herself so much. There were only a few things about which I could not dredge up some sympathy and one of them was the grave responsibilities that went with the "Berkowitz Fortune." I didn't want to hear any more.

"I'll tell you what," I said. "Tell Al I'll be happy to sign that agreement. But you want equality in a relationship, right? Let's make it equal. I mean let's really be fair about this. I'll sign a paper that I have no claim on your money and you sign a paper that you have no claim on mine. Okay?"

"But you don't have anything," she shrugged.

"Oh yes I do. And a hundred dollars is harder for me to get than for you to withdraw ten thousand. That takes you ten minutes. My hundred takes a day out of my life. My hundred is worth more. And the screenplays and whatever else I may write. I think I'm good, potentially. I think the value of what I write will far outweigh the 'Berkowitz Fortune.' I'll sign that I have no claim on anything of yours and you'll sign that you have no claim on me. My money, my royalties, my property, all that stuff will return to the 'Holden Fortune' to keep intact for my children."

"It sounds so ugly when you say that."

"And how do you think it sounded to me?"

"But this is money my *father* made!"

"And this is money *my* children's father will make. If you believe that it's right that your father's money should return to his family and his children, then isn't it right that whatever I make should return to my family and my children? You are not my child. In this equation you're like Lilly. I'm not asking you for anything but equal treatment. If I am to be left out, why shouldn't you be?"

"I wish I never had this money!"

"I doubt that. Very much. But don't worry. You won't lose me. I don't love you for your money, if that's what you're all worried about."

"But you need me. For you to write."

"I don't need you. Don't you know what I do when I'm not home during the day? I work. I make money. I make plenty of money for me to live on. I've done that since I was a teenager with no help from anyone. Except for the rent and the phone, which I'll be happy to pay, you don't spend a penny on me. Don't you know that?"

She didn't reply and the discussion ended there. I think this was the first time I had ever been angry with Barbara. When we went to bed that night I was still angry. I slept with my back to her instead of holding her as I usually did. She knew I had been bitterly crushed when she asked me to sign her agreement, but she couldn't understand the depths of my anger. I don't blame her. I didn't know either. I was fantasizing about marrying her and having another child. Why should I want another responsibility? Where was the committed artist? The writerperson? What was happening to me? I didn't know the answer then, I didn't even know there was a question. But there was and it was about something that was more important to me than I had ever imagined. Legitimacy.

By now, you've probably figured out that I'm illegitimate. My mother and father never married and hardly lived together. That makes me a bastard. But I never heard that word when I was a child and when I did read it and hear it, I never applied it to myself. You can't know what it is to be an outsider unless you are one, but here's the funny part. You can't ever change being black, Jewish, or left-handed no matter how rich you get, but you can change illegitimacy. You can legally be made part of a family. And that's what Barbara was offering me. Marrying Barbara was to me a kind of adoption. It would make me a first-class citizen. My origins would never be questioned with her money behind me. The power of her money was an integral part of what I needed but I had not a moment's fantasy of spending it on myself. That's the paradox Barbara couldn't figure out. How could she? She was as far from my world as anyone could be. She was a Jewish Princess who had had everything.

I talked a lot about money because that's how my illegitimacy manifested itself to me. She thought that was all there was to it, but

114

what the money meant was acceptance. When she asked me to sign that agreement, she was hedging her love and that wasn't good enough. Not for the kind of love she tapped in me. It meant I was good enough to be her stud animal but not good enough for a total commitment. It was like Abraham being asked to sacrifice Isaac to prove his devotion. When the offer is made, Isaac is spared. Isaac was like Barbara's money. When she was willing to share that, I would know I was loved. Barbara knew she could keep me by holding out that carrot of marriage, but she never knew what it really meant to me. I was bound to keep jumping after it, because I didn't know what it meant to me, either. It's the needs you don't know you have that enslave you.

FOURTEEN

It was all forgotten the next day. I began to realize that Barbara completely forgot anything she didn't want to deal with. She erased unpleasant thoughts from her memory as though they had never been there. My first awareness was during a conversation we had while driving to the beach.

"I swear by my fusion," she said. "You are a perfect man."

"Aw, c'mon," I said.

"No. I mean it."

"There has to be something about me you don't like."

"No," she said evenly, "you are perfect."

"Nobody is perfect," I said. "There has to be something, some little habit I have that's not exactly the way you'd like. Some gesture, some word, some piece of clothing I wear . . . "

"Nothing. There's nothing about you I don't like."

"If you said that early on, I could see it. But we've been living together for more than a year. There must be something."

"No, there is nothing."

"I don't mean you secretly hate me," I said. "I'm talking about the slightest negative feeling, or about some tiny thing that I do or that I am."

"Oh, I know what you mean."

"Well?"

"Nothing," she protested. "You are an absolutely perfect man. You have no fault."

"I can't believe that."

"It's true."

Now you might think that would be an enviable position to be in, but it worried me. It was the first hint that there might be a great deal hidden inside Barbara that I knew nothing about. I was soon to see some of it emerge.

I woke up early at the beach house. Barbara was still asleep. I made coffee and walked out into the chilly spring haze. Holding the steaming cup for warmth, I sat down on the end of the deck and watched the morning sun materialize out of the mist. The gray haze of sky blended evenly into the gray ocean lapping lazily at the shore. There was no wind. There was not a single footprint or tire track on the beach, but there was life in the dune. Beneath me, bright green shoots of beach grass speared up through the new drifts of sand we had caught. Bees hovered on the crest of the dune among the white beach plum flowers. Wild roses ventured over the crest to the bare sand of the ocean side. I never realized that wild roses were tough enough to survive the hostile ocean face of the dune, but why would they want to live there? For more sunlight? No competition for the bees? Was it worth that much to them to set those delicate-looking blossoms out in a steady ocean wind?

There was a distant voice behind me. I looked around to the western stretch of beach. The haze had cleared enough for me to see something new. There were three long rows of beach chairs set out on the beach about two hundred yards away. It was the first sign that this lonely beach would have any other people on it during the summer. It was kind of a shock, but then I recalled the agent who showed us the house had mentioned that there was some sort of a beach club nearby. I knew Barbara was not going to like these intruders on her beach, so I walked out with her for her first look. I was not prepared for what followed. She burst into tears and ran into the house. In an instant the house had gone from a dream of happiness to the most awful tragedy. But this was only the beginning.

It was the first warm weekend of the spring and the next day, two by two, all her friends stopped by to admire Barbara's new beach house. Barbara made no attempt to hide her misery. Lian and Carol Wolf tried to cheer her up. They admired the house and land, praised the bargain she made, described how much they had done with their own houses, but Barbara would not be moved.

Through the side window, I caught sight of a group of white-haired people slowly walking to the beach along the wooden walkway some 20 or 30 feet from the house. Barbara saw them, too. She leaped to her feet and ran out to them. I could tell a storm was coming. Barbara turned first to a puffy, blue-haired lady.

"No one's allowed here! This is a private beach!"

"Oh, but we've always—"

"Get out!" she said, waving her arms.

"But Mr. Winnet said—"

"This is *mine*. It's *private property*. Nobody's allowed!"

Barbara had them cowed. They retreated backwards step by step as they tried to negotiate. A bald man in lime-green slacks pointed over his shoulder.

"See?" he said, "we rented the house over there. It's in our lease."

Oh-oh, I thought, they do have a right to use the walkway. But Barbara had them on the run. She was like a giant bird, pecking an intruder away from her nest.

"Prove it! Show me the lease! I don't believe it!"

The last we heard was the bald man's voice fading as he hurried down the path.

"Well, I don't have my driver's license with me . . . "

Barbara came back through the front door. She was triumphant, but the outburst hadn't lessened the fury burning in her eyes. Lian spoke gently to her.

"Barbara, honey, we all have easements. Other people have to get to the beach too . . . . "

"Barbara, dahling," Carol Wolf honked through her Locust Valley lockjaw, "theah is no such thing as a deserted beach, anymaw. At least not two hour's drive from New Yawk."

"I don't care! I can't stand it! I don't want this place. I won't even be able to rent it."

"It's already rented," I said.

"There's people all around. That's not why I bought a beach house!"

Lian soothed, "You've been at our house so many times, Barbara. There's no more people around here than at our house."

"Babe," I said, "we can build a fence so easily against the easement walk. That will give us a private patio, too."

"Then I won't see the sunset! I love the sunset at the beach."

Lian patted her shoulder and said, "There's all kinds of things you can do. And Anton can do them. He's good at building. It won't cost much . . . . "

Barbara didn't want to be mollified. She stalked in and out of the living room picking up her tennis racket and a few clothes.

"What are you doing?" I asked.

"I'm going home," she announced to the room. "Oh, you people can stay. I don't care. I can't stand it anymore. Just lock up. No, don't bother. Leave it open. If I'm lucky somebody will come and burn it down and I'll get some insurance. It isn't worth more than that."

She walked out of the house. I apologized and hurried after her. It was too far for her to walk to the station and she couldn't drive so she sat in Bernie and waited for me. I got in the car.

"Barbara, we have a lot still to do to get ready for the renter. We should stay. And all your friends are concerned about you."

"I can't stand looking at those hideous chairs."

"You remember the joke, the guy goes to the doctor and says, 'Every time I lift my arm like this it hurts. What should I do?' And the doctor says, 'Don't lift it like that anymore. Fifty dollars, please'?"

Barbara stared coldly at me.

"Just don't look over there," I continued, "for a few hours, anyway. We have a magnificent view of the ocean from the living room. Look at that."

"The window is too small. I've always hated that window."

"Well, I don't know what to say. We only have a few weekends until the renter moves in. I think you should be able to hold yourself together for the rest of today and tomorrow."

Barbara clenched her teeth and got out of the car without a word. We walked silently back to the house. She reassured everyone she was okay and said no more about the chairs that afternoon. After the last of her friends had gone, she walked out on the deck and stared at the rows of chairs until the sky reddened into a magnificent sunset. The few people from the beach club had long since gone. There was only a lone fisherman, casting into the surf, his back to the shore. Barbara stepped down the stairs to the beach and then walked over to get a closer look at her enemy. I went out on the deck now and then and watched her walk up and down in front of the hated chairs until the sun went down. There was a cold wind coming off the ocean. It slapped her jacket crazily as her dark silhouette trudged back across the sand. I had a fire going and hamburgers and wine ready for her. The electric blankets were already warming. It was going to be a cold night.

Barbara dropped her exhausted body down on the tattered rattan chairs and soaked up the heat roaring from the fireplace. I set the burgers and wine out on the coffee table in front of her.

"Don't move," I said. "Let's eat here. How're you feeling now?"

"I lost all my money," she said quietly. "This house is worthless."

"Well," I sighed, "have something to eat and a little wine. You'll feel better."

She took a bite of hamburger and chewed it, but then she spit it out on her plate. She took the wine to bed with her. I ate alone and then cleaned up the weekend's dishes. Barbara was asleep when I got into bed.

Next morning I woke before Barbara and made the coffee. I went out on the deck and sat down at the end. I turned my back to the beach chairs and faced the morning sun, which was barely visible in the haze. The beach was deserted from this angle. An exquisite loneliness. I was troubled. I knew Barbara was temperamental. I had accepted that when I entered into this relationship. But she had been completely immature about a couple of beach chairs and some easily fixable drawbacks in a house perched on the most magnificent stretch of beach I had ever seen. If she was going to act like that every time we stepped into the house, we'd be better off without it. This aspect of Barbara made me uneasy, somehow. A gentle hand touched my shoulder. Barbara knelt behind me, a cup of coffee in her hand.

"I was watching you out here," she said. "You looked so calm and at peace with the world. You really love the beach, don't you?"

"What's not to like?" I said. "Look at those roses there, reaching out alone over the crest. The buds look so delicate and yet they must be incredibly tough to survive that wind day and night. They're beautiful."

"I've never seen you so happy," she said. "I'll get used to the chairs and the people. I'll be all right. Don't worry."

She turned her back to the chairs and sat down next to me, hanging her feet over the side of the deck. I put my arm around her. She looked east with me as the sun disc slowly brightened in the haze.

"It's chillier than yesterday," she said.

"Yes."

"You want to go back early?"

"Sure," I said. "There's nothing we can't do next week. Why don't we leave before noon? We'll drive back in the daytime and miss the Sunday night traffic."

"Good," she said. "I'd like that."

We packed a few things and were on the road by 10:00. I felt guilty at

121

having doubted Barbara. She came through after all. She had been disappointed and hurt. Her dream had been damaged. Everything would be fine. I could do a lot of building and fixing to help preserve her dream and, thus, mine. But no matter what we tried or where we went, as Barbara and I were drawn closer and closer together our happiness would always be disrupted by some unaccountable tragedy.

FIFTEEN

It took my lawyer from September to April to get my second wife into court. I flew to Phoenix for the hearing. Robby wasn't in the courtroom, at least not where I could see him. Patricia and her new husband, Harold, were there, though. As usual, she refused any visitation. Then her lawyer presented my lawyer with a request that I agree to let Harold legally adopt my son. For Robin's welfare, of course. My lawyer was taken aback, but that was neither a shock nor a surprise to me. It was the first move Pat made each time I got her into a courtroom. Obliterating my image was not enough for her. Changing Robby's name would erase me completely. I was told he was now registered in school with Harold's name anyway. Pat just wanted to make it legal. The hearing took three days of lawyers, hired psychiatrists, and court reporters. I wonder what poor people do? At the end of the hearing the judge ordered Pat to arrange to have Robin visit with me the next day. Miracle. I hadn't even asked for that.

I drove my rented Volkswagen to the meeting place, an intersection near his school. They were all there already, parked in a dark green Volvo. I parked my car opposite. No one came out of their car for a long while. Then Harold got out of the driver's side and walked around the car. He opened the door and waited, but Robin wouldn't come out. Harold reached in and dragged him out bodily. They started to fight. I could hear them screaming and yelling at each other. Robin had acquired quite a salty vocabulary. Harold tried to pull him toward my car, but Robin wouldn't go. They were almost the same size, so Robin was giving him an even fight. He socked Harold in the stomach quite a few times. Give him one for me, kid. Robin ran away but Harold caught up with him and managed to twist his arm behind his back until he gave up. Still pinning his arm, Harold stumbled with Robin toward my car, but Robin fought every moment he could. I could hear them more clearly now.

"I won't go!"

"You have to!"

"Patricia said I didn't have to!"

"It's the court!" Harold screamed. "The judge says you must! Now get in there!"

One more twist of Robin's arm and he obediently got in. Harold slammed the door on him. My junior high school graduation picture looked back at me: Robin looked exactly as I had when I was fourteen. Complete with glasses. I never knew he had to wear glasses, too.

"Hi, Robby," I said. "How are you?"

He didn't say a word. He looked steadily at me with a glazed, tired stare. His lower lip jutted out.

"Any place you'd like to go where we could just sit and talk?" I said. He didn't say a word or move a muscle.

"Any place you'd like to go where we could sit and not talk?"

He was totally withdrawn.

"Well, let's see what I can find," I said.

I started the car. The car wouldn't start. I switched the key back and forth. The starter motor wouldn't turn over, the relays wouldn't even click. I turned the key in all ways, in all positions, but nothing happened. I couldn't start the car. Nothing. I couldn't believe it. I looked over to Robby's sullen face.

"I can't start the car," I said.

Robby still didn't move or speak. I shook my head slowly.

"I don't understand," I said to myself. "It's rented but it's brand new."

I got out of the seat to have a look at the wiring in the back. I heard Robby's voice. "Here, let me try."

Robby was crossing over into the driver's seat. He was moving and talking. I couldn't pass that up.

"Sure. Please!" I said. "I need all the help I can get."

I checked the wiring and then stood at the door as Robby tried everything he could think of. Nothing worked. I couldn't believe it. Seven years. Seven years I had worked for this meeting and now we were going to spend it sitting at the side of the road with his mother and stepfather parked opposite. Robby switched seats and I got back in the driver's seat. I had the distinct feeling that I was being tested for something. But I thought I had passed that test already. Somehow it was all fitting. Oh well, I only had an hour left with Robby; I might as well relax. I gave the key one more try. The car started immediately. Robby was as amazed as I was.

"What did you do?" he asked.

"I have no idea."

I put the car in gear and drove away. Robby sulked again, but he looked more relaxed than he had before.

"Where do you want to eat?" I said.

"Not hungry."

"It's six-thirty. I don't know about you, but I haven't eaten all day. We're coming to a stretch of road with a lot of restaurants."

"Where?"

"I don't know," I said. "It looks like Taco City."

He chuckled.

"You have your pick of anything," I said.

"Not hungry."

Then he pointed, "See that place?"

"What?"

"That!"

"Mr. Steak?" I said, as it whizzed by.

"Uh-huh."

"What about it?"

"It's okay," he said.

We sat down at a table in "Mr. Steak." Robby leaned way back on the seat.

"Anything the matter?" I asked.

"I'm not hungry."

"Well, I'll order you something. Maybe you'll get hungry."

I ordered two "Mr. Steaks". I began to eat. He stared at the food.

"You're really not hungry."

"I had twenty cokes this afternoon," he said.

"No wonder you're not hungry. No matter."

There was a long pause, then Robby sat up and pointed a finger at me.

"I know all about you," he said.

"Oh?"

"And I don't hold it against you."

"What do you mean?" I said. "What don't you hold against me?"

"Your background," he said.

"What does that mean?"

He shrugged and looked tired again.

"Well, kid," I said, "I am your background, and I don't hold that against you, either."

He had a big laugh at that and then he leaned way back in his seat.

"Are you tired?" I said.

"I've been in the courthouse all day and I have to go back tomorrow."

"How's school?" I asked.

"I don't know."

"You don't know? You do go to school every day, don't you?"

He laughed.

"What happens?" I asked.

"Nothing happens."

"You do homework, right? You take tests, right? You get a report card, right?"

Robby nodded to all of these.

"That's something happening, isn't it?"

"Huh!"

"Did you get my Christmas present?" I asked.

"Yeah."

"What did you buy with it?"

"Nothing."

"What did you do with it?"

"Patricia," he said.

"That was for you. Why didn't you buy something for yourself with it?"

"You don't know anything, do you?" was his sneering reply. "You can't buy anything for twenty-five dollars."

"Ski poles or something?" I said.

"A lot you know."

"One ski pole?"

He laughed and then said, "Why are we staying here?"

"You want the reasons in alphabetical order or as they come into my head?"

"Alphabetical order—backwards," he said.

"Okay, 'Z.' After a day like this, I have no 'zip' left and I don't think you do either."

He laughed. I went on.

"'Y,' ahhh . . . " I tried to think.

"'Why' are we here?" he asked.

"When you say 'why' that begins with 'W' and we're not there yet. 'Y'... I flew two thousand five hundred miles to see 'You' and I have half an hour yet."

"Then why don't we drive it?"

"Sure," I said.

We drove around for a while. Robby directed me from one tourist sight to another, but it was the off season and late and they were all closed. He obviously liked Phoenix and wanted me to like it too. The sun had gone down and it was very dark. I looked at my watch. I had only ten minutes left and I hadn't the faintest notion of where we were.

"It's getting late," I said. "Shall we backtrack?"

"I know this road. Go this way."

"You sure?"

"You don't know these roads," he said. "I do."

"Maybe I better have a look at the map just to make sure. Let me have it, would you?"

Robby held the map out of his open window.

"If you stop, I'll throw the map away."

He laughed as he said it. He was teasing me and enjoying it. I kept driving, but I was a little apprehensive. I did not know much about my son.

"Ahh, listen Robby, you know your mother. If we're not back exactly at seven-thirty, the state police are going to get an all-points and we're going to see flashing lights chase us down the road."

He really laughed at that one. He did know his mother.

"Keep driving," he ordered.

I decided to trust him. He pointed out landmarks in the dark which I couldn't see. I didn't know whether they were there or not. He enjoyed the tease.

"There's the school," he said.

And there it was, through the trees. He directed me through a maze of back roads and then the dark green Volvo appeared straight ahead.

"Do you like hiking?" I asked.

"All right."

"Maybe we'll do that next time. What do you say?"

He didn't say anything. I stopped the car. He got out without a word to me. He got in their Volvo and they drove away. It had gone better than I had ever dreamed. I drove slowly back to my motel. I cried all the way.

In July, my lawyer sent me the final decree with all the visitation spelled out. The first visit with Robin would be in August, a whole week. I wrote to Patricia to make arrangements for the visit. She wrote back that such a visit "would not be convenient" as they would probably be moving before that time. She neglected to mention where they were moving. My lawyer immediately filed for contempt, but they disappeared before we could get them into court. The judge issued a contempt of court citation which I received in the mail. I put it in the file with the others.

SIXTEEN

I met Al and Lilly Berkowitz for the first time when they made a stopover on their way to Capri. They would only be in New York for an evening, which was just as well because Barbara was popping Valium as if it were candy to prepare for their visit. My medication was 100 milligrams of iced Polish vodka.

"It's all going to be fine," I soothed. "I'm sure I'll pass."

"You don't understand. It's like—they know about you, but to see you, and in my apartment? Living together? It's going to kill my father. I don't know what I'm going to say to him."

"Oh, c'mon. At thirty-eight years old? I'm sure Al has considered that you might not be a virgin by this time."

"I'm serious."

"Well, if you're serious, I better zip up my fly."

I pantomimed the symbolic rite of passage accompanied by a zipping sound effect. Barbara ignored it.

"You have to promise me something."

"Oh?"

"Don't ever mention Dr. Alexander."

"I can't imagine why I would, but why not?"

"They have no idea I'm seeing an analyst."

"You've been going for twelve years and they don't know?"

"I never told them. I can't. They would think it meant something terrible. They're so old-fashioned."

I had adjusted to not answering her phone as an amusing quirk of Barbara's, but this sounded rather strange. Well, what did I know? The values held by the middle-class parents of women in my life had often seemed as strange and exotic to me as the culture of some remote Polynesian island. I had happily accepted the gift of their rebellious daughters, but I had long ceased to wonder about their mores.

"I don't think you have to worry," I said. "They may have done and said a lot of things in the past, but parents grow too, you know. Maybe more slowly, but they're different from the way you remember them when you were young."

"Promise me?"

"Of course, Babe. But I'm sure they'll be fine."

And they were. Lilly was a tiny woman, still in good shape, with sort of strawberry hair. Al had a pencil-line moustache and thick black hair which he slicked down flat. He had a pot belly, two-hundred-dollar shoes, and good gold. He was entitled.

I was much better than they had expected. They were obviously relieved when they saw me. Barbara was bursting with pride. Her latest show, "The Superlandlords," was on the air that same evening. She persuaded them to stay on before we went out to dinner. Showing off her man and her program on the same evening, Barbara was in heaven. The film was about the big slumlords of New York City. I got the feeling they had never seen a show she produced before. One thing for sure, CBS commanded a lot more respect than that funny public television channel in Florida they could never get clearly. Their daughter was in the big time. When it was over, Al didn't say anything. Barbara sensed there was something wrong.

"Did you like it, Al?" she said.

"Oh, yeah, yeah, Baby. It was fine. Just fine."

Something was bothering him. She tried to get at it. She wasn't the world's greatest interviewer for nothing.

"Come on, Al," she cajoled. "What did you really think of it? You can tell me."

"Well," he said, "I was just wondering . . . In all of New York City . . ."

He paused, unable to continue.

"Yes, Dad? You can tell me. It's all right."

"In all New York . . . couldn't you find one Christian slumlord?"

She was conscience-stricken.

"I . . . I'm sure there must be, but I tried . . . you know that I really tried!"

He quickly retreated inside himself and patted her reassuringly.

"I know you did, Baby. I'm sure you did. You wouldn't be unfair. I know that. I just thought . . . in a city the size of New York . . . there must be at least one."

Al Berkowitz and I had nothing in common except a love for his daughter. Sitting and talking over dinner, Barbara was plainly happier than she had ever been in her life. I may not have been Al's ideal, but I was Barbara's. That was enough for him. All he wanted for his daughter was to see her happy. Lilly was polite, but Al was genuinely happy to meet me and get to know me. He shook my hand for a long time before he and Lilly left for their hotel. I had been approved. All I needed was my divorce and everybody would be happy.

But my divorce was going nowhere. Margaret wouldn't change her demands for alimony forever and 15 percent of everything I would ever earn. She had managed to keep a job for four months now and she hadn't phoned or appeared at our door or Barbara's office since. All her anger was shifted to the legal fight. She was out for blood, and since the hopeless shrugs of my attorney were hardly encouraging, I looked around for another. Barbara found a militant feminist who she thought would fight the whole idea of alimony for a woman when there was no child from the marriage. This sounded brilliant to me.

The attorney wore her hair in a frizz and blinked at me through red-rimmed owl glasses as we made another financial responsibility statement and submitted it. But Maggie was adamant and my new attorney shrugged as hopelessly as her predecessor.

"There's nothing we can do," she said. "But I think she'll settle for half."

"Half? I can't pay a quarter," I groaned.

I tried to excite her political erogenous zone.

"There has to be a way," I said. "Can't we attack the alimony law? The concept of alimony?" I could see she was getting excited. I had succeeded. Now we'd see some action. "Those laws are ancient," I said. "A woman isn't a chattel anymore. Margaret was an independent working woman when I met her and she is again."

"That poor woman you deserted has every right to the alimony she's asking for," she yelled at a startled me. "She's being easy on you. You should pay her more! And I'd tell you to if I wasn't your lawyer. You can't shirk your responsibilities as easily as that!" She slammed her hand down on her desk for an exclamation point.

My attorney. I couldn't figure it out until we were told that she had recently separated and was chasing her husband for support for their kids. She was venting her justified wrath against me. I sympathized, but knew she would not pursue my case with any particular energy. I looked for another lawyer.

This time Nancy came through. Nancy was Barbara's production assistant, researcher, and hand-holder at CBS. I liked Nancy. She wore her blonde hair long and straight. She looked a lot like Liv Ullman with those same huge, fascinating eyes that never seem to blink. She was a war baby, a sixties radical. She was still a kid, but she was one of the smartest people I ever met. (Listen to me. She was twenty-five years old and I was calling her a kid!)

Nancy had found a lawyer for me who she believed might be a budding genius. She said he had passed the bar only a few weeks before. I went to his office. The address was barely visible through the dirt on the glass door of a broken-down tenement. I walked up the five flights to his office. Well, he's young and hungry, I hoped. Maybe he'll work at it. I went through the battered metal fire door and found myself in the middle of a tenement commune. My new attorney had hair down to his ass and a beard to match. He was smoking dope and offered me some.

We went through the same ritual I had been through so many times before. He went through all the papers I brought and then we went to the inevitable next step: I wrote out a financial statement to the last penny, proving, yet again, that there was no way I could pay what Maggie demanded.

"I can't possibly pay this, Mr. Buck," I said for the nth time.

"Call me Bucky. She'll settle for half," he said, as sagely as his predecessors. What do lawyers do, anyway? This lawyer sucked air down after his grass while I started the whole boring litany.

"I only knew this woman for five years. We had no children. To pay her alimony for the rest of her life . . . . It just isn't right. It's not fair!"

And Bucky shrugged, just like they had all shrugged, and said, "The law in this state says she has that right, and unless you can come up with an effective countersuit charging her with terrible things she did to you, there's nothing you can do. You'd better resign yourself to it. I would not be doing my job as your attorney to advise you to pay legal fees for something you can't possibly win. And you have some money. Or you will have. It looks like your career is just starting."

"That's just it. I'm writing more and more. I have to look forward to long periods of no money coming in . . . "

"You're a writer, huh?"

"What I'm trying to tell you is I'm trying to write. There won't be any money coming in for long periods—"

"I'll tell you what," he interrupted, "you go home, sit down at the typewriter and write about your marriage. Write anything you want. Anything that comes into your head, no matter how unimportant or outrageous it might seem to you. Everything! And then send it to me."

I did. I mailed him thirty single-spaced pages. We had a meeting at his place a few days later. He was excited.

"You said on page eleven that you asked her to have a baby once and she refused. Is that true?"

"Of course. She was terrified."

"Hmmmm."

"Don't you believe me?" I asked.

"You never mentioned it before."

"It didn't seem important. That's the way she was. I was very depressed when my ex-wife disappeared with my son the last time. You've got to understand, I had three kids who were gone from me. I spent a large chunk of my life on my kids and I didn't have a single one of them with me."

"So that would make it fairly recently that you asked her, right?"

"Well, I'm not sure when—"

"*Be* sure. Sounds fairly recent to me. If it came after your last hearing then it would be . . . during that summer. Wouldn't it have been somewhere around then?"

"Well, I suppose . . . " I stammered. "Yeah, yeah, it could have been."

"Was it definitely?"

"Why does it have to be so definite?"

"Because if it was within twelve months from the time you left, we got a case and a good countersuit. I mean good! New York is an old-fashioned state. A wife refusing to have a baby happens to be grounds for divorce that a man can bring against her. And from what I figure you had to have asked her sometime within the last eleven months. Now, I don't want to influence you as to the date, but you have to be *sure*. Do you understand?"

"I understand."

We sure had a case. After the countersuit was filed we all met in Margaret's attorney's office. She challenged everything else in the countersuit, but she made no attempt to disagree that she had refused to have a baby. That request had more of an effect on her than I had realized. She lied about a lot of other things, but she wouldn't lie about that. I had to respect her for that.

I asked them again for my business stuff. I needed my corporation checkbook for my growing freelance work. Her attorney hemmed and hawed again about not knowing where any of my records were, but Maggie shut him up and told me she was sure she could find it. She was so sure she arranged to meet me the next week and give me the checkbook. I don't think she had any sudden kindness; she was facing the possibility that she might not be awarded legal fees now that I had a strong countersuit. Any time we met in her lawyer's office she would have to pay for the appointment now. She was meeting me halfway because I finally had a case. I breathed a lot easier.

We met in a singles bar around the corner from the old apartment. It was called "The Red Baron" or something. It was a warm day and Maggie wasn't wearing a coat. She had always worn a frowzy coat and looked kind of beat in her lawyer's office, but we were alone now. She looked sleek and trim in a perfectly tailored pair of new jeans and a loose black sweater. She had lost all the puffy fat she had accumulated while we were married. She looked just like she had when we met. I ordered a drink for her and she handed over the checkbook.

"Thanks," I said. "How are you doing?"

"Oh, fine."

"You look great."

"Ugh! I feel awful. I must look a wreck."

"You know you don't. Separation seems to agree with you."

"So they say," she said.

"You lost a lot of weight."

"You did, too."

We sat on the high stools and sipped our drinks for a few minutes in silence. It's amazing how far you can go from someone you know so well. She crushed out a cigarette and lit another. She eyed me curiously.

"You don't smoke any more?" she asked.

"No. I started playing tennis and I found I didn't have any wind, so I quit."

"Was it hard to stop?"

"Nothing to it. Tennis gave me more pleasure than the pipe. I didn't miss it at all."

"I should stop," she said. "It's a filthy habit."

There had been almost constant conflict between us through all the years of our marriage and separation. But now we sat calmly, with a common purpose and there was no conflict for the first time. With the few words we exchanged, I could feel the chemistry that had brought us together was working again. We were strangely vulnerable in this unexpected hiatus. We were so intimate for that moment that something slipped out of me that I had wanted to say for a long time.

"I'm sorry I hit you."

"Oh, it wasn't anything. You didn't have to do it quite so hard, though."

"I didn't think you'd get the message otherwise."

"Maybe you should have done it years ago."

That is the one reply I had never expected. I had no answer for it.

"You might have saved what we had," she said, staring out the window. "We might have had a chance."

"Yeah . . . maybe so. Maybe that's what you want in a man and it's good we're apart because I'm not that kind of man. I wasn't good for you and you weren't good for me. But that's past now. I'm glad we could sit here and talk peacefully. And thanks for the checkbook."

She turned to me, "How long will it take you to send the money you owe me?"

The spell was breaking.

"Soon. As soon as I can."

"When will that be? I'm behind in the rent and the gas and electric."

"About a week or so. Checks have to clear."

"I'm really desperate," she said.

"Yeah. It won't be long."

Things were back to normal. I could cope with this. I held up my glass.

"Cheers."

"Good luck," she said.

SEVENTEEN

My attorney in Phoenix soon found Harold. He was working in a private school in a little town in Connecticut. There was still no address for Robin, so I called Harold at his school. I told him I had a contempt of court decree and would bring Pat into court if the visit wasn't arranged immediately. I got a letter from her inviting me to take Robin on a visit the next Saturday and Sunday.

Pat had set our meeting place in a parking lot behind the town library, a small white clapboard house on a quiet corner of a well kept green. There was a tumble-down graveyard in the middle of the green surrounded by a low iron railing. As I drove to the back of the library, I saw the green Volvo standing in the parking lot. I parked Bernie across from it. Robin got out of the Volvo and came over to my window. It was still a shock to look at him; the resemblance was so startling. I rolled my window down.

"Hi, Robby."

"I have all my needs!" he shouted. "Why don't you stop bothering us! I don't have to go if I don't want to!"

"Robby, there is a court decree that says you have to. You're going to cause your mother and Harold a lot of trouble if you don't come with me."

Pat got out and joined us. "He doesn't have to make the visit if he doesn't want to!" she shouted. "Why don't you stop bothering us!"

She took him back to the Volvo and they drove away. I followed. She led me on a scenic tour of western Connecticut for about twenty minutes and then she parked in front of the town police department. I imagine they didn't give her much help because when she finally strode down the steps she was white with anger. I followed her on the scenic tour again. I was in no hurry. She stopped on a deserted road. I pulled up behind her. Robin got out and came to the window again.

"I have all my needs! Why don't you stop bothering us! I don't want you! Now get out of here!"

I got out and walked behind him to their car. I tried to talk to Pat but she rolled her window up and looked straight ahead. Robin got in and she drove away, leaving me standing in the road.

I drove to the only address I knew, the school where Harold worked. As I entered the grounds, I saw the Volvo with Arizona plates parked near a cottage just inside the entrance. I knocked at the cottage door, but there was no answer. I looked in a window. The cottage seemed empty. All the furniture was pushed to the center of the room and covered with drop cloths, as though the room was being painted. I called at the window but there was no answer. I tried the front door. It was open and I called inside, "Hello?"

Pat ran around a corner of the room, screaming, "Get out! Get out! You have no right here! Robby doesn't want to visit! He has all his needs right here with us! He doesn't want you!"

"Then I assume you're cancelling the visit?" I said.

Robin appeared and joined her shouts, "Get out of here! I don't want you! Get out!"

Pat pleaded with me. "Can't you please stop bothering us?"

"You're doing this all to yourself," I said. "For seven years you've done anything you could to stop me from visiting my son. It's all over now. If you don't make this visit, I'm going into court next week with the contempt decree from Arizona."

"There's nothing I can do," she wailed helplessly. "He won't go!"

"You brought it all on yourself. You created this and you'd better start changing it now. You can get Harold to force Robby to make the visit, just as he did in Phoenix."

"I brought Robin to the place for you to pick him up. That's all I have to do. If he doesn't want to go, he doesn't have to! That's what my lawyer says!"

"Well, see what he says when you're in court. You're not getting away with that again. I'm going to sit in my car for ten minutes. If you don't have Robby make the visit in ten minutes, I'll leave but I'll be here tomorrow for the second day's visit. And if you don't want to be in contempt of court I strongly advise you to have Harold with you, since he was able to force Robby to make the visit in Phoenix."

I went back to my car and waited the ten minutes but there was no sign of them. I went back to New York more determined than ever that this would finally stop.

On Sunday I drove into the parking lot and sipped my coffee while I waited. The little town was deserted this early. Pat drove into the lot and parked opposite me. Robin got out of the car and walked up to my window. He recited the words he said before without a change in syllable or inflection: "I have all my needs! Why don't you stop bothering us! I don't have to go if I don't want to!"

Pat got out of the Volvo and walked over to us.

"Robby, please!" she begged. "Don't do this! You have got to go with him!"

Each minute of yesterday's scene replayed. Pat cried and begged, but Robin refused to go. Finally I had had it. If Harold could do it, so could I. I got out of the car and joined the yelling. "How dare you disobey your mother like that! And Harold! Get in this car! Now!"

He turned and ran. I ran after him and grabbed his arm. I pulled him to the car while he punched and kicked me. Pat now turned on me. "Let him go! Let him go! Take your hands off him!"

I managed to get Robby to my car. Pat ran back to her Volvo, opened the door and honked the horn again and again, screaming, "Help! Help! Help!"

I hopped into the driver's seat. The car started instantly. Good old Bernie. I threw it in drive and pulled away as fast as I could. I didn't believe what I saw in front of me: Pat was driving the Volvo straight across my car to block me from leaving. I hit the brake. Too late. Wham! With barely a shudder, Bernie lifted the Volvo off the ground. He made a dent in the side of the Volvo and Pat was okay, but she had succeeded in blocking my way out of the little parking lot. Well, she asked for this one. I floored the pedal. Bernie's big V-8 engine roared and pushed the Volvo sideways across the parking lot. Good old Bernie! Pat screamed and honked the horn for help. Robby sat goggle-eyed, not moving or saying a word. When I had enough room, I backed up and the Volvo bounced down on all four wheels. I drove past Pat and out of the lot. She tried to chase after me, but both tires on the other side had been pulled off the rim and the Volvo bucked down the road on crumpled tires before she gave up. It had taken a little work, but I had the visit at last. I headed for New York on the Merritt Parkway.

"I was thinking we could take a ride on the Circle Line boat around Manhattan first. What do you think of that?"

Robby's jaw stuck out. He didn't say a word.

"We had a nice visit that other short time in Phoenix. There's no reason why we can't do it now. So, just relax, we'll be in New York in a—"

Lights flashed behind me and a siren howled. In this saga, nothing surprised me. I pulled over to the side of the road and parked. I sat in the car waiting. Two helmeted cops stalked around Bernie. They had guns in their hands, pointing right at me!

"Officer," I said, "I know what's going on. It's all a—"

"Outta that car! *NOW!*"

"Officer, this is my son—"

"I wanta see your hands!"

I froze. He was serious.

"See your hands or we shoot!" one cop said, while the other shouted, "Out! Now! Or do we pull you out!"

I'm not an experienced criminal and I never went to their training school. I had no idea what they considered a threatening gesture. I couldn't move.

"Listen," I said, "I'll be happy to get out, but I have to put my hands down to open the door. Is that all right?"

He didn't say a word. His nickle-plated six-shooter pointed right between my eyes. The second cop had his gun on me from the other side. I moved my hands as slowly and deliberately as I could and gently opened the car door. I got one leg out and the other cop opened Robby's door and yanked him out. The cop pulled me out, threw me against the car, and spread-eagled and frisked me. Many other police cars had answered the call and I was soon surrounded by flashing red and blue lights twirling gaily in the morning sun. Their sirens sounded like a cat convention slowly howling down to silence. The Connecticut Highway Patrol had stopped me, and in addition the town police arrived, the police from Westport and Newport, a sheriff from somewhere, and other cars with lots of lights and no markings. The last to arrive was a fire company's bright red sedan. I remained spread-eagled on the car with a gun to my head while they all argued over who had jurisdiction. Two young cops won me and led me to their car.

"Look, officer, I'm the boy's father. I have court orders for seven years giving me visitation. I don't have them with me, but—"

"Would you get in, please?"

I got in and they started driving.

"Ahh, excuse me," I said. "May I have your names please? I'll need a record of this."

The cop who wasn't driving turned to me. "I'm Officer Kreiger and this is Officer Samuels."

Kreiger pulled out a little card and read me my rights from it. That done, he relaxed. "Say, Mr. . . . " he began. "I'm sorry. What's your name?"

"Holden."

"Mr. Holden, the call was for a kidnapping and this is one offense where an officer can shoot first, you know."

"I didn't know that. Thanks for not shooting me."

"Oh, that's all right," he said. "See, normally I'd put handcuffs on you, but you know, I see you're all right, and I figure it's one of these crazy marital things, but when the arrest is for kidnapping, we have to follow a strict procedure. I would have done the same thing if I was the one who pulled you over."

"This'll be the third time she's called the police, but it's never been so spectacular."

I was mugged, fingerprinted, and held while they figured out what to do with me. Pat would have to tell them there was a court order for the visit. I imagine she did because I heard a man's deep voice yelling back at her. From the look that Officers Kreiger and Samuels exchanged, I guessed they knew the voice's owner. There was a long, loud yelling discussion and then a beefy old cop in a sport shirt appeared and he was mad! He asked the two officers about my car and left the station with a big black tool box. He came back later carrying little plastic bags with tiny flecks in them. Something was up. The two officers went to lunch and came back. I was still waiting. The big beefy cop came out again and handed me a stack of summonses and warrants. I leafed through them. Assault with a deadly weapon (Bernie). Assault and battery against Robby. Malicious assault with an automobile. Leaving the scene of an accident, and many, many more. I looked up at him.

"I'd like to file some complaints against her, too," I said.

"You can't!"

"How can you not allow me to make a complaint?"

"Because I said you can't!"

"May I have your name, please?"

"Goodman. *Chief of Police* Goodman. Now get the fuck outta here!"

I paid the bail, and at three o'clock in the afternoon I was a free man. It had ended with a bit of a shocker, but all I wanted was my day in court.

I got my day in court a few weeks later but it didn't do me any good. Since all those other charges were connected with the dispute over Robby, the judge put off hearing them until we settled the visitation question. I thought it had been settled years ago. The visitation dispute was referred to the Domestic Relations Section. A hearing would be set sometime in the future.

"But—but—but—" I stammered to my lawyer. "How can they do this? What about this Arizona decree I'm holding in my hands? What about the full faith and credit from state to state they told me about in Arizona?"

"Oh, a judge doesn't have to recognize another state's decree if he doesn't want to," my lawyer assured me. "In the long run it'll be better for you. Domestic Relations will uphold your visitation rights."

"In the long run? In the long run he's going to be an adult! What about contempt of court? Can't we press that? The only one who can cancel a visit is the judge. It's written right here. She's in contempt."

"Domestic Relations is only concerned with the child's welfare. They don't penalize parents."

"But they're penalizing my son by default! Doesn't anyone realize that she has avoided visitation for seven years and gotten away with it? She's going to go on doing it in the same way unless some court stops her. It doesn't matter what Domestic Relations says, the only way she'll make a visit is if she's forced."

"There's nothing you can do about it now," he said. "Domestic Relations will be sympathetic."

Well, they might have been sympathetic, but they were very busy. The soonest time for a hearing was six weeks away. I telephoned Robby a number of times, but Pat said he refused to come to the phone. I wrote to him and sent him a check for his birthday. He didn't reply but he cashed the check. I showed the check to Barbara. He had endorsed it, "Robin Holden" because that's how the check was made out, and underneath he had written another endorsement, "Robby Stoner": Harold's last name.

"How awful for you," Barbara said. "You wanted to see him so much. There must be something you can do."

"It's been years. Courts don't seem to help. She does just what she wants. At least I know where he is. We'll see what happens with Domestic Relations."

When the time for the appointment came, Pat simply cancelled it. A second appointment was made for three months away. Another year had gone by.

Because of Pat's cancellation, a court session was scheduled for the other charges. By this time I had filed countercharges of false arrest and many others. It looked like both sides would agree to drop the charges and it would all be forgotten. I drove up to Connecticut for the night court session.

A lot of time had gone by since I set out to try to get visitation with Robin and I had done quite a bit of thinking. I had always assumed that I was fighting Pat, that once Robby was out of her influence, even temporarily, he'd relax with me the way he had on our short visit in Phoenix. I thought that once he knew he had a court protecting his right to see me, he'd have the security to open up and we'd have a relationship. Every kid wants a father, right? I never knew how far the alienation had gone. Even though our visit in Phoenix had been calm and pleasant, his stepfather had to twist his arm to make him go. And then Robby fought furiously to avoid making visits both days in Connecticut. For the first time it became clear to me that it was Robby who was fighting me, not Pat anymore.

And that shouldn't have been strange to me. After all, I was the son of an absent father. My mother had tried to get my father picked up by the FBI to prevent him from visiting me. If he hadn't moved fast, he would have been in the detention camps for years and then deported. Pat's battles were nothing compared to the heavyweight ones I grew up with. Seeing Robby with Pat, I saw myself with my mother again with a clarity I had never had before. Anytime I had manifested a resemblance to my father or any male, all her anger at being abandoned suddenly focussed on me like a death ray. I soon learned not to act like my father, or any male, if I had any hope of getting love from

143

my mother. The result was that I systematically destroyed the image of a growing male inside me when I was young, and when I got older I continued to do little things like destroying the source of my creativity in exchange for love from the women who succeeded my mother. I imagined that Robby must have gone through a lot of that since he was a mirror image of me. He would have done anything against me to prove his loyalty to his mother.

I wanted to love Robby and experience him and have him love me, but in practice all he experienced with me was awful pain. He was now fourteen years old. It was obvious that the alienation was complete. He didn't want to see me and he would do anything in his power to prevent it. So where did that leave me? I seemed to have only one choice. I had decided to stop all my legal actions to force visitation.

The tiny country courtroom was crowded. The old frosted glass globes gave off a yellowish light. Robin entered with Pat and Harold. He was wearing an old-fashioned plaid mackinaw. It was like seeing a worn, deckle-edged snapshot of myself as a kid, except that I was always a happy kid in my photographs. Robin's jaw jutted out and his eyes burned at me. He was ready for a fight. I could only look at him for a moment. It was too much. They sat way in the back, as far from me as they could. When my lawyer showed up, I told him what I wanted to do. After a few minutes with Pat's lawyer, he came back.

"It's all settled. There is one thing more."

"Yeah?"

"Your ex-wife wants you to allow her husband to legally adopt your son."

"That is out of the question," I said.

I watched them leave the courtroom. Robby was triumphant at his mother's side as the three of them walked out. It might be the last time he would ever see me, but he didn't even glance back.

I thought I was doing the best thing for him, but no amount of rationalization can change the sick feeling in your gut when you consciously leave your child. I would never see Robin as a boy and maybe not ever again. I would continue sending him checks and writing to him, keeping all the doors open I could, but any relationship would have to wait until sometime in the future. In the meantime, life had to go on. I had a career that was starting to move and I had Barbara. That's a lot more than most people get in one lifetime.

144

EIGHTEEN

I took Barbara to see O'Neill's *Moon for the Misbegotten* when it opened on Broadway. She was fascinated by it and quickly made arrangements to shoot a series of interviews with Jose-Manuel Quintero, Colleen Dewhurst, and Jason Robards, describing how their lives and careers had long been associated with O'Neill's work. There was a cancellation in the CBS schedule and these interviews were selected to fill the spot. They had to be cut and on the air in a week. Barbara's executive producer decided that videotape was the only means fast enough, but CBS had only recently got their CMX editing computer working and no one knew too much about it. In my many gigs over the past year, I had become something of an expert with this hardware and I offered Barbara any help I could.

We sat together in the CMX room for three days around the clock putting this show together. This was the first time we had worked together since our days at WNET and it was fun. This was what I had imagined our relationship to be from the beginning. We would have two independent careers, but they would intertwine now and then so that each of us could use our individual strengths to help the other. Barbara and our two careers was all I had now. My family had never cared whether I was alive or dead. My children were scattered across America and it seemed to be my fate never to have them. When I walked out of that Connecticut courtroom I cut the last tie to my past. Barbara was my love, my family, my parent, and my child all in one. At that moment my relationship with Barbara and the possibility of our marriage was the only stability I had in the world and I would do anything for her to cement it.

"I *hate* flying!"

Barbara's fingernails dug deeper and deeper into my wrist as our plane left the ground and headed for Miami. After we were safely in the air she grimaced at the marks she left on my skin.

"Oh, I'm so sorry," she said, "but that comes with the territory. Anyone who has ever flown with me can show you the scars. The closer the firma, the lesser the terror."

It had taken a lot of Valium to get her off the ground and she was flying on her own now. She didn't need an airplane. She was terrified of flying and even more terrified to be seeing her family in Fort Lauderdale. We were going down for Thanksgiving.

"I dread this. All Lilly talks about is marriage, marriage, marriage."

"Well, that's what parents like them do."

"You have to do something for me."

"Sure, Babe. What is it?"

"If they ever ask you, I . . . I told them you've only been married twice."

"Twice? Why'd you tell them that?"

"The way they talk about you . . . . Al always says, 'Why do you want to marry a two-time loser?' Two marriages are bad enough, but three they'd never accept."

"There seems to be a lot of talk about marriage," I said. "Anyone I know?"

"It's them. They never let up. Don't they understand that I could be very happy remaining single? Why can't people just live together?"

"Because love isn't static. Two people in love are drawn closer and closer. You can't be casual about someone you really love. Marriage is coming together as close as possible."

"It's nothing but an archaic ritual."

"Sure it's a ritual. But you make a ritual of living together. You celebrate it every day."

"What's so important about a piece of paper?"

"It's not a piece of paper, it's a commitment. You're weaving your love into the social fabric. When you live together you're always leaving yourself a fire escape, a way to get out. You don't worry about getting away from someone you really love."

"You should talk, with your track record," Barbara said.

"Listen, marriage is one thing I know a lot about. I also know what it isn't."

"Didn't bring you anything but misery."

146

"How can you say that?" I said. "You think I was chained and handcuffed each time I got married? You couldn't hold me back. Every one of my marriages was probably the best time in my life when it was new. It wasn't the marriages that were bad, it was the breaking up. I was only a kid when I got married at seventeen. We grew at different rates and in different directions. We changed. We had to separate."

"That doesn't sound like your ex-wife I saw."

"The stronger the bond, the more force it takes to break it apart. I've been the breaker and the breakee. It wasn't fun either way. But there was nothing wrong with the marriages and there's certainly nothing wrong with you and me getting married."

"Not to mention Al and Lilly," she said.

"Well, if something you want coincides with something they want, it's even better, isn't it? But you have to make up your own mind. I know I'm prejudiced. Or maybe it's habit. If you sneeze around me, I'll say 'I do!' instead of 'Gesundheit!'"

Barbara laughed. The plane landed.

Al put us up in an expensive Miami Beach hotel and we went up to Fort Lauderdale for dinner. Lilly cornered me right away. "So, ahh, when is your divorce coming through?"

"Maybe soon now," I said. "I have a new attorney and he's drawn up a strong countersuit. They're starting to negotiate at last."

"Is there any trouble?"

"No. She wants all kinds of alimony and I don't think she's entitled to it. We were only married a few years and we never had any children."

"Huh!" she said. "When you get your divorce, have you thought about the wedding? We'd like to have it down here if you both—"

"Mother," Barbara snarled through clenched teeth, "can't we talk about something more pleasant? I'm eating!"

"What's so unpleasant about getting married?" Lilly said. "You love him, you live with him, you tell me it's going to be forever, what difference does a piece of paper make? You're married already!"

"Mother!"

Al blustered to the rescue.

"C'mon Lilly! Leave them alone, for God's sake! They're here for a vacation."

There was a long, embarrassed silence. Al broke it.

"The hotel treatin' ya okay, An'n?"

Al always left the "t" and the "o" out when he said my name.

"Just fine," I said.

"The manager's a good friend a' mine. Anything you want, let me know."

"It's great, Al. And I appreciate it, your paying for the trip and the car and all."

"Stop it already. You don't pay for nothing down here. You're in the family. This is the only way I get to see my daughter, didn't you know that? Have some more wine."

Al was all right. He was a good man and a generous father. I wouldn't mind being his son-in-law.

Before we left Fort Lauderdale, Barbara and I had dinner with Shana, another one of her surrogate mothers. Barbara had many older women as friends, each of whom, she would confide to me, she wished had been her mother instead of Lilly. Barbara gave me a tour of Shana's condominium, discussing every item in it with an enthusiasm she had never shown before for household impedimenta. My nodding assent to Shana's "good taste" somehow put a seal of approval on her. Shana had a decorator's card and commuted back and forth from New York. By the end of the evening Barbara had hired Shana to completely redecorate our Central Park South love nest.

With all the marriage talk, there had been no further mention of an agreement for me to sign away any claims on the "Berkowitz Fortune." Or maybe Barbara had told them one thing and neglected to tell me. It was hard to know what Barbara thought about certain subjects, like marriage. But it was obvious something was going on. When we went to bed our last night in Miami Beach, Barbara said, "Well, they approve of you. They even like you . . . sort of. They'd be much happier if you had a lot of money, but you're a lot better than they anticipated. They always expected me to bring home a hippie or someone artistic and strange."

"You will please give them my thanks for that left-handed compliment? Sounds more like Lilly. Oh, they're okay. They mean well. What about you?"

"Huh?"

"Do you approve?"

"You know I love you," she said.

"Yeah, I know that, but do you . . . ? What do you think about us getting married? You never talk about that."

She waited a long moment and then I realized she was breathing heavily. She had fallen sound asleep in a moment; not surprising with the drinks and wine on top of the Valium it took to get her out of the door. Wow! It looked like it really might happen. If Margaret would only agree to a divorce, there was a good chance I was going to marry a millionaire! A millionairess!

NINETEEN

Barbara had mentioned fixing up the apartment ever since I moved in, but I never took her domestic fantasies seriously. Now she decorated with a vengeance. One week after another, the place was painted, the floors stained white, and red carpet laid in the bedroom. I put up white shutters and designed and built a semi-enclosed modern bed for her. It was big and white and boxy with hidden shelves inside. Instead of a headboard, I built a compartment for storing blankets with a slanted front that was just the right angle and height for sitting up in bed. Barbara had always loved to watch pro football in bed and she went into another world if the Dolphins played. She settled into her new bed the moment I set it up. She scrunched her hips around and found her comfortable space. I swear she was nesting, like an elegant long-legged heron come to rest on her Bauhaus bed.

I had built into the bed everything she could need. When Barbara was home, she spent most of her time in it, snuggled comfortably in her spot, telephoning, watching television, reading, or writing. Shana tactfully did not comment on my bed, but worked it into her decorating plan, even designing a spread and pillows for it. It was the only piece of furniture Barbara declared off-limits. Everything else— furniture, lamps, tables—was thrown out and new pieces ordered every day. Shana was charged to find the best of everything. Money was no object. And why not? It was for us. Our being together for the future was a fact now. When the dreaded word, "marriage," crept timidly into her friends' conversations, Barbara didn't shut them up as she used to. They began to accept what none of them had dared dream before: Barbara had finally found a man she wanted to live with and the relationship had weathered the test of time. The only thing, apparently, that stood in the way of our marriage was that I was still married to Margaret. My divorce seemed as distant as ever.

One of my editing gigs turned into a writing job. I had talked them into making a syndicated version of the BBC *War and Peace* series which I would, of course, cut. We would need narration written for thirteen hours of openings, closes, "the story so far," sales tape synopses, all the verbiage that makes a TV picture work. That kind of narration gets no credit, but I jumped at it. It would be over a hundred pages of money writing and I could recycle a lot of it for the endless promos I knew they were going to need. All my prior writing had been of the notoriously capricious muse-generated type. Professional hack writing to order and to time was excellent discipline for me. I attacked it with every onomatopoetic participle I had.

I had no sooner started to write when Barbara came to me with an emergency. Her latest show was only half cut and her editor was going on vacation in two weeks. Luckily, it was the Christmas season and the rest of the staff was going on vacation too. They gave Barbara permission to hire a freelance editor to finish the show and she wanted me to do it. My writing was going very well and I knew I could squeeze it in. I finished the narration in a week, delivered it, and started cutting on Barbara's show the same day. Her editor, Gilfredo, was the supervising editor of the series. He had initiated the cutting so he was going to get the screen credit, but I didn't care. Barbara needed me and I wanted to help her.

Barbara called this show *Shadows Behind the Golden Door*. It was about East European Nazis who were alive and thriving in America. It's a TV staple now, but it was practically a forbidden subject then and very touchy. The station manager was so goosey about legal problems that we took to saying, "There are those who have alleged that it is a good morning," when we met in the hall. Barbara had an instinct for important stories and this was a story that needed telling. We worked night and day, restructured it, wrote a new narration, and Barbara finagled more money out of the budget to take the correspondent out and shoot new openings and closes. I even matched the original, something I hadn't had to do in years. We got it to the lab and mixed the tracks with enough time to make the air date the following week.

Once the pressure of the *Shadows* show was off her back, Barbara relaxed and we had a marvelous secular Christmas of good restaurants, friends, and theater. We spent Christmas Eve at the theater watching Archibald MacLeish's *J.B.* with Charles Nelson Reilly and

Vincent Gardenia. We sat in my favorite spot, the front row of the mezzanine, and looked out over a sea of yarmulkas and babushkas. Almost the entire orchestra was occupied by orthodox Jews who were also enjoying their non-Christian Christmas.

Barbara invited Dale and Samantha to the apartment to watch the broadcast of the *Shadows* film we had just finished. In case I had forgotten, Barbara reminded me again not to mention Ben and Lian in their presence. She didn't have to worry. It was getting to be second nature to me now, as it must have been to her. Dale had just flown in from Hollywood. He wore a white jump suit under a fur coat. He was never without his good grass. Sam wore a black dress with her usual decolletage down to her navel. They were fascinated by the show. After the last fadeout, Sam and Dale and I applauded. Barbara was proud of herself. She deserved to be.

"How did you get all the information on these guys?" Sam asked.

"Oh, it's in the public record. You just have to search for it. Nancy, my researcher, did a lot of it. She's dynamite."

"There's something special about this show," Sam said. "There's a quality of . . . I've seen every film you've ever made, Barbara, and there's something special about this one. I . . . of course!"

Sam turned to me, her face lighted up with her discovery.

"I didn't see your name in the credits, but I'll bet you had something to do with it. Am I right?"

"Well, ah . . . he did, he did work on it," Barbara said before I could think of what to say.

"No, no, no! Wait a minute. I know your work, Barbara. I'll bet Anton did a lot on this show. How about it?"

"Don't start trouble, Sam," said Dale.

He took a long toke and retreated. Barbara's nose was plainly out of joint. I had no desire or need to share Barbara's spotlight. I hadn't said a word and my name was nowhere in the credits but Samantha pressed for her answer.

"This was something I worked on a long time," Barbara said. "My editor had to go on vacation and Anton did recut it completely, but what made you suspect?"

"I knew it!"

Sam was elated at her discovery. She threw her arms around Barbara, squeezing her into her vast, motherly bosom.

"Barbara, I'm not belittling your work. I love you, darling. I've seen every film you've ever made and I think you're the most talented producer in television, but I remember the very first time you and Anton made a picture together. Of course I didn't know about him then."

"Neither did I," said Barbara. "I had no idea we'd be together."

"I thought about it," I said.

"I never forgot the show on the aged. There was a special something to it. It was in the other shows you made together at NET. And I told you that, then, remember? You said this special man in your life was cutting your shows. That's how I guessed. This show is different from the other shows you've been making at CBS."

"Sam . . ." warned Dale.

"What I'm trying to say is that you should always try to work together."

"Is that a nice way of telling me I'm not good enough alone?" Barbara said.

"I remember those shows, too, Barbara," Dale said. "I know what Sam's talking about. There's no shame in collaborating if you get results like that."

I was getting very uncomfortable. I took Barbara in my arms.

"Now wait a minute," I said. "I just cut it. Barbara put the ideas together, did all the research and fought for it at CBS. This is the last kind of show they want on the air. I know I'm good and I know I can structure footage that Barbara shoots. We enjoy working together. But it's not in the same league as pulling an original concept out of the air, giving it form, and battling to get a controversial idea accepted. There's a big difference."

"It didn't hurt George S. Kaufman to collaborate," Sam said. "That's all I was trying to say."

Samantha wouldn't let up. She was obviously jealous of Barbara's career and she had clearly been trying to undermine Barbara's accomplishment in her show. They called each other best friends, but there was always that barely repressed hostility between them just below the surface. I stopped participating in the discussion and our conversation soon faded into the sweet haze of Dale's dope.

Barbara got a special Christmas present that year: an Emmy nomination for Best Writer for her *Superlandlord* show. Ever since I had met her, Barbara only wore slacks and tops or a jump suit. Now she dug into a deep corner of her closet and pulled out one high-fashion, dressy outfit after another, searching for the perfect thing to wear for the Emmy Awards dinner. I lay back naked on the bed and watched.

"Where'd those come from?" I asked.

"Oh, they've always been there. Lilly bought a lot of them for me in Paris and Rome. We've never had an occasion before, but now . . . . What will I say if I win?"

"Whatever you want. You know, you thank everybody and—"

"How can I thank those cretins at the station? I made that show in spite of them. Oh, I'll never win anyway. What am I worried about?"

"You have a very good chance. You saw the other shows up for it this year. They're just standard news docs with no bite. You have a very good chance."

"A woman? In that 'old boy' network? Not a chance."

"The times they are a-changin', Babe. You're a minority group now. They need women to fill their quota. Now if you were black also . . ."

"I'm not the only woman producer around."

"No, but you're the best."

"Whatever. We'll go anyway. I want to see all my old friends. I'll think of something to say if . . . "

She shook off the thought and quickly held up a black dress over her body.

"How do you like this one?"

"I don't know. I'd have to see it on. Try it."

She went through them one after another, looking at me for an instant reaction. My main reaction was a lazy erection watching her dress and undress over and over. She kept going back to a favorite of hers, a glossy peach-colored two-piece thing like formal pajamas. The pants were tight around her hips and then flowed out loosely over her legs. She tried it on again.

"What do you think of this, really?"

"I think it's sensational. You keep going back to it. You must like it."

"Oh, I don't know . . . I used to love it, but . . . "

"What's wrong with it?"

155

"The fucking zipper always opens, see? This is one-of-a-kind and they sew it by hand. It's so tight that it opens up by the end of the evening and my ass hangs out."

"Let me see it."

I slipped off the bed to my knees and examined the zipper closely. Her body moved nervously under my touch. She wasn't feeling sexy, it was a different nervousness. She was preparing for the hunt, and for the rewards of the chase.

"It will lock closed if you snap it, like this."

"It won't stay."

"It should stay long enough for a speech. And it's a great outfit. What else have you got?"

"Nothing but this. And there's no time to get anything else. It'll have to be. I'll get Manny to sew this little bit."

She slipped the pants to the floor. I naturally had to kiss that naked tush. With the dressing out of the way, she became conscious of my presence and all her nervous energy flowed instantly into another channel. She pushed me down onto my back and straddled my thighs. I got hard right away and she guided me inside. Her pleasure was so fast and full that I wondered if she was faking it for some reason. She got up and started the shower right away.

"Wait, what about you?"

"Oh, I'm fine," she said with an alley cat grin.

"So fast?"

"I didn't have a climax. Not in the regular way. But I don't need it. It's different lately. There's something I never felt before, a deeper satisfaction when you come inside me now. At the moment you come, my whole body feels right. And I have this feeling all day long now. There are moments, quiet moments . . . even in my day, in between phone calls or something, and then I realize that I'm carrying you around in my body all day long. It's a marvelous feeling!"

She showered and dressed quickly as she spoke. "Nancy and I were talking about you after you came back from court without your son. Now that you won't see him any more . . . "

"Yeah?"

"We were talking about how ideal it must be for you to have a child. How marvelous it must be for them."

"What do you mean?"

"Oh, we were picturing you taking a little blond-haired boy for a walk in the park and how they ask questions all the time and what a delight you must be to a little boy because you always have an answer. That's what Nancy said, 'Even if he doesn't know, Anton always tries to think. He always has some answer.'"

"Hmmm," I hummed.

"It was a perfect picture, you walking with a little blond boy asking you questions and you giving answers all day long."

Barbara put her arms around my neck. She was dressed, I was still naked. She got serious.

"I want you to know, you're the only man whose baby I ever wanted. I have never felt this way before. But I'm too old, of course. It's too dangerous after thirty-five. But I want you to know, if I could, if I thought I could, I would want to have your baby grow inside of me."

Wow. What a feeling. I mean, I've had kids, but no woman ever said that to me before. I felt not only wanted but necessary. We were coming together in ways I had never dreamed possible with Barbara. This new desire stirring inside her might soon be our child. If she was moved to try, I was sure we could make a good baby together. With our love, it would be a completely wanted child.

"It isn't impossible," I said. "Lian must have had her last kids when she was nearly forty."

"Yeah, and she had to get a caesarean and Mike tied her tubes right there. He wasn't going to let her try again. It nearly killed her."

"It's much safer now, though, and Mike seems to be able to help any woman." I gently squeezed her hips. "You're in great shape. Probably the best shape you've ever been in your life. This would be your last chance."

Barbara looked in my eyes a long moment and then kissed me goodbye. She picked up her shopping bag stuffed with books and papers for her current show. Suddenly her knees buckled under her. She gasped for air. An anxiety attack. I tried to help her, but she stumbled into the kitchen and frantically searched the refrigerator for something to drink. There was only beer. She washed down two Valium with a can of Miller High Life and recovered quickly.

"You see? There it is again! I could *never* have a baby while I have these anxiety attacks. And they've been getting worse and worse lately. If it wasn't for Nancy, I wouldn't be able to get through the day." There was a pathetic despair in her voice as she continued, "I don't understand. I have everything a woman could want. I have a success-

ful career, a marvelous man who loves me, my back is all healed . . . .
The more happiness in my life, the worse the anxiety gets. It's not
fair!"

There was so much noise in the huge ballroom at the Emmy
Awards dinner, that I could hardly hear the M.C.

"Best writer of a documentary . . . Barbara Gordon!"

Barbara didn't react to the announcement. I wasn't sure I heard it
right, either. A spotlight swung to our table and Barbara was in the
hot blue center. Then she knew. She stood up abruptly, her chair
tumbling back. I reached for it as she sidestepped her way around me.
The zipper of her glossy peach pants was completely open. Barbara's
ass was indeed hanging out.

"Barbara, wait!"

She didn't hear me. I held my arm across her path but she flung me
aside like a swinging door.

"Babe! No! Wait!"

She didn't know that I existed. She turned into the spotlight. No
one could see the open zipper yet. I jumped up and chased her as she
pushed her way through the next row of tables. Samantha appeared
and threw her arms around Barbara, immobilizing her for a moment.
Barbara wasn't aware of Samantha, either. She kept struggling to get
to the stage where the Emmy was. As Samantha hugged and kissed
her, I put my arms around her, too, hiding her back as I pulled and
clasped the damn zipper, hoping it would hold. Barbara wriggled free
from both our arms and bolted for the rostrum for her acceptance
speech.

All her previous laurels had been shared with others. This was the
first time Barbara had won an original award. I had never seen her so
happy, so high. She thanked all the right people, including the
cretins. I clapped so hard my palms stung. I'm sure the applause was
louder than for any of the previous winners. Barbara had a lot of
friends. We were all with her up there on the stage. We all reached for
her on the way back to the table, shaking her hand, patting her back,
hugging her, kissing her, and loving her. She was in heaven. This is
what she lived for. That shiny gold statuette was more important to
her than me or any of her friends, if you can understand that. And we
loved her for it. I loved her for it.

TWENTY

The apartment was almost finished. It was bright with morning sunlight, white stained floors, white wicker, white everywhere. The plants I had brought into Barbara's life were flourishing in their new home. Their full leaves stood out boldly against the white walls and floors. Barbara and I were drinking coffee. I was about to leave for a meeting with Maggie, her attorney, and my attorney. Barbara looked unusually apprehensive.

"You seem nervous, Babe."

"Be careful. She's dangerous."

"Well, this is nothing to worry about. It's just a preliminary hearing to make a property settlement. We still have to go to court later for the divorce."

"When will that be?"

"Who knows? I'm sorry, Babe. I know this waiting is a drag for you, but it's got to be done. It'll be over soon."

Barbara silently sipped her coffee. She looked depressed as I left for the hearing.

We all met in a little room on the sixth floor of the State Supreme Court Building downtown. The lawyers mumbled greetings but Maggie and I said nothing to each other. There was a mountain of our claims and counter-claims at the end of the conference table. Behind these documents sat a little guy in his shirt sleeves. He had a sharp nose and iron-gray hair. He looked sixty-odd years and tough. It said "Special Referee" on his door and I thought he must be one of those unknown people who arbitrate for a living. He introduced himself, "Good morning. My name is Irving Greene . . . " (It said "Honorable" on his name plate.) " . . . I'm a special referee for this action for divorce between Margaret Holden and Anton Holden. Are the plaintiff and the defendant here?"

"Yes."

"Yes."

He flipped casually through the two years' worth of legal wrangling in front of him.

"I notice there's been a history of disagreement between the two parties here."

Nobody spoke. We all knew that.

"But it seems to me that you're in complete agreement in one area."

Maggie and I stared at each other. What could we possibly have overlooked?

"You both want a divorce. Is that correct?"

We both nodded, the attorneys agreed. No one knew where he was leading us.

"Well, I'm a special referee, but I have the powers of a Supreme Court judge in this action. I can grant you a divorce, if you both want one."

Nobody spoke. He looked at each of us.

"Well?" he said.

The lawyers and Maggie and I looked at each other. We didn't understand. He repeated as though he was talking to a roomful of idiots.

"If you two both want a non-contested divorce, and there are no children of this marriage, I can grant it. Absolute and final. Right now. Today. How about it?"

A no-fault non-contested divorce in New York? This was something new. Apparently the state was experimenting with it. Our attorneys had never heard of the possibility. They conferred with Irving and were convinced. My lawyer asked me if I wanted a divorce.

"Of course! Are you kidding?" I said.

I heard Margaret saying the same thing to her lawyer. They sent Maggie and me out in the hall to talk over how far we'd go with the money settlement. She was still holding out for a percentage of my life forever.

"You'll never get it," I said. "You want to pay lawyers the rest of your life? Or do you want to stop fucking around and get it over with? I say let's go for it right here. What do you say?"

She thought a moment and then said, "Okay."

Okay? Simple as that? She couldn't have said that two years ago? I didn't say anything, though. I know when I'm well off. Pay the ten dollars, right?

After the Honorable Irving Greene had arbitrated with subway unions and the Rockefellers, we were a pushover. He steamrollered us through a property settlement in minutes. I helped a little. I let her have everything except my old Moviola. Thirty minutes later we were through. I had a divorce. It was a miracle. Years ago, I had been through New York's farcical adultery trials with wife number one and I'll tell you, civilization is marvelous. I called home right away. Barbara was still there.

"Babe! You'll never guess! I have a divorce!"

"Huh?"

"Surprised? It's true. I have a divorce! It's all over! We can get married now."

I thought she would be overjoyed. She wasn't. She sounded panicky.

"How . . . ? How did that happen? I thought it was only a property settlement. I . . . "

"Don't ask. I'll explain when I get home. I love you! I want to marry you, Babe! I'm coming home right now. Isn't it fantastic?"

"Ahhh . . . yeah, sure," she said.

"I'm coming right home. We have to celebrate! I love you!"

I bought a bottle of Dom Perignon and taxied all the way uptown. It was a glorious, sunny February day.

The apartment seemed empty and silent when I got home. Barbara was nowhere around. I thought she'd be waiting to celebrate with me. "Babe?" I called. I heard a muffled reply from the bedroom and went in. The shutters were closed. It was too dark to see clearly. Barbara was in bed, completely hidden under the covers. I was too excited to wonder why she would be sleeping in the middle of such a day. I nudged her gently to wake her. "Babe?"

She mumbled from under the covers. I got two glasses from the kitchen and sat on the edge of the bed. Barbara slowly emerged from the covers as I opened the champagne.

"I have a divorce at last! Isn't it wonderful? A real, legal, binding, absolute divorce! And it's not a bad settlement. It's a fixed amount of alimony. When I'm paid up, I'm rid of her. That's all I ever wanted."

I popped the cork and poured out two glasses of champagne as Barbara sat up. She seemed not quite awake yet. "It's all over and our life is just beginning." I put one glass in her hand and toasted, "To you and me, Babe."

She took a sip and immediately threw it up on the bed. She dry-heaved and gagged. I took the glass from her and patted her on the back. My eyes were used to the dark and I saw her clearly for the first time. She didn't look well. "Are you all right, Babe?"

"I got . . . horrible cold." Her jaw was slack and wobbling. I could hardly make out what she was saying.

"A cold?" I said. "You were fine this morning. How could you get so sick so fast?"

She pulled her face up to me and touched her nose to mine. "Can't breathe!" she groaned. She began to sway comically. I thought for a moment she was making it up, but she had no control over her jerky movements. "I feel awful," she murmured.

"I'm sorry, Babe. I didn't know you were sick. Can I get you something?"

"Un-unh," she groaned and slowly burrowed backwards into the warm tunnel of blankets. Her voice faded after her, "Gotta sleep. Don't wake me . . . up." She slept all that day and through the next night.

I realize now that after I telephoned Barbara with the sudden, shocking news of my divorce, she had probably taken every Valium in the house and who knows what else to wash it down with. How can I declare that so confidently? Well, they call Valium a good muscle relaxant. By the time I got home and Barbara tried to sit up, every joint in her body wobbled as loosely as though she were a rubber marionette without strings. I've never seen anything like it. She had no control over her muscles at all. I was so high with my good news, that I didn't question Barbara's odd physical behavior then, but the picture stayed with me. This was only two o'clock on a Wednesday afternoon. Barbara had been perfectly fine when I left her that morning. She was neither a late sleeper nor a midday drunk, but she was so zonked out I doubt if she could remember that day's existence at all. And I didn't understand what was happening. Back then no one knew much about Valium, and I had no way of knowing how terrified Barbara was of this marriage she both desired and dreaded.

In the two years we lived together Barbara functioned quite well balancing the demands of her career, me, her parents, CBS, her anxiety attacks, and her Valium. She not only functioned, she regularly produced award-winning TV shows, which is something few people can accomplish cold sober. I would not describe Barbara as having a "drug problem" during that time. But everything changed after the day I brought home my divorce and I was ready, eager, and able to marry her. She suddenly had to resolve all her ambivalence about marriage and she couldn't. Barbara had developed plenty of defenses against marriage, but she had no defenses against the new desires that welled up inside her body once it had been freed by her back operation. I believe that for the first time in her life a part of Barbara wanted marriage and even children, too. To suppress those desires she had to battle herself now, and Barbara Gordon was a formidable opponent.

While she slept drugged through that sunny February afternoon, my joyous celebration slowly faded as I drank the last of the champagne all by myself. Everything had turned topsy-turvy. This was only the first of many such days in the year to come.

PART III

TWENTY ONE

With my divorce in hand, I assumed we were going to get married, but Barbara wouldn't say yes and she wouldn't say no, either. She finally did say that it would have to wait until she got a break in between shows. Then she took on extra shows in mid-season and the break never materialized. She exhausted herself with work. We hardly saw each other. When we chanced to meet for dinner we barely had time to eat, and as we passed through the bedroom door she would pop two Valium and be unconscious in minutes. Many times she didn't have a chance to take her clothes off before falling asleep and I would have to undress her.

I was too busy, too. Time-Life liked the narration I had written and they gave me a chance to write for their syndicated animal show. I had cut a few episodes of that series, but the screen credit as writer was much more important to me. In the caste system of movies and television, editors are listed "below the line" in the budget. That means labor, by the hour, along with truck drivers and grips. Writers are listed "above the line." That means talent, along with the director, the producer, and the stars. You can't carry the rubric "Editor" and go around waving a screenplay. It doesn't matter how good it might be; no one takes you seriously.

It was a good show with none of that cloying anthropomorphism most animal shows have. They liked my script and gave me another one to write immediately after. It was about spiders. What did I know from spiders? In two weeks of research I knew a lot. All that time I had put in was paying off in much more than money. I was a professional writer with an "above the line" credit on a first-class syndicated show. I worked my ass off.

Barbara and I didn't see each other for weeks on end, but when we did it was obvious that our magic relationship had changed. After I got my divorce problems seemed to appear everywhere. There are times when you do everything right. And there are times when you can't do anything right no matter how hard you try. There are times in a relationship, usually the beginning, when you could be in jail for armed robbery, for instance, and your lover will say something like, "Oh, he's just a little wild. You have to get to know him. He's really a lot of fun." And then there are times in the same relationship, usually the ending, when if you set a pencil down on a table a millimeter in the wrong direction it becomes a capital offense even worse than murder. I was musing about this phenomenon while making love to Barbara one night. My head was nestled in between her lovely legs just like always and I was kissing her just as I always did but she was not responding the way she always had before.

"You're going too fast," she said. "More gently. Higher . . . no, no, no, not that high! Lower! If you just wouldn't rush into it like that. I wish you'd start gently."

Start gently? I did, but it seems like an hour ago. She must have forgotten. There are times when your lady does not fall head over heels, panting passion and coming over and over again with rhapsodic groans. There are times when it takes work; times when you find yourself staring at your lover's pubic hair; times when you find yourself counting those hairs . . . one by one. But you really love her and it isn't unpleasant. It's very soft and warm and tasty and there are a lot of sensual memories associated with this place (from *way* back, right?). But you're older now; your back is stiff. So, trying not to miss a precious moment, you ease yourself into a more comfortable position. You try to lay flat and be careful you don't put any weight on your hardon—but oh, it doesn't matter, it seems to have got soft. Hope she doesn't notice. Now if I can just keep this rhythm up . . . Oops.

"Oh, don't stop now! How can you . . . ? I was just about to . . ."

Well, how was I to know? She's been "just about to" all night. Luckily I can't talk with my mouth full.

"No, you've lost it again," she said.

I don't think women realize that at such times their little bit gets much littler and softer and hard to find in there.

"Oh, it's all right. You can stop. I just don't seem to be able . . ."

Stop? My undying love (and ego) will not permit. I'm the greatest lover in the world, right? Onward! I'll just have to ease up a little. She must be numb by now. My jaw is.

"Harder! Harder!"

Well, okay. Harder.

"Don't rush it so much!"

Harder, but don't rush it. O-kay. I eventually synchronized with her distant drummer. I was comfortable now and in that position I could catch my breath when I needed to. I began to get lost in the mechanics of making love. And it is sort of soothing, like worry beads, I suppose. Some men need to have their hands busy. When my tongue is busy at a familiar task it helps me to think.

So we might never get married. So what? That was only a fantasy, after all. Just an overreaction on my part to losing my son. Barbara had given birth to the only child she would ever have. Her Emmy was delivered and we stood it on the low shelf above the bed. I could see the winged gold statuette right above Barbara's tightly closed eyes. Emmy's outstretched arms offered a globe of shining, intertwined circles over us morning and night, sleeping and making love. Emmy would be the offspring of our relationship. Emmy and all her cousins. Barbara and I would win them one by one.

"Ahh. That's it," she said, "now faster . . . "

There you go, Babe. I can feel it starting deep within you. It's going to be a tough one for you. I can feel that, too. You're fighting it, going incredibly tense inside. Soon, Babe, you'll get the release you're fighting so hard for. Love making is difficult when you're angry and depressed.

Since my divorce, Barbara had seemed angry with everyone around her. She was angry with CBS, angry with the shows they wanted her to do, and she was constantly getting into fights with her crews. She was trying to film a piece about a small-town woman mayor who had just discovered she had a hopeless cancer. It's not the kind of subject I would associate with Barbara, but she was forced to take it and then to her surprise she formed an intense love for this woman.

The woman's name was Jean Walling. Jean was a strong-jawed woman in her fifties with short white hair. She was a giving person who had naturally moved into taking care of her community after her children had grown. She had upset the "business as usual" attitude of her little town's city hall and the party was talking of nominating her for the senate seat. She represented everything Barbara stood for, every political fantasy Barbara ever had. Jean was trying to fight her cancer emotionally and physically and still be a mayor every day. She had been told her cancer was hopeless, but this lady mainlined hope. It was infectious. Jean really thought she could beat it. Barbara thought so too. Barbara seemed to confuse Jean's life-and-death struggle with her own life in some strange way. She believed that this film she was making would help Jean cheat death.

Jean's tragic story meant so much to Barbara that, without asking me, she had pulled strings at CBS and Gilfredo had agreed to hire me to cut the film for her. She couldn't bear the thought of any editor at the station jeopardizing this film. I hesitated before answering. I was right in the middle of my spider movie and there didn't seem to be enough time to make both air dates. Barbara finally persuaded me and I agreed to start cutting hers at night while I finished mine during the day. I overlapped the two shows for a week or so of long nights, but it was always exciting to cut one of Barbara's important films. The film-making chemistry between us still worked. A structure evolved that neither of us had expected and a powerful little movie began to take shape, which Barbara called *A Gift of Time*.

As I made each cut I watched Jean's every gesture a hundred times over. I got to know her intimately. One night the cumulative effect of the hours of screening suddenly hit me. I realized that I was watching this woman die in front of my eyes. I took Barbara aside to show her. In the speeded up time of cutting, we could see Jean deteriorate during the days since Barbara began filming. Her color turned waxen, her flesh tightened, her gestures and her walk had changed. It was unmistakable. And Jean did soon die, just a few days before air time. I grimly cut in a title we had prepared for just this possibility and added the date. It was almost like her grave marker on film:

MAYOR JEAN WALLING DIED
IN MIDDLESEX HOSPITAL
NEW BRUNSWICK, NEW JERSEY,
ON APRIL 25, 1975

A lot of love went into that film and a lot was drained out of Barbara and me. Barbara was depressed for weeks afterwards, but I don't think it was entirely about Jean's death. The looming prospect of marriage was very like the death of a little girl whose name was Barbara Gordon.

Tonight was the first time she wanted to make love since Jean had died and it was hard for her. But I knew her body well, she was finally

170

getting to the edge of her climax. She was unbearably tense now. She couldn't hold back much longer. She came with a scream almost of pain. Her taut stomach jerked and shivered, flowing into a release that took with it, at least for the moment, all of Barbara's anger and despair.

There you go, Babe. Let it all come. There . . . . Her breath came in convulsive gasps. Her hands grabbed at the air. Above her, Emmy watched in golden silence, offering her shining globe only inches from Barbara's fingertips.

TWENTY TWO

In the months following, Barbara's anxiety attacks took a puzzling turn. She began having them on weekends. She would leave the house on some innocent errand and ten or twenty minutes later she'd be back, gasping for breath, shaking and sweating, and then she'd collapse on the couch. Nothing I tried seemed to help her now. I was mystified because I had always connected her attacks with conflicts at work and, as far as I knew, Barbara had no conflicts with Bergdorf's or Gristede's or Manny the cleaner. I was the only person she was with on Saturdays and Sundays and I still didn't associate her anxiety attacks with me.

There was a conflict between us, though, and it was rapidly turning into a very bitter fight. Barbara never resolved her disappointment over the beach house so we had decided to remodel it to change those features she disliked. We were working from a design of mine which involved completely removing the old low roof and raising a high, sloping one that would open up the ocean view. The old ocean wall would be replaced by four patio doors that would go from one side of the house to the other, with windows above the doors that would make a glass living room wall almost 12 feet high. This would give an ocean view from anywhere in the house and the hated beach chairs couldn't be seen.

We contacted three Ukranian brothers who had rebuilt her friend Roxanne's beach house. We wanted them to start right away. Barbara wrote out a check for half the amount in advance. That had been back in October. Barbara and I were new to housebuilding and we found that it wasn't so simple to remodel a house in the sleepy little village of Quogue. At each permit hearing we thought was the last, we'd be told that there was always one more needed before we could start building. It wasn't until sometime around March that we finally got our permit to begin work. I gave the go-ahead to the three brothers.

I was eager to watch my design take shape, but I suddenly got very busy on an important job. I had taken an assignment as a producer, writing and supervising the editing of a Bicentennial documentary, another fusing of my writing and editing. It was a salvage job I took over from their first producer. They were over budget, behind schedule, and the fee wasn't that great, but that's how you get opportunities. I would have a current screen credit as a writer-producer, another step out of the cinema's working class. Screen credit is very important in this gypsy business. Sometimes it's the only proof you have that you have existed.

Weeks went by before Barbara and I both had a long enough break from our busy schedules to drive out and see how the beach house was coming along. They should have been nearly finished by this time, but as we turned onto the dune road Barbara screamed, "There's no house! My house is gone!"

It did look that way, but as I drove closer we could see a few walls still standing. We walked around to the beach side. It looked like a bomb had gone off inside the house. The roof and three walls were torn off and the debris was piled shoulder high around the perimeter. Fifty years of shingling and painted split lumber was piled where it fell. Barbara was in shock. They might not finish in time for the summer rental, which was supposed to pay for the remodeling.

It took me a while to locate them and my worst fears were confirmed. The permits had been delayed for so long that they gradually spent the down payment. They would finish the job, but someone would have to go with them to supervise.

"You've got to be there every day," Barbara said, "or they'll fuck off like they did up to now."

"You're right. They might. Except that I don't have the time to do it."

"But you have to. I can't. I have my job."

"Yeah, well, you seem to forget that I have my job, also," I said.

"But that's not as important as renting the house."

That line jolted me. It took me a moment to reply.

"Did I hear right? *Your* job is too important to leave? *Your* job is more important than the house, but *my* job is not as important? Is that what you said?"

"You don't expect me to leave my show, do you?" She said that with

174

the kind of assurance you reserve for answers like, "The sky is blue." I still couldn't quite believe it.

"But you expect me to leave *my* show?" I said.

"You have more talent than to waste your time on a piece of shit like that."

That got to me. "It may seem like a piece of shit to you," I replied coolly, "and it may very well be a piece of shit, but it's my life and my career and I'll decide whether or not it's a piece of shit."

"But this is our dream house!"

"No, Babe. Stop kidding yourself. It's not *our* house. It's *your* house. You own it. We're not married. We don't share the money. We're talking dollars and time and careers now, not dreams. I gave a commitment to these people. You can't ask me to walk out in the middle."

"But what are we going to do?"

"They may finish on time yet. And if they don't, I'll be through with this job soon. I'll come out here and do it and at most you'll lose a month's rent."

"I can't afford that. How will I pay the mortgage?"

"Then hire somebody to do it!" I yelled. "You have enough money!"

"Can't you just quit that fucking job?"

"No! You quit your fucking job! It's your house!"

It was our first real fight. It was ugly, but in a way I was glad it was happening. It woke me up to the realities of living with Barbara without being married. This kind of conflict was bound to happen as long as she persisted in pretending that her money didn't exist. There would always be decisions in life that she could make and I could not afford.

But Barbara didn't take frustration easily. Her weekend anxiety attacks got worse and now even her Valium wasn't working as it used to. She had taken to washing it down with beer. An unusual thirst seemed to accompany these new attacks. She gulped her Miller High Life after the Valium as though she hadn't had a drink in days. Soon that wasn't enough either, and she'd have to take more Valium and more beer until she was doped up enough to leave the house for her weekend errands. I was accustomed to Barbara's attacks by this time and at first I didn't think much about it. And the beer didn't seem unusual. It was mid-day Saturday or Sunday and the sun was over the yardarm, oh, maybe sometimes a few hours early, but it was no big deal. It was like having a light drink with lunch. But I did get concerned when these weekend attacks became a regular occurrence and I asked her what her doctor was doing about it.

"I don't know!" she said.

"Don't you ask him about it?"

"I do, but lately all he does is make me act out these strange hostility games and . . . "

Her voice trailed off and I could hardly hear her.

"Hostility games?" I said. "What does that mean?"

"He makes me scream, 'I hate! I hate! I hate!' And then I make like a machine gun . . . "

She held her hands out, pointing her fingers like she was holding a machine gun.

" . . . and then I scream and yell and fire my machine gun— DADADADADADADAT! DADADADADADADAT! I shoot at all the people around me! DADADADADADADADADADADADADADADADADADAT!"

Barbara really got into it. She sprayed the apartment with imaginary bullets. I couldn't help noticing that I was in some of the crossfire.

"DADADADADADADADADADAT!"

Seventy-five dollars an hour for this?

"DADADADADADADADADADAT!"

After she had emptied one cathartic clip and the noise died down, I ventured to ask, "Ahhh . . . who are you shooting at?"

"Oh . . . oh, just the people who are *on* me every day, pressuring me. He says I'm doing fine, that there should be a breakthrough, but I don't feel any different. Oh, by the way . . . what are you doing Thursday morning?"

I was immediately alert. Barbara reserved "Oh, by the way . . . " only for news of cataclysmic potential. "Thursday?" I said. "I'm always busy on this show. Why do you ask?"

"Doctor Alexander wants to talk to you."

"Your shrink? What's it about?"

"It's very important. I want you to come with me on my next appointment."

"Ahhh . . . sure. I'd be happy to."

Her psychiatrist? Well! Aside from Barbara's Valium prescription and an occasional cryptic reference like that machine gun, I had no knowledge of Doctor Alexander, who by this time must have known a great deal about me. Now I was being summoned to the holy of holies. I felt as though I was approaching for an audience with him. No, by the time Barbara and I were in the cab Thursday morning, I felt like I was approaching for an audience with . . . Him.

"He" was an ordinary man, thin, with a hawk nose and soulful eyes. He was quite likeable, but he looked weak across from Barbara. I wondered who really ran their sessions. We shook hands and I sat down in a squooshy leather chair and waited to see what this was all about.

"Barbara has indicated that there is a problem between the two of you," he began. "She thought perhaps I could help. It's about the beach house. Barbara doesn't understand your refusal . . . your apparent unwillingness to help complete the renovation before the summer."

So that's why she wanted me to see him. It was like having "Daddy" resolve an argument. I wondered what she thought he could accomplish. Barbara and I had had this discussion quite a few times in the last weeks and I wasn't about to change my mind. This was becoming a symbol of our whole relationship, or at least of her ambivalence. I didn't care what her hired gun would say, I wasn't going to give up any part of my career for a piece of real estate that wasn't even mine. I left Maggie to get away from that kind of shit.

"Barbara is exactly right," I said. "'Refusal' is the better word. I did refuse. Yes."

"Can you tell me why? I'd like to hear your point of view."

"The disagreement is that before we found out about the house, I began work on a project of my own which I can't leave. It's my first credit as a writer-producer in a long time. That's very important to me. Also, the executive producer is one of the men I do a lot of work for at Time-Life. If I walk out on this job he'll never hire me again. That's where most of my income came from last year."

Barbara turned to the doctor, "He doesn't need the money. All he has to do is write. At home or at the beach. I'm happy to support him. He knows that."

"Babe, you're the nicest thing that's happened to me in my life, but

177

I never asked you to support me. I have to make my own living. What would I do if something happened to you tomorrow? Like the way Jean Walling died so—"

"Don't say that!" she blurted out.

"Damn it! I have to say it! Suppose you're out shooting in Alaska or somewhere and something happens to you, you're unconscious in a hospital. How could I fly there with no money? How could I help you? How would I pay the rent? How would I live? What would you expect me to do, call Al and ask him for a handout? Do you think he would give me money if I wasn't married to you?"

She didn't answer.

"Babe, you must see the postition you're trying to put me in. What do you expect me to do if we aren't married and I have no work or money of my own?"

I waited for a response but she stared sullenly into her lap.

"I have to have a life and a career even if we are married. But when we aren't married it's an absolute necessity. You can't ask me to give up my next year's income for the house if we aren't married."

"I always thought of it as our dream house," she said sadly. "I thought you felt that way, too."

"I enjoy the house but it's too rich for me. I can't afford that kind of dream. You can. You can't ask me to make such a sacrifice for your house."

"But it's *our* house."

"No, Babe. In no way is it *our* house. I stay in it with you, but it's *your* house. *You* own it. The rent goes into *your* bank account, it pays *your* mortgage, and the equity eventually returns to the ever-loving Berkowitz Fortune like you said."

"No!" She was flustered. "I . . . I was going to put the house in both our names. I always meant to."

"Well, when that happens—*if* that happens—it will be a marvelous, generous act, but my love, you do have a way of avoiding those kinds of commitments. And that's okay! I love you the way you are except that you want all the perquisites of marriage with none of the responsibilities."

"It sounds like such a threat," she muttered. "If I marry you, you'll fix the house. That's . . . that's *blackmail!*"

"Blackmail? . . . Oh, Babe . . . I don't know what to say to that."

She stared at her lap and didn't move. Doctor Alexander's cool voice broke the long silence.

"Barbara . . . ?"

She didn't respond.

"Barbara, you asked him here to explain and I think he's done that. Certainly from his point of view, he's justified in looking at the situation the way he has."

Barbara exploded at him. "I know you want me to get married, too! It's a conspiracy! You're both in it together!"

The doctor cleared his throat and continued, "It may not fit into your plans, but you do have to make some decision for him. If you don't make a decision about marriage then he is absolutely right in taking care of himself first. You would do exactly the same in his position."

Barbara clenched her mouth shut and stared at him as though she had been betrayed by her most trusted ally. Doctor Alexander seemed to get smaller and smaller in his chair. He glanced at his clock.

"The hour is up, I'm afraid. Before you go, Barbara, do you need another prescription?"

"Oh yes."

She responded to that all right. Before we left, I had an opportunity to observe the Valium-dispensing machine. He gave her whatever she asked for. He had no idea he had given her a prescription for a month only last week. I knew because I had filled it for her. I was beginning to count, and for the first time in our relationship, I was beginning to worry about it.

But no amount of Valium could resolve our dispute over the house. Barbara got madder and madder. She asked me again to quit, but I was adamant. This was going to be a showdown. She was going to have to face the reality of our relationship sooner or later and stop being so damned ambivalent. With her house and her money involved, she couldn't avoid it this time. The conflict hung this way until one day I walked into the apartment and found Barbara leaning weakly in the kitchen doorway holding a handful of small yellow papers. Tears streamed down her cheeks.

"It's gone . . . all gone . . . . " She let the papers slip from her fingers one at a time and they fluttered slowly to the floor. "Everything's gone. . . . " she said.

There was a posed, melodramatic look to her performance that made me almost laugh for an instant, but her tears were real. I went to her. "Babe, what's wrong?"

179

"It's gone. There's nothing left."

"Gone? What?"

She explained through her sobs as best she could, "I knew they shouldn't have bought so many . . . . All my money was in UDCs and now . . . they're worthless! All Al's money is gone!"

When Barbara said "UDC" I knew immediately what was wrong. The first waves of New York City's default were felt in the market's sudden panic over the state's Urban Development Corporation Bonds. Overnight, holders of these bonds learned that they might be worthless. Barbara had gone through all her computer stock transfer receipts which were the small yellow papers now scattered all over the hallway. She had just discovered that her broker had bought her two hundred fifty thousand dollars' worth of these bonds.

"I'll have to sell the house," she sobbed. "If anyone wants it!"

"No, Babe, not the house. You won't have to do that."

"The land is valuable. I have to. I can't pay the mortgage."

"No. The rental will pay the mortgage. It pays for itself just like you always said."

"Not with two walls and no roof it won't."

I felt like King Shit right about then. Something snapped inside me. All my former resolve disappeared in Barbara's tears. Suddenly my work didn't seem as important as the hurt she was feeling. It was my responsibility that the walls and roof had been torn down to make way for the rebuilding. Barbara would never have gone into that alone. It was my responsibility and it was up to me to do something about it. She had given to me when I needed and I owed her for that. I put my arms around her.

"Babe, I'm going to fix the house. All those things I said before—"

"It's all right. I respect your life and what you said."

"Please, Babe, listen to me. I meant what I said, but this is different. We didn't know this when we were at the doctor's. Sometimes it takes an outside force to resolve personal differences, but that doesn't make it any less sincere. I'm going to quit and the house will be done."

"No!" she said. "You don't have to. I understand. I'll sell the land for whatever I can and I'll be rid of it. It was just a silly dream."

"Barbara, I don't want you to lose your dream house. I never wanted that. I'll get those guys out there and it will be done on time. I can't do anything about the bonds, but you can relax about the house at least. Do you hear me? Babe, please stop crying for a moment and listen to what I'm saying. The house will be okay. I'm going to take care of it."

I wiped away her tears and kissed her. "Babe, I want you to understand something. You have to know that I love you . . . without your money. The money has nothing to do with what I feel. Maybe there's some good in this if you understand that."

I held her face up to mine. "Now you're broke," I joked. "Welcome to the working class."

Tears welled in her eyes and she started to cry again, but this time she was happy.

I quit the next day. They weren't too happy about it. I didn't expect them to be. I searched out the three brothers and we went on a shopping trip for the lumber, the windows, the doors, and all the supplies. We started construction on the house immediately. Barbara stopped me one morning before I went out to the beach to work on the house. She looked serious.

"I want to talk to you," she said. "I've been thinking a lot about what you said in Doctor Alexander's office about Jean. I realized that I could . . . What happened to her could happen to me without warning. I have to live life right now. When I said the house is ours I really meant that. It doesn't belong to Al or Lilly or the fucking Berkowitz Fortune. You are the most important person in my life and I want you to know that."

She handed me a piece of yellow lined paper written in longhand. It was a will, witnessed by Nancy, leaving the beach house to me if anything happened to Barbara. I read it over and over as she spoke.

"I listened to all you said at Doctor Alexander's and you were right. It takes something like those UDCs to see life clearly. All Al's money doesn't mean anything next to the happiness you give me."

I fought back tears as I read the will. I was not prepared for anything like this. Barbara took a book out of her shopping bag, *The Algonquin Wits*. She was researching a show she hoped to do on them. She took the will from me and folded it.

"If anything happens to me, Nancy knows where it is."

She opened the book to a sad picture of Dorothy Parker, slipped the will alongside and closed the book on it.

"It'll be in here until I have time to draw up the papers because . . . as soon as I finish these two shows . . . " She paused a moment then went on, "I want to get married. But I'm not going to have a big

181

wedding like Lilly wants. I don't need anyone but Nancy. We need a witness and Nancy is special. She loves you a lot and I don't know how I could have survived this year without her. I put in for a vacation in October. They were happy to give me a month off with no problem, like you always said they would. We'll get married and go to Europe for a honeymoon. We'll just drive around like you always wanted."

We fell into each other's arms. I couldn't hold back my tears any longer.

"Babe, I never doubted you. . . . " Along with my tears came wrenching sobs. "It is *our* house. It'll be beautiful. You'll see." I bawled like a baby.

ARISE YE PRISONERS OF STARVATION.
ARISE YE WRETCHED OF THE EARTH . . .

I was singing to myself as I escorted Barbara up the long wooden walk for her first look at the completed beach house.

FOR JUSTICE THUNDERS CONDEMNATION.
A BETTER WORLD'S IN BIRTH

"What's that you're mumbling?" she asked.

"Nothing. I'm just feeling good."

Barbara was knocked out the moment she opened the door. The new ceiling soared to 12-foot-high windows that overlooked an unbroken view of the ocean. The living room looked huge and bright and airy. And most spectacular of all for Barbara, none of the beach chairs could be seen.

"You did it!" she said.

"For you, love."

We rented it to the first person who saw it for a preposterously high sum.

There was one weekend left before the summer rental and we gave a housewarming party at the beach house for all the friends we hadn't seen in the course of our last very busy year. All the neighbors from up and down the beach stopped by. Samantha and Dale stayed for the weekend with their two kids and Nancy slept on a couch. Meyer and Ruth drove from Connecticut. Meyer was the only one of our friends who Barbara confided to about her money. He was an ex-lefty who had become a wealthy capitalist. He reassured Barbara that her bonds would be safe, although no one knew quite how, yet.

Barbara was determined to have all her friends share in her happiness and she invited Ben and Lian, too. After all her mystery in keeping them apart, Dale and Ben acted as though there was nothing special in both of them being there. They were aware of each other, though. They studiously avoided each other's presence as they melted into the rapidly growing crowd which spilled out to the deck, drinking, laughing, and chatting, with screaming children tearing across the deck to the beach. It all revolved around Barbara, who had turned from helpless dependent guest into queen bee hostess. She talked excitedly about our plans to marry and then go to Europe for a relaxed month's honeymoon.

I wondered how I could ever have doubted her. She had gotten over all her anger about the beach chairs, all her fears of the money and losing the house and she had even overcome her considerable ambivalence about our marriage. Having resolved our first serious conflict so happily for both of us, it seemed as though Barbara's anxiety had lost its power over her.

But it was only a temporary respite. A much deeper conflict was beginning to emerge that neither of us suspected. As the day of our marriage neared, it threatened to destroy the most important part of Barbara's life: her career.

TWENTY THREE

Since I had walked out on my last job in order to finish the house, I was unemployed for a while. But I had started writing again and Barbara briefly realized her cherished fantasy of working and supporting her artist-in-residence—me. My part of the unwritten deal was to do all the shopping, cooking, and housework, which suited me just fine. I had done that stuff with all my wives and girl friends without thinking. I never knew what a conventional mother was, so I never expected any of my wives to be one.

Now that I was doing all the shopping, I noticed that I regularly bought six-packs of beer with the groceries and they regularly disappeared from the refrigerator during the week, although I didn't drink them. I opened my eyes and saw that what had begun as Barbara's response to an immediate need had become a habit. Barbara was taking two Valium and a beer the moment she got out of bed every morning, whether she had an anxiety attack or not—unless she now had anxiety going from the bedroom to the kitchen. Once aware of this, I realized that Barbara had gone on to yet another stage. I had lately watched as she habitually slipped two cans of Miller High Life into her elegant bag each morning as she left for work. I didn't say anything. I didn't want to think about what I saw happening. You fight this kind of knowledge about someone you love. It takes an outside incident to force you to see what you've known for a long time.

Barbara called me into the station one night to take a look at her current film. Gilfredo had made a rough assembly but she wanted my opinion in private. There was nothing unusual in this; I had done it many times since Gilfredo and I had become friends. He didn't mind. While I threaded up the picture and track on the Moviola, Barbara tried to explain the thesis of her show. As she talked, she seemed to get more and more confused and suddenly she burst into tears.

"I've been filming this shit for weeks," she cried, "and I still don't know what this show's about! Gilfredo, well he's the best they have here, and I love him, but he can't make any sense of it either!"

She sobbed quietly, unable to go on. I couldn't imagine why she was so upset. She had never mentioned anything at home.

"Don't worry, Babe."

I put an arm gently on her shoulder. It was like old times in a darkened cutting room together.

"Let's take a look. See what you've got so far."

We began to screen the footage. I was not prepared for what I saw. The master interviewer I knew so well was gone. In her place was a somnambulent Barbara going through the motions. Her questions made no sense. She wasn't listening to the responses. Her speech was garbled and sleepy-sounding. She couldn't handle the people she interviewed. They twisted her around as though she were an amateur fresh out of journalism school. Most of the footage was unusable. Ironically, the subject was the abuses of institutional psychiatry, such as psychiatric testing and the epidemic use of drugs for psychiatric treatment.

"I'm going to call it *Who Owns Your Mind*," she said. "I have more shooting days but I don't know what to shoot."

She spoke rapidly and waved notes from the stack of research Xeroxes she had on the floor.

"This is the doctor who made Maisie's original diagnosis which got her fired from teaching. Then I have an interview with the head of the Psychiatrist's Association of America. That should be high comedy. Or low farce. Hi, comedy! 'Lo farce! And someone from the Board of Ed. But I don't know what to ask them or where they go in this structure. It isn't coming out the way I thought and now I'm not even sure if it was a good idea or what. I screen this over and over with Gilfredo and it doesn't make any sense to me."

I didn't know quite how to bring up what was on my mind. All I could think of was the beer and Valium she took every morning when she got up and the two more beers she always took with her to work. As I rewound the film, I tried to think of a gentle way to say it. There was none.

"I see a lot there," I said. "A good show, in fact. With some more shooting you can focus right in on it. The concept is great, but the structure, the editing isn't the problem . . . . How can I say it?"

She waited for me to go on, honestly not knowing what I was going to say. She hadn't seen herself on the screen as I had, or maybe she didn't want to.

"Babe, I know you've had a lot of pressure lately and you've been taking a lot of Valium. And I know a lot of cans of beer go out every morning tucked in your bag . . . "

"And that's only for the 'before lunch' Valium," she said. "I'm so rushed, sometimes I get called to a meeting and Nancy doesn't have time to get me a soda, so I need to have it handy. You don't know what I've been going through."

"Are you drinking a lot?"

"I have a drink or two for lunch sometimes, and then to unwind for dinner I may have one. Why?"

"Are you taking anything else besides the Valium?" I asked.

"No, just the Valium."

"But you're taking a lot of it now."

"Well, I wouldn't call it a lot," she said.

"I've been watching you take two when you wake up every morning."

"I'd never get out of the house if I didn't."

"And then a couple more before lunch," I went on, "and maybe some at lunch or in the afternoon and definitely I know you always take two at night."

"Ye-e-ah, I suppose so, but what does that have to do with this *meshuggina* show?"

"Did you watch the same footage I just did?"

She looked blankly at me.

"Barbara, look at yourself."

I ran the film back and played it again to show her particular scenes of herself as I talked.

"I know you, Babe. I fell in love with that woman on a Moviola screen. I've watched you on film for thousands of hours. I know how you work. You make your best shows flying by the seat of your pants. It's that spur of the moment stuff that's your best, grabbing every opportunity, thinking in mid-interview, never letting them get by you . . . . Listening is what you do best in an interview, but here . . . here, look at this shot. He completely ignored your question and you didn't follow through. He's running the interview exactly as he wants. The Barbara I knew would never let him get away with that. Look. You're not handling him the way you usually would. You're not even listening to him."

I ran some more shots.

"Here, listen to your voice in this one."

She listened carefully to her slurred speech and watched herself on the screen as though for the first time. She didn't like what she saw.

"I know you, Babe. This is not you. You were stoned out of your mind during these interviews."

"On a few beers?"

"Beers and Valium all day long from the moment you wake up."

"But Valium doesn't do anything to you. It's just for anxiety."

"I don't want to get into that. I don't know anything about it and I don't want to know. All I know is what I see on the screen. Don't you see what I see? You want to go on the air like that?"

I pointed to the still running film. The on-screen Barbara was swaying in her chair, almost rocking. Her eyes were half closed. Barbara listened to herself in silence.

"I'm not trying to be moral about it," I said. "Shit, I like my vodka and my wine too much for that, but I never let it get in the way of my work. When I'm writing I can't even have a glass of wine because I can feel it affects my thinking and I don't like that."

"But Valium's not like that," she said earnestly. "It's medi-*ca*-tion! I know what it's like to feel high on grass or alcohol. I'm not high on Valium. I don't feel any different. I don't feel high or anything."

"Maybe 'stoned' is the wrong word, but it's the only word I could think of to describe the way you are on that film. What would you call it?"

"I . . . I don't know, but I know that Valium has no effect . . . "

"Babe, stop kidding yourself. You wouldn't bother to take it if it had no effect. You've been taking it for years because it does *something* for you. Whatever that something is, you're taking too much Valium, and beer, and booze with it. I don't care what you call it, you can see that *something* on the screen in front of you if you'll only look at yourself honestly."

Barbara turned away from her image on the screen and stared silently at the opposite wall.

"You asked me to come here to give you my opinion of this footage. I wish I didn't have to say it, but my opinion is that if you want this show to go on the air, and make any sense, then when you go out shooting the next interviews, on those mornings at least, you have to lay off the Valium and beer. Do whatever you want afterwards, but not before shooting."

"How will I get out of the house?"

"I'll help you however I can, but you've got to pull yourself together. You're fucking up your career now. Do you want that?"

There was a long pause.

"Don't listen to me," I said. "Here, look at yourself again."

I started to run the film fast for another look. She held my hand, stopping the Moviola.

"You don't have to," she said quietly. "I don't want to see myself like that ever again."

She thought for a long time.

"I'm not sure I can do it."

"Babe, you're talking about three, maybe four isolated mornings that you'll lay off the Valium for only a couple of hours. If it's that difficult for you, you ought to do some serious thinking about yourself. Cause that's in the nature of a problem. But that's for after this is on the air. Unless you want to scrap the show."

"I couldn't do that!"

"You have an air date and a professional reputation to consider right now. Is a couple of hours of no Valium worth risking that?"

"Can you be with me for the rest of the show?" she said. "Could you cut it? If you cut it for me you could check the dailies and go over the questions with me and help me see where I'm going."

"Of course I would, Babe, but Gilfredo's cutting this, isn't he?"

"I cried on his shoulder last night. He knows I want you. He'll get them to hire you again. I know it's only news editor's pay, but . . ."

"Don't think of that," I said. "Of course I'll do it."

"But you're writing again and I'll be taking you away from your writing. That bothers me more than anything."

"Babe, you have an air date. That's an emergency. I'm not doing anything that can't wait a few weeks. You and I are going to get married. We're a part of each other. I help you now and you'll help me when I need it. That's what our relationship was supposed to be from the beginning."

With that assurance, she broke, "Stay with me for this one, please! Don't leave me alone. I don't think I can make it without you."

I held her in my arms and tousled her ragged hair. "I'll be here, Babe. Don't worry."

Barbara came through. She needed a little help from her friends, but that doesn't take anything away from her. I structured a possible film using as much of the footage as I thought would still work and sketched out what she would need for the gaps. Nancy set up more interviews and we wrote a new narration. I was in the cutting room while Barbara was out shooting with Nancy, so I don't know whether she cut down on the Valium or not. She didn't tell me and I didn't ask. She came back with good footage. We made the air date with a decent show and that's what was important for the moment.

But seeing her career threatened like that, the seriousness of the problem was finally brought home to her. She was truly scared this time. She talked about it one night soon after at the beach house. We were relaxing after a marvelous fish dinner she had insisted on cooking for us. She was almost taking refuge in her rare domesticity. We sipped our wine with the fireplace at our backs and the moon hanging in the high windows overlooking the black ocean. It was one of those nights when everything good in our relationship came together.

"You know," she said, "I've always been such a terrible workaholic. I never let myself take a vacation, a real rest before." She shrugged. "Before you, it didn't matter because vacations were never fun anyway, not as much fun as work was. Work was all I knew. But now I have something to work for, for the first time in my life. You notice I haven't had an anxiety attack since we've been out here at the beach?"

"I noticed."

"That's how I want it to be always. No work is worth those anxiety attacks. So I'm making a fiat and this is what it is. This is what my new life must be from now on. I must always be able to stop working and sit here in our house and watch the ocean and eat a fish with my pussycat. This is what I work for now. Don't ever let me forget that."

"Don't worry, I won't."

"It's my fault we put off the trip to Europe for so long, and I'm sorry. I didn't want to."

"No, don't say that. You were busy."

"My work always came first, but never again. You come first now and they can go fuck themselves at the station if they don't like it. I want this good feeling with you to last. This is my new life. I want to be married to my pussycat and have a honeymoon in Europe and nothing will spoil that."

We had put off this trip to Europe for years, but now it was really going to happen. We made reservations in small but very expensive hotels in London, Paris, and Venice. In between Paris and Venice we planned to get a car and a Michelin Guide and to drive all over France and eat. We would go from place to place as our fancy took us. No pressure, definitely no tours, and as much tennis as we could find. I had always fantasized that life with Barbara would be like this.

Neither of us had a credit card. We went to Barbara's bank and she withdrew ten thousand dollars for expenses. She handed me five thousand in traveller's checks for me to sign. I was dumbfounded. Not what I would call a "budget vacation." Her executive producer loaded Barbara with a lot of last-minute chores at the station. She was frantically busy right up to the night before we left, so we put off our marriage. We were just as happy to have the honeymoon first and get married after. Plane and hotel reservations couldn't be cancelled as easily as a marriage, it seemed.

We saw the beach house from the plane as we flew to Europe. It was only a tiny dot, but the coastline was distinctive enough to recognize even from this height. Barbara waved out the window.

"Goodbye house," she said. "Don't float away while Anton and I are gone."

We gained altitude over Block Island. Then Martha's Vineyard and Nantucket slipped away beneath us and there was nothing but open ocean ahead. The bright blue sky quickly faded to a black, moonless night.

TWENTY FOUR

I had rarely been able to take vacations in the past. When I had, it was only for long weekends, so I never had the opportunity to find out the truth of the folklore that warns that a vacation is the acid test of a relationship. Barbara and I had the money and time to relax and satiate ourselves on whatever took our fancy. I had no reason to anticipate anything other than a marvelous time. One of my last stops before leaving New York was at the drugstore to fill Barbara's vacation Valium prescription. The pharmacist knew Barbara from her prescriptions and even he remarked on the amount she was getting. Good old Doc Alexander had obliged her with what looked like a pint bottle. She was taking no chances. She knew herself a lot better than I did.

We had both been sure that a long rest from work would relieve Barbara's attacks, but her anxiety followed her all the way to Europe and it got worse. Any time she had to leave the safety of a hotel room, Barbara swallowed so much Valium and booze I thought she would turn into Rubber Woman. In London she panicked at the West End theater crowds on our first night out. After that, she refused to go anywhere there might be crowds. In Paris she became terrified of heights: when I proposed the Eiffel Tower or Montmartre she refused to go. This from a woman who lived on the sixteenth floor of an apartment building in mid-town New York surrounded by teeming crowds.

Ghosts followed us everywhere. Barbara regaled me with detailed stories of her miseries associated with every place in Europe. She seemed to have visited every spot on her many trips with her parents and had a uniformly awful time in each place. She couldn't share my enjoyment because of her depressing memories. She stayed in bed for much of the trip, afraid to leave the safety of the hotel room. She insisted that I go out by myself and have a good time, but there's a limit to how many long, lonely walks you can take. She did go out in Paris, but not for sightseeing. She had developed a horrendous toothache. Oh, it was real all right. It had been plaguing her for years but she had never had time to take care of it. Paris was mostly the inside of a dentist's office, surgery, and another legitimate reason for massive doses of wine and, of course, even more Valium.

Barbara relaxed for the first time when we drove out of Paris into the French countryside.

"This is all new to me," she said. "It's wonderful. Al and Lilly never drove through the countryside like this. They always flew and never went out of the cities. I've been to Europe so many times and I've never seen anything like this."

I had rented a new Peugeot so that the drive would be easy on Barbara's back. We carried a Michelin Guide instead of a road map. We were going to eat our way to the Riviera. Just before lunch we'd stop at a village and buy a bottle of wine, fresh bread, and cheese. I had to perform a comic pantomime many times before I learned the word for "corkscrew" in French. For some strange reason it wasn't in the phrase book. After a few days the car stank of cheese, but it was a magnificent smell to carry with you along the back roads of France.

Even with its rows of new condominiums, the Riviera was another place full of Barbara's ghosts. She sank back into a deep depression until I moved us to a hotel on the Cap D'Antibes. She felt better there because it was new to her. We played tennis on an antique clay court overlooking the Mediterranean. Instead of chain link fences, the courts were separated with high arbor vitae hedges that looked more than a hundred years old. A missed ball would zock in the dark green needles. From an adjoining court we heard an anguished cry, *"Regardez la balle!" "RE-GAR-DEZ LA BALLE!"* We both fell to our knees in tipsy laughter. Semper tennis.

We made love a lot on the Cap D'Antibes. We had a lot of laughs and some good times, but it didn't last long. Barbara's terror caught up with her on the drive to Venice. Is there a fear of the highway? Highwayphobia? Well, Barbara got that now. There's only one road from the Riviera to Milano. It goes through mountains and over deep gorges. We'd drive under a porcelain Mediterranean sun and suddenly plunge into a pitch-dark tunnel. A few minutes later, a blinding hole would appear at the end of the darkness and we'd roar out of the tunnel to find ourselves a thousand feet in the air on a road that seemingly had no guard rails. It was like being shot out of a cannon. Her prior fears were nothing compared to this. She was scared shitless. She gripped the dash with one hand and dug the fingers of her other hand deep into my arm. She tried to scrunch down in the seat, but she seemed even more frightened there. She was like this during the entire drive of three hundred kilometers from Antibes to Milano.

We were doubling back from a side trip to Sirmione, the ancient island town in the Lago di Garda. It had been a longer distance than I thought and Barbara had to go to the bathroom badly. When she took a lot of Valium and booze she had great difficulty holding her urine. She had been in the habit of peeing on the floor in Bernie on long drives, but she wanted a bathroom now and there was no place in sight. The woods on both sides of the highway were deserted, and she was scared of the woods now. I searched off the road and then back on the narrow highway, but I couldn't find a bathroom for her. Finally, a tiny gas station appeared in the woods. It was open and it had a john and a jane. As soon as I parked, a dog the size of a Great Dane came up and thudded his huge paws on the car window. Barbara cowered in her seat, terrified of the dog. Dogophobia now. The dog was only interested in the cheese smell that permeated the car. I got rid of him by throwing the last of the Gorgonzola far away and he disappeared into the woods after it. But even with the dog out of the way, Barbara refused to get out of the car.

"No!" she yelled. "I won't! I won't! I won't!" I had been listening to this same voice all across Europe, but now something inside me snapped. I went over to my side of the car and got in.

"Listen carefully," I said. "You are going to get out of this car now and you are going to that ladies room and do whatever you have to do. Because if you don't get out now and go to the bathroom," I said, "I am going to turn right around and drive straight to Milano and get on the first plane and I don't care if you don't pee till we get to JFK."

She didn't move. She looked up at me in sullen anger.

"I mean it," I said. "Don't test me. I'll turn around right now."

Without a word she got out of the car and went to the bathroom.

Something had been released inside me because when Barbara got back in the car and we continued to drive, I let loose a monologue that I must have been unconsciously thinking about for a long time.

"Remember how you told me Ben and Lian used to drive you out to

195

Sag Harbor and you had to sit with the kids in the back and it drove you crazy to be cooped up in a car with two whining kids? You remember what that sounded like? Well, that's exactly what you sound like on this trip. I feel like I've been escorting a five-year-old spoiled brat who whines and complains and has a temper tantrum anytime she doesn't get her way. This is no vacation for me. I'm not taking any more of your crap! You got that?"

Barbara listened in stunned silence. She had never heard this kind of outburst from me before. I had always deferred to her feelings and tempers. Her behavior wasn't any different from what it had been since my divorce. Her anxiety and her complaining were familiar, but at least I had some relief when she'd go off to the station. Now I listened to it twenty-four hours a day, and after two weeks I had gotten pretty sick of it.

I must have been saving this up for years because once I started I didn't stop and Barbara didn't open her mouth all the time I talked. As we drove, I went through the catalogue of her illnesses, her back, her vertigo, and her anxiety. Her original back attack came in her first weeks at Vassar. It was her first time away from home, a frightening time for anyone. She fell off a bike and then her mother had to come and feed her and take care of her like a baby. The back injury was real, but it fit right into her need for dependency, and she nurtured her invalidism. Whenever there was something she couldn't face she'd fall down, have a back attack, and get depressed. Or, reversing the order, get depressed and be so drugged that she'd fall down and hurt her back. But they always went together and they always produced the same result: her mother or Samantha or some other friend, lately me, would feed her, and carry her and dress her and clean up after her. No matter what the cause, her attacks all had a similar result: they reproduced a helpless infant's existence for her. When her back had deteriorated to the point where she could no longer work she got an operation, and within weeks she began falling down in supermarkets. That same theme kept coming back again, "falling, falling," so much like her original falling off the bicycle. It was like never learning how to drive. A brilliant, accomplished woman who could learn anything for her career in twenty years couldn't learn to drive because she didn't want to learn. When she got tired someone would always have to come along and carry her back home.

"Don't you see the thread?" I said. "You're just like a little girl who says, 'Cawwy me, Daddy.' Then she grows a little and she's too heavy to carry. She gets tired and says 'Cawwy me' and no one carries her. Then she learns to turn on all the charm she can to seduce the nearest male someone, 'Cawwy me? Pwease?' But she's too big to carry so she stamps her foot and grits her teeth and she's furious and seductive by turns and all she can do is yell, 'Cawwy meeeee!' Didn't you ever see a little girl like that? It seems to me every little girl goes through that sad stage at least once in her life. But a part of you is stuck there at five years old. You've been taking the same medicine for all your illnesses and going to the same doctor for I don't know how long and you suffer and never do anything about it, because you don't want to lose that last dependency. In many ways you're the most un-independent woman I ever met. Maybe it goes along with being a career woman, I don't know. Maybe you need some dependencies in order to be independent. But you're destroying your life with this just as you destroyed it with your back."

Barbara didn't say a word as I drove and talked. Once I had yelled at her, once she knew I wasn't going to stand still for that shit, her anxiety and terror of the roads magically disappeared. The drive to Verona and then to Venice was uneventful. She was polite and didn't show any terror or anxiety. It was a pleasure.

Our hotel room in Venice overlooked the end of the Grand Canal and the Lagoon. Before I opened my bags I sat at the window and watched the water traffic for a long time. Barbara joined me and the pigeons.

"It's fantastic," I said.

"Isn't it? The most beautiful city in the world. I wanted you to see this. I insisted they reserve one facing the water."

"It was worth it," I said.

"I'm glad you're happy. I could never enjoy it when I was here."

She was off on another ghost story.

"Al and Lilly again?" I said.

"Oh, yeah, they were terrible, always fighting. But the first time I was here was even worse. They had sent me to Europe just before I was going to go away to school. I went with my roommate Bernice and she fell in love with Cesare the gondolier. He was a student or something. He looked ordinary to me. No one I'd ever fall in love with. When

Bernice introduced us he told me he had never known a Jewess before. It was the only time I had ever been called a Jewess. It was a strangely exciting word to me."

She paused a moment as though recalling that excitement. Then she shook the memory away and went on.

"Well, Bernice disappeared with him and left me alone all the time I was in Venice. Here I was in the most beautiful city on the planet and I was miserable the whole time. Bernice came back an hour before we were supposed to leave. I asked her what she was doing all this time and she told me how love was the most incredible thing in the world and I should try it and I would understand. While we talked she took a long hot bath. Cesare didn't have one in his apartment. Her body was all red and scratched up and even bitten. I was so naive about sex then, I couldn't understand why she would want to be with someone who did that to her. Then she told me she wasn't going to leave with me. She was going to stay with Cesare. So I had to go to Florence and Rome all by myself. And I wrote postcards to her parents from every place, lying for her while she was with Cesare and I was all alone. I never had such a miserable time in my—"

She suddenly stopped her dismal reminiscing. She was quiet for a long moment as though she just remembered something. She looked up at me.

"I want you to tell me again what you said in the car," she said.

"Huh?"

"About my back and the vertigo and anxiety attacks. About my wanting to stay a child with them. No one ever said that to me before."

"That's too bad," I said.

"No, it's good. That made more sense to me than all my analysts put together ever did. Please?"

"I don't know. What do you want me to talk about?"

"Just what you said before. I've been thinking about it a lot. I see my whole life for the first time. Everything fits in somehow. I'm sure of it."

That's all Barbara had to say and I was off again. But this time it wasn't a release of frustrated anger. I talked all about babies crying and mothers holding and how that relates to anxiety. Barbara made me go further and deeper because she wanted to listen. She hung on my every word and kept telling me that I made more sense than all her high-priced analysts combined. She was turning on the teacher in me, the father. She knew how to hook me.

I talked for hours. She seemed soothed, almost drowsy by the steady sound of my voice. It got very late. After all that talk, one gets hungry and thirsty and here we were in Venice, one of the world's food places. When I mentioned leaving the hotel for a late dinner at Harry's a visible shiver went up Barbara's weary back. Her anxiety again. Harry's was another place full of her ghosts. She swallowed a handful of Valium with a glass of water but she couldn't get up from the bed. All my anger and annoyance had dissipated in my talking. I felt for her.

"Look," I said. "We don't have to. I'll bring something back."

"No. I don't want you to do that. No more. All those terrible things that happen to marriages, they happen because men are so insensitive, so childish. You're none of those things. You really are Mr. Right. If I marry you those awful things I'm afraid of will never happen. You are the only man I could ever marry. You're valuable to me. I have to conquer this fear for you. I'm going to go out with you tonight if it kills me."

She could barely walk but she did it. She fought her brain and made her legs stand up and walk out of the room. She fought her psychic reflexes that told her only fear. She overcame them and walked shakily out of the hotel with me. She held up a plastic umbrella to shelter us against the fine drizzle that polished the dark-gray stones of the Riva Schiavone.

Harry's wasn't a long walk, only three bridges from our hotel. We had dinner and started to walk back. The night was clear and black, the drizzle had stopped. The water of the Lagoon lapped softly nearby. Barbara walked slowly and tremulously, her umbrella dangling from her wrist. Her other arm was over my shoulder for support. She was exhausted from her effort. We got as far as the gondolier's landing when she stopped, her body wavering.

"I . . . I can't go on," she said.

"What's the matter?"

"I can't walk any more!"

She started to sob softly.

"I thought I could overcome it," she said. "I thought it was all going to be better . . . and it's worse than ever."

"Life doesn't happen that way, Babe," I said quietly. "Miracles happen from work. Long, hard work. Don't worry. You did fantastically. I'm proud of you. Try again now. You can do it. I know you can."

She struggled. Her body swayed precariously, but her feet stuck to the stone.

"I—I can't move my legs," she said. "It's like in a dream where you have to run but your legs are rooted in the ground and you can't move them."

Barbara hung her head in shame, feeling a failure. I didn't know what to do. Then she looked cautiously up at me. Her wet eyes looked teasing and guilty, as though she might get caught at something.

"Cawwy me, Daddy?" she asked softly. "Pwease?"

She looked like a naughty little girl sharing a forbidden secret and she got to me. I swept her up in my arms and carried her back to our hotel across the three bridges.

I teetered up the few steps into our hotel lobby and flopped us both down to rest on a large old-fashioned velour sofa. Barbara had enjoyed her ride. She was still drunkenly mischievous. She stretched half on, half off the sofa and laid her head back in my lap. She waved her hands, leading an invisible orchestra and sang to their accompaniment.

A CANOPIED BED HAS SO MUCH CLASS,
AND SO'S A CEILING MADE OF GLASS,
IN OUR LIT-TLE DEN OF IN-IQ-UI-TY.

"Look!" she said, pointing up.

The ceiling was all mirror from one end of the lobby to the other. It was a quite beautiful antique mirror reflecting the marble pillars and marble walls and marble floor. I came back to our reflection on the pale green sofa and saw that Barbara was nuzzling into my lap. The lobby was empty except for the desk clerk and he didn't seem too interested in us. I laughed quietly at Barbara's playing around, and then she zipped open my fly and with one deft motion lifted my cock out and slipped it into her mouth. She lay very still, listening. I was embarassed. The sweeping arms of the couch hid my lap from the desk clerk, but anyone coming in the door could see us clearly. The desk clerk caught my eye. He nodded and smiled and I nodded back.

Barbara started to work, watching herself in this role in the mirror. I couldn't take my eyes off the front door. Then she stopped for a moment and said, "No. Up there. Look at us. Are you embarrassed?"

"No. No."

I looked up and it was a curious feeling like watching someone else and having the feeling at the same time. Barbara had gone for an erotic area that was new. I couldn't make any noise, which added another tension to the excitement. I groaned slightly. The ever-solicitous desk clerk responded immediately, "Signore?"

"Nothing," I said.

Barbara didn't stop. I couldn't hold back anymore and there was a moment when I didn't know or care if anyone walked by or if a hundred people were sitting in an audience watching us. I came to my senses in a moment and felt immediately self-conscious. I quickly zipped up again. Barbara was wearing her alley cat grin.

"If you want to give me a present I would really like sometime," she said, "a mirror on the ceiling over our bed is the one thing I would want more than anything in our little den of iniquity."

I made a mental note to do just that for her birthday or for Christmas.

Venice was our last stop in Europe. We drove to Milan and flew back to New York on the same day. Barbara plunged into work the moment we got back. She had a new documentary about the Port of New York Authority to do. It didn't have Barbara's usual bad guys, innocent victims, and wrongs to set right, but she was committed to it and it had to get on the air as soon as possible. She said we couldn't get married until she had a hiatus in between her shows. I had been patient with her this far, I could wait until the hiatus. But my outburst at her in Italy had opened up a long repressed awareness about Barbara and our relationship. A chain reaction of emotional events began inside me that would lead to an explosion I was powerless to stop.

TWENTY FIVE

Soon after we got back my older sister organized a family Thanksgiving dinner at which my mother would appear and the four of her children had to attend. I was surprised because my mother traditionally refused such assignments, but thought maybe she was mellowing in her old age. Barbara took this opportunity to meet her, since she assumed my mother would naturally want to attend our wedding. We all met at my cousin's house in Pelham, just north of the Bronx. It was an old-fashioned lower-middle-class house, pleasant and full of children and relatives, but as we walked into the modest living room, Barbara looked around her as though she was entering Indian territory.

It always surprised me to see how small my mother was. I saw her so rarely that my image of her was from memories formed when I was a teenager and younger. Her hair was as long and dark as it had been then. She never cut it. She wore it in two braids wrapped around her head in a sort of coronet. In these later years she braided in a colorful ribbon. She wore a layered assemblage of clothing in vivid patterns and shades of purple. She spoke with somewhat of an English accent. She had been born in New York, but the accent wasn't phony. Her mother and father were solidly British and so were many of the important people in her life, like my stepfather. Barbara didn't know what to make of her, but she screwed up her courage and invited my mother to our wedding, a curious reversal of roles now that I think of it. My mother's reply was not what Barbara expected.

"I cahn't think of a more dreadful way to waste a perfectly good day than to have a wedding," she said. "Cahn't you think of anything more original?"

And with that my mother abruptly turned away, ignoring Barbara for the rest of the evening as though she had ceased to exist. I assured

Barbara that it was nothing personal. My mother had done that with any woman I was with for as long as I could remember.

As we drove back, Barbara tactfully expressed concern about Al and Lilly's projected reaction to my bohemian mother. She was greatly relieved when I told her that my mother was dead serious and she'd never show up for anything as normal as a wedding.

In their various ways, I'm afraid my family embarrassed Barbara. When we were in England, we had taken a side trip to Sussex to visit my stepfather. He lived there with a woman he married after he left my mother. He was a British subject and England was the furthest refuge he could find from her revenge. I took Barbara to see him so she could meet one of the influences of my life. He still looked like a young Leslie Howard with that frayed corduroy appearance of a barely surviving British intellectual. He was pleased to see me and showed off his latest work. He was writing popular history books for children, something that I gathered didn't pay too much. He was worn-at-the-elbows poor, still having trouble making ends meet, and he had to be more than sixty years old. He was his usual charming self, but Barbara had been as uncomfortable with him as she was with my mother. My family was poor and I'm afraid Barbara couldn't overcome an inherent lack of respect for that. She was a limousine liberal and, try as they might, those people don't know what it's like to be really poor and they never will.

When we all lived together my stepfather wrote his poetry and plays and my mother published her little poetry magazine for its small but devoted audience. They had scant concern for anyone outside themselves, but I'd take their life any day over that Fort Lauderdale condo crowd. I've been comfortable and I've lost it all too many times to count, but no matter what happened I was beginning to realize that those two people had engendered something of value in me that I could never lose, something that endured and grew, and that was a love of the language of the mind. No amount of Barbara's money was as important as that.

Barbara had gone back to loading up on Valium and beer every morning in order to get out of the house, but she seemed to be back to normal, or what normal had become for Barbara since my divorce. Then it transpired that her show was going to have to be cut over the Christmas holidays, and, as usual, Gilfredo had to take his annual vacation and, as usual, Barbara didn't trust anyone else with her film.

She asked me to cut it and, as usual, I automatically said, "Sure Babe, whatever you need. It's important for your career." And then as I began cutting, she asked me to help her write the narration and I was happy to do that, too. Then she wanted me to go out on location with her to contribute any ideas I had when she shot the interviews and Jim Jensen's standups, and I did that, too. But I saw this year rolling around exactly like the last year and I was beginning to get very tired of it.

I stopped at the corner of Tenth Avenue and Fifty-seventh Street and waited for the light to change. I was walking alone to CBS to put in another day of cutting on Barbara's film. My foot was poised to step off the curb. I was immobile for a reflective moment and in that moment I saw myself clearly. I didn't like what I saw. I was back where I was three years ago, exactly as I had been when I met Barbara. I was a news editor again, the absolute bottom of the craft, working for shit money on one of her documentaries.

I had no interest in being an editor. If I had I would be cutting the best features I could and going after Oscars. Not so long ago, I was a hot new film director. All I had needed then was enough time to write and develop properties for myself to direct. Where had all that gone? Why wasn't I at my desk writing my own stuff? I had gotten side-tracked with Margaret and I was getting sidetracked again with Barbara. Having me cut her shows had become nothing but a habit for Barbara. It had become a habit with me, too, and I didn't like it. Here I was going to a fucking news editing room, cutting 16 mm spaghetti shot by rotten newscameramen, salvaging Barbara's shows and writing her scripts for her at home when she was too spaced out on Valium and booze to think coherently. I was totally anonymous while she got a series of great reviews and awards. How had this happened? I had begun this news editing gig to help Barbara out in a couple of emergencies. She needed me and I was happy to do it. We were going to be married. Our lives and our careers intertwined. But did they?

Ten months had gone by since my divorce. Barbara had said again and again that she wanted to marry, but somehow at the last moment always avoided it. In that brief moment as I waited for the light to change I knew that Barbara was never going to marry me. She would avoid it forever. The avenue traffic slowed and stopped. The light turned green. I stepped off the curb a changed man.

TWENTY SIX

With that new realization, I saw Barbara's daily behavior with an objectivity I never had before. It seemed to me that she was becoming increasingly unstable in a manner I could not explain or put my finger on. It was as though she was twiddling with her lid immediately prior to flipping it. I couldn't envision exactly how, but I had the distinct feeling that I might find myself on the street with only a moment's notice. And if that happened, I suddenly realized with alarm that I was virtually broke. A rather large chunk of the money I made had gone to Margaret and my son and their respective lawyers. I had been casual about money with Barbara. I enjoyed the security she so generously offered and so I had always insisted that I pay for parts of our life like theaters and taxis and restaurants and for two people who ate out daily in Manhattan, that added up to a lot of money. I stopped doing that now. I made sure Barbara had money with her any time we went out. I was happy cutting her show at CBS now and I stashed all the money I made in my bank. To any outside observer, however, our life went on as happily as it had before.

Barbara's birthday was on the nineteenth of December. I had drawn plans for her mirrored ceiling, bought the mirrors and materials, and hid it all in my closet. I was working on the Port Authority show but I came home for a long lunch to prepare her birthday present. I got all the materials out and worked all through lunch installing the mirrors on the ceiling over the bed. When we got home that night I told her her birthday present was in the bedroom. She looked all over and couldn't find it. She never looked up. I refused to tell her where it was. She finally flopped down on the bed but she was lying on her side and still didn't look up. I left the bedroom and I heard a long, "Oooohhh" from her. She was enchanted by the time I got back into the bedroom. She repeated the scene from the hotel lobby in Venice, except those two people above us were naked now, floating above us in erotic poses. She got no end of joy out of her present.

I was happy to give it to her, but a deep anger was slowly building inside me. It surfaced unexpectedly a few days before Christmas. Barbara and I were in the editing room.

"I can't think of a good enough Christmas present for Nancy," Barbara said. "That girl saved my life this year. I don't know what I would have done without her. I want to show her I appreciate all she's done."

"How about a trip to Europe?"

"What? I'm serious."

"So am I," I said.

"But that's expensive."

"Not a whole trip. Get her a Laker ticket to London. With that incentive she'll save the rest. Didn't you see her reaction when we were planning our trip? She's never had a vacation. She made her way through school working in a factory. And then taking care of her sick family. She's done nothing but work all her young life. She'd flip out."

"That's still a lot more money than I had in mind," Barbara said.

I exploded and yelled at Barbara as loudly as I could.

"What is she, a fucking servant you get a lace handkerchief for?"

Barbara was shocked. I have a loud voice and she wasn't used to hearing me yell. My voice must have seemed even louder in the tiny room.

"You just told me she saved your life," I went on. "She doesn't need this job, you know that. She loves you. She turned down a better paying job to stay with you. You know that, too. What do you think her work is worth?"

"Oh, more than I could ever repay."

"No, you're wrong. You can repay her. Very easily. She gets a straight salary working on this unit, no overtime. Count how many hours she put in for you, how many nights around the clock, how many Saturdays and how many Sundays every single week this last year. What do you think her brain is worth? Even at a buck an hour her time will come to quite a bit more than the three-hundred-eighty-odd bucks that the ticket costs. Think of it as a bonus. Think of it as an award you got because of her. Or, think of it as saving your life. Any way you think of it, you got her cheap!"

Barbara got out her checkbook and hastily signed a blank check.

"Ah, y-you take care of it, will you? I'm going to be awfully busy this week. I've got to go now."

She handed me the check and hurried out of the cutting room. I think I heard her crying as she closed the door, but I didn't care.

I bought Nancy's ticket but I wanted the present to look bigger. I bought a bunch of travel guides with walking tours and a *Europe on $15 a Day*. I put her ticket inside the book so she wouldn't see it right away. When Nancy opened the present she was confused at first. She thanked us both, but I could see it didn't quite make sense to her. She could see what the books were and she had to assume they were for reading, maybe fantasizing about travel, but that's not something you ordinarily get someone as a present unless they're traveling. The real thing was too far out of her ken to even speculate on. She opened the book, took the ticket out and stared at it for a long time. She began to sob deeply, trying to fight the extent of her feeling, but she couldn't hold it in for long. She cried with a kind of hysterical joy. Years of tears poured down her cheeks. She threw her arms around Barbara who was a little embarrassed at Nancy's overwhelming reaction. Then Nancy flew into my arms, her tears wetting my sweater. I kissed her and hugged her.

"You got a ticket to ride," I said.

"Thank you both . . . so much. . . . " she choked.

She cried in my arms for a while and then staggered back to her typewriter. She tried to work, but she burst into tears again. Barbara was self-conscious with Nancy's effusive gratitude, perhaps because I had shamed her into it and she felt a little guilty. It wasn't like me to lose my temper like that, but it bothered me that she considered Nancy's talent as a service due her by some divine right, some sort of *droit de seigneur*. Or maybe my anger wasn't about Nancy. Maybe it had to do with someone else, a man who was emerging for the first time in a long while.

I was thinking a lot about myself lately. I was planning a long writing spell, one that would last me the rest of my life, with no more interruptions. I had earlier mentioned to Barbara that when we were married I would like to consider moving into a larger place so I could have a room to myself, but she always filed such talk into the black hole labelled "Marriage." It had become obvious that if I wanted a private space to write in, I'd have to get it myself. That was no problem. I could rent a little tenement over on Ninth or Tenth Avenue very cheaply. I didn't need much, only space for a table and a typewriter and a studio couch. Another fantasy soon knocked on the door of my imaginary writer's rat nest. She was an impressionable colt of a girl fresh out of college who would visit my "studio" now and then. She would want to be a writer and I would take her under my wing and other parts of my anatomy. She would be a lot like Cathy, I thought. I rather liked that fantasy. It gave me a lot to think about while I worked.

Perhaps this is nature's way of telling us that two people who have cleaved together are now cleaving apart. But relationships change slowly. I still had lingering fantasies of marrying Barbara and she had said nothing to dispel them. Since we were working closely together, I'd jog her memory now and then, "Hey, Babe," I'd say, "whatever happened about us getting married?" and she'd reply, "I'm too busy to discuss *that* now." Other times I'd say, "This show is just about over. It looks like you'll have a break soon. Don't you think we should make some marriage plans?" and she'd groan, "Oh, I'm too tired tonight. Just let me get this show out of the way. Then I can relax," and she'd pop two good old Valium, take a long drink of her Miller High Life, and forget it was ever mentioned. I got another freelance gig and I stashed away that money, too, as I waited patiently for the hiatus between Barbara's shows. But the hiatus never came. Barbara was already deeply involved in her next film and she was still too busy to talk about marriage.

By this time, however, I had some money in the bank. You remember those English novels of the eighteenth and nineteenth centuries where the hero or heroine always had a "small annuity" left them by some maiden aunt? It wasn't enough to make him or her into a rich snob, but it did serve to move the plot smartly along, since the characters didn't have to spend their time going to work every day. I had saved up my "small annuity" and the hero of my story could now make his next move. It was more than a year since I had come home with my divorce. It had been four months since we got back from Europe, the last time she had said we were going to marry. It was clear that no vacation, no beach house, no rest, no hiatus mattered a damn to Barbara. My patience finally ran out. She was always too tired to talk about it at home, so I called her at her office.

"Judge Sirica for President Headquarters!" Barbara answered.

"Hi, Babe. It's me."

"Oh, hi. I've only got a minute."

"Can you make lunch today?" I said.

"Lunch? What do you mean, 'lunch'?"

"I'd like to take you to lunch at the Slate. There's something I want to talk over with you."

"I'm kind of busy," she said, "but I can be home for dinner by— Fuck! I'm going to be late again. What's on your mind?"

"I'll tell you when I see you."

"You sound serious."

"It's nothing bad."

"Is something wrong?" she asked.

"Nope. Nothing unusual."

"You can't even give me a hint?"

"No," I insisted. "I'll tell you at lunch. I don't want you to hang up the phone and run off to work and forget all about it. And I don't want to talk to you at night when you're tired and you fall asleep in the middle of what I'm saying. I want you to hear exactly what I have to say and I think that lunch is the only time I could get your full attention. I want your undivided attention for this."

"It's that important?"

"It's that important."

"Well, maybe I could . . . Nancy!" she yelled. "When did I make that lunch with Gleason?"

I could hear Nancy's voice indistinctly, then Barbara's muffled conversation. She must have covered the phone with her hand.

"Are you still there?" she asked.

"I'm still here."

"Let me see . . . "

"I'm not in a rush," I said. "I don't want you to be crowded. Doesn't have to be today or tomorrow, but I would like lunch with you as soon as you can give me a solid hour with no interruptions."

"I can make it today. One o'clock at the Slate?"

"Terrific."

The Slate was only a few blocks from CBS. It's a pleasant, dark hangout of New York movie and TV people. I waited for Barbara in the second-floor restaurant and waved to her as she walked up the last steps. She saw me and tripped on the top step. Falling again. Her old emotional theme. She grabbed the banister and pulled herself up. I stood up as she walked unsteadily toward me.

"Hi, Babe," I said softly.

I kissed her. She was trembling. When she sat down at the banquette she knocked over the glass of bread sticks, scattering them across the floor.

"Oh, I'm sorry!" she gasped.

She bent down and hurriedly tried to pick them up. The waitress took over and cleared them away. I ordered Barbara a drink and sipped mine. She seemed frightened.

"What's this all about?" she said.

"I have a lot of things to say. Don't worry. It's nothing horrible. I don't see you much lately. You manage to make lunch appointments every day, so I figured that would be the best way I could talk to you for an hour. Let's order and get that over with, okay?"

"Sure."

She looked furtively over the menu at me. We ordered and her drink arrived.

"There," I said.

She waited for me to begin.

"This is like something from Kafka," she said.

"No, no, no. Not at all. I wanted to talk to you about our marriage."

"Is that all?" she said, obviously relieved. "You had me so scared. I told Nancy and she's scared, too. She can't wait to find out. We couldn't imagine what was wrong. I thought this was serious."

"It is serious. It's very important to me. I just want to ask you one simple question."

"Yes?"

"The question is, do you want to be married to me, or not?"

"Well, ahhh . . . "

I waited but she had nothing further to say.

"You've been saying we were going to get married for some time now," I went on, "but it's been a year since I got my divorce and you keep putting it off. I understand you have a certain ambivalence. I understand that. I've been very patient with you, but I think by now you owe me an answer. You want to be married? Fine. You want to stay single? Also fine. I want to know what your feelings are right now. Today."

"Couldn't you have picked a better time for this?" she said.

"There hasn't been a better time for three years, and if I leave it up to

you there never will be. You don't have to give me a date. This isn't
going to be written in stone. You can change your mind any time you
want. You tell me today you want to marry and then next week tell me
you changed your mind, you prefer to be single and live together?
Fine. At least I'll know where I stand for one week. Right now I have
no idea where I stand at any time and I can't go on this way. So, how
about it?"

"Huh?"

"What is your answer?" I said.

"Answer to what?"

I might as well have been talking to the wall.

"Do you want to marry me or not? I want to know. It's important to
me."

"Well, I . . . oh, well, if you're that serious, I'll have to think about
it."

"You've had three years," I said. "You know I'd like to marry you. I
won't pretend that I don't. But I fell in love with you single and I'll
love you just as much if you want to stay single and just live together.
All I want is an answer from you. Do you want to marry me or not?"

She stared at me without saying a word.

"You realize," I went on, "that if you don't answer it will be the
same as if you answered no. Do you understand that?"

After a long moment she nodded.

"Now," I enunciated as clearly as I could, "do you want to marry
me or not?"

I must have waited a full ten minutes in complete silence. I took sips
from my drink. The waitress came with the food and put all the plates
around. Barbara just looked at them and still didn't utter a sound. She
sat motionless and looked bewildered. I looked at my watch before I
finally spoke.

"That's your answer then? Silence?"

I waited a few minutes more, but she had nothing to say.

"I have to assume then, that you don't want to marry me. You want
to remain single and live together. That's what you want, right?"

She made a barely perceptible sound.

"Well, that's what I have to believe right now. Your lunch is getting
cold."

She took a tentative bite. I began to eat. She saw that I had nothing
more to say and she relaxed and ate some more.

"I'll have to hurry," she said. "I should be getting back soon."

213

I couldn't believe her indifference. It was all over for her as though nothing had happened. She hadn't said, "Gee, I'm sorry, I couldn't . . . " or, "Everything will work out," or, "It's not you, it's only my insecurity." She acted as though nothing had happened. My pain came out in a verbal assault.

"You can talk now, huh? But for me? Nothing! I found out what I wanted to know, all right. I sure know now what I'm worth to you. First thing I ever asked you for and you didn't have the consideration to give me a fucking answer. You don't even think enough of me to say 'no' to my face. I'm not even worth that to you. I think that's pretty low, Babe."

She had hurt me and she knew it, but there was nothing she could say.

"I gotta tell you something, Babe. Some things you have come to take for granted in our relationship are going to change."

"What do you mean?"

"For one, I'm not going to cut another show for you. Editing means nothing to me. I have to get back to writing and I can't be sidetracked anymore. The second is that I need a place to write. I can't do it in the bedroom. I'm going to get a little apartment on the West Side."

She panicked. "No! You don't have to do that. I don't want you to spend the little money you have. You can write at the beach house."

"It's two hours away from New York, there's no heat, it's freezing-ass cold except for the summer and in the summer it's rented."

"Well, if that's all you want, you can put heat in. I'll pay for it."

"That's what *you* want. What about what *I* want for my career? When we started living together, I thought we were going to share, but it isn't that way at all. What's important to you comes first. I won't live that way another day. I offered myself to you to truly share and you didn't want to."

"That's not true! I never said—" She checked herself.

"There are times in life when you have to take responsibility for what you do. 'In dreams begin responsibility,' Babe."

"I want to! I want to! But why does it always have to be marriage?"

"I didn't ask you to marry me! I just wanted an answer, yes or no! That's all. You say I'm the most important thing in your life, but I'm not even worth an answer. Then you act as though nothing at all had happened."

"I don't know what to say. What do I have to say to make you happy?"

"Answer me," I said again. "Yes or no? Just answer. That's all I want."

She opened her mouth but no words came out.

"Forget it," I said. "Finish your fucking lunch."

"I can't eat any more."

"Then let's go."

I paid and cabbed her back. We didn't say a word to each other. She was near tears when I dropped her off. I was too hurt to care. I know I shocked her when I said I was going to get my own place to work in. She needed to be shocked. She had everything she wanted in life: her career, her beach house, her money and her man. I only wanted my own little piece of the world, too.

I walked back home and took a detour up and down Ninth Avenue. I looked for rental signs and soaked up the neighborhood. The noise, the tattered little shops, the old people in the doorways, the dialects, the kids, the trucks, and the fruit and vegetable stands all looked as comfortable and inviting to me as Montmartre must have looked to generations of Parisian artists. This was where I belonged. It had been childish to imagine that a relationship with Barbara would get me a legitimate ticket into the first-class section of the world.

I met Barbara later for dinner at Fuji. She never said a word about our lunch discussion. I imagine she had buried the uncomfortable thoughts under layers of Valium. She was doing it even now with a couple of drinks and a couple more Valium. When we got home, she downed two more Valium with a can of Miller High Life and fell asleep fully dressed. She didn't stir as I undressed her and she was still unconscious when I left the apartment next morning. I had an appointment near Third Avenue and it was Saint Patrick's Day. Fifth Avenue would be blocked off. I strode out into the crowds going to the parade. I heard a distant troop of bagpipes skirling over their big bass drum. It was a sunny day and I felt good. I always enjoyed walking to my appointments. It was the nearest thing to a sport I had when I was a kid. I had sometimes walked the entire length of Manhattan just for the pleasure of it.

My job was pretty much over. They liked the treatments I wrote, and they were going to use the promotional tape I was making today to pitch a series to network. If we made it, I had a chance to write an episode or two or three. Good feeling. I carried those good feelings through the day and then I came back home to the one thing I had never anticipated.

PART IV

TWENTY SEVEN

Barbara was home. That was unusual, because she rarely got home before eight or nine. Even stranger, she was in the kitchen cooking dinner. She walked the few steps from the kitchen toward me, wiping flour from her hands with a dish towel. Her eyes had an unusual intensity. I put down my briefcase and kissed her lightly.

"I have something to tell you," she said.

I couldn't imagine what, but it was something big. She was very nervous. She clasped her fingers together tensely and then relaxed them again and again. She spoke rapidly without stopping for breath.

"When we talked at lunch yesterday," she said, "and you were disappointed in me, I was crushed. I cried as soon as I got back to my office. I couldn't stop crying all day. Nancy kept everyone away from me."

I reached out to her.

"Babe, I'm sorry," I said. "I was hurt, I shouldn't have been so hard on you."

"No! You were right! I know everything I've done. You do anything I ask and all I do is hang on you. I'm ashamed of myself. I want to be your woman. When you asked if I was going to marry you, I wanted so much to say, 'yes' but it wouldn't come out. No matter how hard I tried I couldn't make myself say it. And you were so hurt. I couldn't bear the thought that I hurt you. You, the one good thing in my life. I thought about it all day today. I couldn't go to work. No matter how much I thought, I came up with the same answer every time."

Barbara reached up with both hands and cupped my face. She touched my lips with her fingertips as she spoke.

"There's only one answer for me," she went on, "and I can say it now. Yes! Yes, my dear sweet darling, I want to marry you and I'm going to marry you, right away!"

I was astounded. Romantic phrases did not come easily to Barbara. I had never seen her like this. She was glowing. Tears swelled in her eyes.

"And if Mike says it's safe," she continued, "I want to have your baby."

"Oh, Babe . . . "

I took her in my arms and held her. I didn't know what to say. It was taking a long time to sink in. I had just put all thoughts of marriage out of my mind forever. Now my life was taking a hundred eighty degree turn once again and my brain was spinning as fast as it could to catch up.

"And I have something else to tell you," she said.

More? I was still absorbing the first surprise.

"There is a reason why I can say 'yes' to you today and you'll be so proud of me. Once I knew that marrying you was the most important thing in my life I knew I couldn't come to you hooked on Valium like a junkie. It's been destroying me and I don't want it to destroy us. I knew I had to get a grip on myself like you said. I have to grow up some day and this is it. This is the day! I've gone off the Valium. I quit today. No more. Never again. I haven't had any Valium all day and I don't want any. I'm never going to have another Valium again. I don't need it. I have my Prince Valium and this is the beginning of my new life with you. I want to come to you clean. We'll be married right after. It should only take a week or so and then I'll be free of it. And no more anxiety. Isn't it wonderful? I feel better already!"

She searched my face for approval.

"I think it's fantastic," I said.

Barbara seemed disappointed that I wasn't sharing her elation, but I was too confused to say much else. If she had gone so far as to give up her Valium for me, that meant she was serious this time. I kissed her while I searched for an appropriate answer.

"This is the kind of thing you celebrate," I said, lamely. "Can I get you something?"

I rummaged in the kitchen for a drink.

"I don't think I should," she said.

"A glass of wine, maybe?"

"No," she said, "no wine or anything. I think I should just stop everything."

I put my glass down, feeling guilty.

"Maybe I shouldn't," I said. "Will it bother you?"

"No! No! I don't want any. Isn't it wonderful?"

"It's marvelous," I said. "I'm still trying to take it all in. It's kind of a surprise to me, all so suddenly."

We sat down in the living room. She talked rapidly with a great deal of pride about her decision.

"It's been coming for a long time," she said. "I first thought about it on those bad days in Europe. I thought a vacation, to relax, would help, you know, but the anxiety followed me there, too, and it was worse than it ever was before. That really scared me. The way I was in Europe. I don't think you knew what I was going through."

"I had some idea."

"I've thought a lot since then. I called Alexander today and told him to go fuck himself. I told him I wasn't ever going to see him again. I don't want anymore doctors. I have you. You're better than any doctor I ever had in my life. You know me better than anyone. All the things you know. I trust you. And you're so strong. With you, I know I can beat this. Can I count on you?"

"Are you kidding? You're doing all this for me? Can you count on me? Of course, I'll be here for you. Whatever you need."

I held her by the shoulders and looked closely at her for the first time.

"How do you feel so far?"

"There's a humming in my head that comes and goes," she said, "and I'm a little scared sometimes, but it doesn't seem to be anything I can't handle."

"Are you going to be able to go to work?"

"Work? Fuck the show! Fuck CBS! I'm going to stick this out until it's over and then we're going to get married and if that screws up their schedule, fuck 'em! We're going to have a big wedding and all the people I love are going to come. I'm making a fiat right now. This wedding is going to be a blast 'cause I want everyone to know that I *want* to marry you. It's a celebration. You're worth the world to me. And I don't want you to ever again think you're not worth it. Because you're worth more than my whole life. What do you think of that?"

"Babe, I said all those things yesterday because I believed them and because they were true. I was mad and unhappy and I exaggerated, but that was yesterday. It's not yesterday anymore. I just want you to know that no one has ever given me as much as you just offered to me. No one any time in my life."

She was breathing heavily. I held her again and she quieted down. Images were flooding through my head. There was so much that I couldn't think clearly. All I could see was her determination and her courage. It was the old Barbara I was seeing. A courageous, stand-up lady. She was the lady I knew from long ago.

Barbara seemed fragile as we ate the dinner she had prepared. She jumped at the slightest sound and periodically she'd have a shivering fit as though she was freezing cold. I helped her into bed and turned on the TV set. I got out her heating pad and tried to relax her the way I did when she had a back spasm or an anxiety attack. I helped her out of her clothes and began to gently massage her back. It seemed to soothe her so I kept it up. Starting from her lower back, I massaged all up along her spine, up her neck, and then her head. She rolled over sleepily. I softly rubbed her cheeks, her mouth, her eyes and her throbbing temples. She stopped her intermittent shivering. Then I moved my hands down her neck, her chest, shoulders, breasts, gently around her stomach and then her legs, working along both legs to her toes. She was soon asleep. I turned the TV set down. Now that I wasn't touching her, she began to toss fitfully. She made tiny sad cries that broke my heart. Something was tormenting her in her sleep. I massaged her gently again, rubbing her shoulders and continuing down each of her arms, working her sleeping pain out through her fingertips. I touched her as softly as I could, trying not to wake her, maintaining the steady rhythm of my hands on her body.

I knew nothing about Valium, but I could see that this was not going to be easy for her. Barbara was assuming that she'd be free of her anxiety when she was free of the Valium, as though the Valium had been the cause of it. I knew better than that, but I felt there couldn't be anything wrong with her getting off such heavy drug use, no matter how safe it was supposed to be. Once she was out of that Valium haze, she'd be able to see herself more clearly and perhaps get to the heart of her anxiety.

I woke up suddenly, still dressed, with my shoes tangled in the blankets and my glasses still on. I must have nodded off. Barbara was just leaving the bed, pulling a blanket over her shivering, naked body.

"Where are you going?" I said.

"Living room. I can't sleep."

She started shivering again. She pulled the blanket around her, but it did no good.

"C'mon," I said. "I'll rub your back. It worked before."

"No. You need your sleep."

"Me? Ha. I'm not withdrawing. You need all I can give you and a lot more. I'll be all right. C'mon."

She came back to bed. I gently rubbed and stroked her. Her skin was hot and dry. Eventually I nodded off only to be awakened by Barbara jolting awake from her nightmare. We spent the rest of the night this way. I massaged her until morning came. She seemed to relax as the sun slowly filled the apartment.

"You look better," I said. "How do you feel?"

"Better. Some of it is gone. I'm still shaky but not the way I was last night."

"Good. Good sign. You're gonna be okay. But only because you're so brave."

I kissed her.

"Keep it up," I said. "We'll see you through it."

I started cleaning last night's dishes and put up some strong coffee. Then I thought better.

"Should you have coffee?" I said.

"I don't know."

"How does your body feel? Do you have an appetite, a taste for coffee?"

"Yeah, I think . . . I'm more thirsty than anything."

"Oh shit. Of course. You're going to need lots and lots of juice. Don't forget you're used to drinking a lot, beer, wine, alcohol. You're going to need a lot of liquids. And lots of good food and lots of vitamins."

I began to write out a grocery list of the healthiest food I could imagine.

"We've got to get you super vitamins. Lots of B's. I'll go where you always got your Valium prescription and get vitamins there instead. That's symbolic, huh?"

"Do you have to leave?" she said.

"There's not much in the house. I was going to get some food and then I'll get vitamins on the way back. Is something wrong?"

"The burning in my head is gone, but I'm scared to be alone. Other than that, I feel okay. I'm weak. I didn't sleep. I want to rest."

I stroked her head.

"Easy, Babe. Don't worry. I have an appointment after lunch, but I'll be here all morning. I don't have to go out. The grocery delivers and the doorman likes nothing better than to run errands for a tip. We could hole up here forever and never have to leave."

I had no idea how significant that remark would become. I called in the groceries and had the doorman pick up a morning *Times* and a carton of cigarettes for Barbara. I would get the vitamins on the way back. I made breakfast and when the groceries arrived I poured out some V-8 for Barbara and filled the refrigerator with the gallons of various other juices I had ordered. I cleaned up the dishes. Barbara rested. She seemed weak and tired, but other than that she looked fine. She had no more shivering fits while I was there.

I went out for my appointment and on the way back I bought every vitamin and mineral collection I could find at the pharmacy. I made dinner for us. Soon after dinner, Barbara's withdrawal symptoms began again. She lay in bed but she still couldn't sleep. She would have brief shivering seizures and then begin sweating. She clenched her jaw, suppressing her pain until it was over. I massaged her hot body all over. It was all I could think of doing and she seemed to relax at my touch and fall asleep. So far, her symptoms fit my limited knowledge of drug withdrawal. It wouldn't be any pleasure trip, but this was nothing Barbara couldn't handle with her determination. Her skin returned to normal temperature as I continued to massage her. I nodded off.

Deep in sleep, I heard Barbara crying for help only inches from my ear. I groped Morpheus a little as I struggled to wake up. When I opened my eyes I saw Barbara's face close to mine. She opened her mouth and pointed inside, groaning from the pain of her effort. Her gum was red and swollen right where the Paris dentist had done the temporary root canal. The same tooth that had erupted in Paris was exploding now. Barbara howled in pain. I knew what she was going through. I had had a couple of abscessed teeth. Barbara must have touched it off when she chenched her jaws so tightly during her withdrawal seizures.

"Oh, fuck!" I said. "In all this time you haven't taken care of that tooth?"

She couldn't speak properly because of the pain.

"I was hoo busy! Owww!"

"Damn it, Babe! He told you to have that temporary thing fixed the minute we got back to the States. You picked one hell of a time!"

It was almost midnight. I pulled myself out of bed. There was still time to get something for her. I got some ice for her tooth before I left. She seemed frightened when I turned to leave, but I shrugged it off assuming it was her panic over the toothache. I couldn't imagine anything worse than the instant awful pain of an abscessed tooth on top of what she was already suffering from her withdrawal. I bought a couple of drugstore toothache remedies, but they didn't help. She cried all night. I kept putting ice on her jaw. It gave her some moments of relief but not a lot. Neither of us slept.

By next morning, Barbara's cheek was swollen out enormously from the infection. She could hardly speak and her pain was constant, but she refused to go to her dentist. She was genuinely terrified of leaving the apartment. But it was Friday. I couldn't let Barbara go through a weekend of this. Then I remembered Tina and Horace. They were special friends of Barbara's, although we rarely saw them. Horace was a doctor and his office was right around the corner in a medical building full of dentists. He might know of a dentist who would take her. And Tina worked in his office as his assistant. I was sure Barbara wouldn't be afraid to see them. That's assuming Horace would agree and could find a dentist. But he was my only chance. I called him and when I told him it was a real emergency, he arranged to have a dentist friend take care of Barbara that afternoon.

Finding a dentist to take her on a Friday afternoon was an accomplishment. Getting Barbara there was something else again. I cajoled her into getting dressed, but she wouldn't walk out of the apartment. I thought at first she was just overreacting as she always did when she complained, but she was serious. She refused to leave.

"I'm too scared to go," she said. "You get me something instead."

The pain hit her every time she spoke.

"We tried all that stuff," I said. "It doesn't work. You have an abscessed tooth. Today is Friday. Do you think I'm going to let you go through this pain all weekend? You've got to go to the dentist!"

"No!" she yelled and grimaced with the pain.

I held her by her shoulders.

"Listen to me, Babe. Your tooth is only going to get worse. And it's on top of the pain you have from the withdrawal. I can't let you do this to yourself. I am going to carry you out that door if I have to. Do you understand me?"

She thought a minute.

"I don't have makeup on. I look terrible."

"Horace is your friend. He won't care. And Tina will be there, too."

"Let me put on makeup."

"Okay, but hurry. I told him we'd be right there."

Barbara stood in front of the bathroom mirror and put on her lipstick as I watched over her shoulder. Her face was pasty white from no sleep. Her lipstick was a wavy uneven line on her lips but it seemed to make her feel better.

She walked with me to the front door, but then stopped. She wouldn't move. I wasn't going to let her (or me) suffer her pain all through the weekend. I picked her up and carried her out. She grabbed the door frame and held fast. I had to pry her fingers off but when I went for her other hand, she grabbed on again with the free one. I finally got both her hands off, slammed the door and carried her on my shoulder, kicking and screaming to the elevator. This was more serious than I had thought.

She quieted down by the time I got her to the elevator and stood her on her feet. Her terror must have been some funny reaction to the withdrawal. I had never seen her like that before. Barbara was trembling as she got in the elevator. Louie pretended not to see. She was shaky, but she walked with me around the corner to Horace's office.

Horace was a black man from Barbados. His lilting English colonial accent was always soothing. He must have been fifteen years older than Tina, but he was still vigorous. Tina was tiny, small-boned, and white. They were worried about the way Barbara looked. She was haggard and drawn from so little sleep on top of the withdrawal. Horace gave her a brief examination and then Tina took Barbara down the hall to the dentist's office. While they were gone, I told

Horace about Barbara's Valium withdrawal. He knew about her drugs. He had never liked the way she took so much and he was glad she was stopping. He felt that Barbara should have no trouble getting off Valium. I didn't want to explain what I had gone through to get Barbara out of the door. I thought it would all pass in a few more days of withdrawal. Horace gave me a prescription for vitamins and a list of foods she should eat. It was just what I had bought for her the day before.

Tina brought Barbara back to the office. She looked better now. She clutched my arm for support as we prepared to leave. Tina seemed apprehensive about letting Barbara out of her hands.

"She'll be all right," I said.

"And you," Horace said to me. "How are you?"

"Me? I'm not withdrawing from anything. I'm fine."

"Are you sure?"

"Sure," I said. "I haven't slept much in two days, but aside from that . . ."

"Ah."

"Hey, I'm only human."

"That's what I'm afraid of," he said.

The dentist must have shot Barbara up with some powerful pain-killer because she fell sound asleep the moment she lay down on our bed.

TWENTY EIGHT

Barbara woke the next morning with alternating hot fever and shivering seizures. She would begin to shake uncontrollably. She'd grab onto something to try and stay upright, but the shaking was too intense. She'd fall helplessly and I'd carry her into bed. Sweat poured from her whole body. The only thing that seemed to help was when she lay in bed and I continually massaged her. As long as I touched her and stroked her, she quieted down somewhat. It was the nearest thing to rest that I could give her. She seemed to relax and fall asleep. But when night came it didn't work anymore. As soon as she fell into the regular breathing of deep sleep, she would suddenly scream awake and sit bolt upright, her whole body shaking. This happened again and again, all night long. The moment she'd fall asleep, some nightmare would shock her awake.

The doorman got us the Sunday *Times*. Barbara tried to read to get her mind off the withdrawal but she nodded off immediately and bolted awake again, with a cry. She soon put the paper aside. She stayed in the living room walking around or sitting up on the couch with her head in her hands. I tried to talk to her, but now it seemed my voice and my touch had become irritating. She wasn't unkind, she was genuinely bothered and she really wanted to be alone. I caught catnaps in the bedroom only to wake again at her cries. Whatever it was, the nightmare would never let her alone. The night passed into the day this way and then into the next night with no change. I got some sleep, but Barbara didn't rest the whole weekend.

The ringing telephone woke me up the next morning. My eyes were stuck together and I searched for the phone. The service picked up on the second ring. Fuck 'em. If it was important they'd call again. I got my eyes open. It was gray daylight and Barbara was awake, sitting by my side. She looked barely conscious, trying to stay awake.

"How are you doing?" I asked.

She answered in a weak voice.

"I . . . I'm going to shake this. I'm going to do it."

"Have you slept?"

"Don't need to. I'm going to make it."

The phone rang again. It was Nancy. I handed Barbara the phone. She put it up to her face and then she started to shake. She opened her mouth as though gulping for air. There was a terrified look in her eyes. She snatched the phone from her ear and covered the mouthpiece.

"I can't," she said. "I'm afraid I'm going to break apart, shatter. I'm going to lose control. Please! You take it!"

I took the phone from her and she fell back into bed.

"How's Barbara's withdrawal coming?" Nancy asked.

"She's having a rough time. She hasn't slept in . . . I don't know. What day is this?"

"Monday. That's why I'm calling. By some coincidence, I was at a party last weekend and I heard of a woman drug therapist who helps people withdraw from all kinds of drugs. She's supposed to be very good. Do you think she could help Barbara?"

"Anything! Anything. Can you get her?"

"I'll see what I can do."

Nancy came through as she always did. The therapist showed up that night. She was in her late twenties, a motherly sort of grown-up hippie. She was slightly plump with a long black ponytail. She looked a lot like Samantha. Her gathered full skirt made her full hips look even bigger. I gave her a rundown on what had happened to Barbara so far. She nodded as I spoke, apparently very familiar with these situations.

Barbara never looked up while I talked to the therapist. She was sitting on the couch where she had been for most of these past three days, still holding her head in her shaking hands. She was wearing a wine-colored robe I had given her for Christmas. It was tailored and looked good on her tall figure, but now it was all crumpled. Her eyes were swollen, her skin pasty, and her hair unwashed. She looked very thin. The therapist didn't seem surprised at her condition. She sat down next to Barbara and put her arms around her shoulders.

"What's your name?" she asked.

Barbara didn't reply. The therapist looked up at me.

"What's her name?"

"Barbara," I said.

"Everything's going to be all right, Barbara," she said. "I'm going to take care of you now."

"Anything I can do?" I asked.

"I'll need some towels. Cold towels."

"Water? Ice?"

"Ice first. Then water. She's burning up. Run a bath."

I got what she asked for. She wrapped Barbara's head in cold towels. She held Barbara and began to massage her pretty much the way I had, but Barbara seemed to be able to relax with the woman. We carried Barbara to the tub and set her down gently into the hot water. She wanted to be alone with her so I made a dinner of hamburgers and potatoes while she bathed Barbara and then got her into bed. The therapist was a vegetarian and wouldn't take the hamburgers, but she wanted a plate for Barbara. She fed Barbara spoonful by spoonful the way you would a baby. It was the first real food Barbara had taken in days. This woman knew what she was doing. Barbara accepted the food hungrily from her and then she fell asleep cradled in the therapist's arms. They slept together in the bed and I fell asleep on the couch.

The next morning I crept into the bedroom. The therapist was awake. Barbara was still sleeping in her arms.

"Can I get you something?" I whispered.

"I'll take care of it. Just leave us alone. If you could leave the house it would be better. It's easier for her to have somebody around she doesn't know. Someone without ties to the old days, you know."

It sounded wise to me. What a relief. The therapist did all the work of Barbara's withdrawal. For a whole week she held her day and night. She massaged and caressed Barbara's naked body and sang softly to her all day long. At night she slept with Barbara and held her cradled in her arms as though Barbara was her helpless infant. I slept on the couch in the living room. Now that the therapist was with her and obviously doing so well, I took the opportunity to take care of the chores that had been stacking up. I restocked the groceries, did the wash, and got the laundry and dry cleaning. My job was over, so I went downtown and registered for unemployment again. When I had a chance, I hit some tennis balls in a practice court that was near the apartment. It felt good to move around the court again even if it was only for half an hour. I couldn't wait until Barbara was back on her feet and we could play together like old times.

The therapist had to leave on Sunday night. She had been with Barbara for seven days. Barbara seemed to be well over the withdrawal. She was sleeping soundly. She had signed a lot of blank checks just in case and I made one out for the therapist. Before she left, she cautioned me to make sure that Barbara got plenty of exercise so her blood would circulate and she'd get used to her body without the Valium. I assured her that was no problem. The withdrawal had turned out to be tougher than anyone had suspected, but Barbara never gave up. I had a new respect for this woman I was going to marry . I slept happily all night on the couch so as not to disturb her.

Barbara looked wonderful the next morning. She took a bath while I made breakfast. She brushed her hair and there was color in her cheeks.

"How are you feeling?" I said.

"A little shaky, but good. Better than I have in a long time. I can't wait to start living again."

"Good. I have an outing planned. We're going to play tennis today at the Wall Street bubble."

"Aren't you rushing it?" she said. "I don't know if I'm up to tennis. Couldn't we start tomorrow?"

"The therapist said you need exercise and that I should make sure to get you out of the house. You're sleeping now, the withdrawal is over, and to regain your health a little moving around is called for. There's nothing you love more than tennis. To further interest you, I am even going to let you win."

"What? You never let me win. I can take you any day!"

That got her interested. I booked a court and got the car out of the garage. It was chilly, so Barbara changed into her new brown velvet warm-up suit.

"Leaving the house without Valium," she said. "I'm not sure I can do it."

"Got to start sometime. I'll help you. Here."

Step by step she walked the length of the hall, got into the elevator, and then walked unsteadily through the lobby. We got in the car and Barbara relaxed as I headed downtown.

"You see?" I said. "You just left the house with no Valium. It can be done. You just did it. This is only your first day, too. We're going to do a little every day from now on."

She started to writhe uncomfortably in the seat.

"Something is happening to my stomach. Take me back. I'm scared! I have to get back."

We were on the FDR drive and that wasn't so easy.

"Do you feel sick?" I said.

"No, it's something strange. A weird feeling I never felt before."

"But you're not sick?"

"No. It's very, very strange."

"Can you play?" I said.

"It went away. I think so."

The Wall Street courts were the best in the city. I had had no trouble booking a court. It was eleven o'clock on a weekday and they were relatively deserted. The bubbles were new and clean. They had been built on a pier in the Hudson River. It was chilly inside. Barbara kept her warm-up suit on, but I stripped down to tennis shorts. She stared at me in an odd way as we started to play. She wasn't fully co-ordinated yet, but that was to be expected. All the more reason for her to start moving around. She stopped playing and yelled something to me. I couldn't hear over the steady roar of the fans that kept the bubble inflated. We walked to the net.

"I want to go back," she said.

"It won't mean anything if we go right back. Let's stay out for the hour. You don't have to play hard."

We played again, but her heart wasn't in it. She shouted something again. I still couldn't hear over the roar.

"What? What?" I yelled.

I walked toward her. She was holding the racket between her legs and moving it around as she walked toward me. She moved close enough so I could make out her words. Her voice was somewhere between a growl and a purr.

"I can't play anymore," she said.

"Why not?"

"Because all I want to do with this racket is to shove it up me. It's driving me crazy to hold it. I can't stand it anymore. If you don't take me home right now and fuck me, I'm going to shove this racket right in."

233

She stared at me with burning eyes and proceeded to do what she had threatened. I thought better of tennis and decided that we might perhaps substitute a different form of exercise. Certainly an exercise she wanted to do was much better than one where she had some reluctance. We hadn't touched each other sexually since she began her withdrawal.

When we got home, she stripped off her warm-up suit and laid down on the bed while I quickly undressed.

"Quick, quick," she said.

She started rubbing her stomach, or, more properly, her womb, which seemed to be lower now than I had ever seen it. It was slightly swollen, more rounded than usual. She spread the lips of her vagina wide open. The inner membranes were swollen out and pulsed with the rhythm of her blood. She kept her unblinking eyes levelled at me. My shoelaces tangled as I tried to open them. I gave up and left my shoe on.

"Fuck me quick," she said. "I can't stand it anymore."

I did. It was unbelievable. It seemed to be unbelievable for her too. It was unlike anything I had ever experienced. Her vagina seemed to have a mind all its own. I thought she would squeeze out every single sperm, every drop of fluid in my body and leave me a shrivelled hulk. It was like one long steady violent orgasm for her. Her inside gripped me impossibly tightly and would not let go of me until she was exhausted. Her orgasm kept on going, her body kept convulsing long after I was too exhausted to move. And with typical male humility, I must confess that I had nothing to do with the degree of Barbara's unexpected sexuality. I was mostly an observer hanging on for dear life.

"What happened to me? What was that?" she said.

She could hardly breathe.

"That, my dear, is the big 'O.' The next time you hear a feminist question the existence of a vaginal orgasm, you have just experienced the answer. Or, more romantically, it's what the woman in the Song of Solomon meant when she said, 'my bowels were moved for him.'"

"I never felt anything like that before. Not even with you. Oh! I think my IUD came out!"

She felt around for it.

"No, it's still there. I don't think I could go through that again."

"I don't think I could go through it again either," I said. "Not right away ."

"But why did it happen now?"

"The therapist did tell me that your body might feel very different now that you're free of the Valium."

"But Valium has nothing to do with sex."

"Maybe not in normal doses, but you were taking that stuff from morning to night. So for the first two weeks in a lot of years you haven't had your brain pickled in Valium. I think you nearly O.D.'d on female hormones back there."

"That fucking Valium!" she said.

"No, that *non*-fucking Valium. Can you imagine what the rest of your life is going to be like without Valium?"

We stayed in bed and made love all that day. We were like new lovers again.

TWENTY NINE

I had thought our love making was a harbinger of Barbara's increasing good health and vitality, but for the next few days all she wanted to do was to stay at home and read a psychology book the therapist suggested for her. It was a paperback volume of transcribed therapy sessions with a California guru who was fashionable in the late sixties and early seventies. His therapy was a little Freud, a little Jung, a little Zen, a little "space," a little environment, but mostly just the common sense you get from living a long time with your eyes open. Maybe when you talk sense to a bunch of superannuated California adolescents they are likely to perceive it as Eternal Truth.

Barbara read it avidly, convinced that it held the key to all her troubles. I was a bit skeptical, but I didn't say anything.

She needed a lot of rest, too, after all she'd been through. Exercise could wait a few days. She was eating well and she was relaxed and the book kept her busy so she didn't mind when I went out.

But she soon began to have trouble sleeping again. This wasn't like her earlier Valium withdrawal. She had no more of those symptoms. Her alternating fever and shivering seizures never came back, but her nightmares did. Now her nightmares came back while she was awake and they were heralded by a physical phenomenon I had never heard of. Barbara described to me how she would get a sort of electric buzzing in her brain around the area of her right temple. Then with her finger, she traced a path this electric spark traveled as though it was on a wire from her right temple all the way across her forehead to come to rest at a spot in her brain just forward of her left temple. When the spark hit her left temple it would set off the same indistinct but terrifying nightmares that had haunted her before. I sat with her and watched as she traced the path of the spark in her head and then clenched her teeth and squeezed her eyes tight shut from the intolerable buzzing in her head.

"If it's that serious, don't you think you ought to see a doctor?" I said.

"I don't need any doctor. They're the ones who gave me the Valium in the first place. I feel fine now. This will pass. Everybody thought it would be bad, even Samantha. When I told her I was going to quit cold she warned me not to do it. And you see? It was rough for a while but I'm fine now. Wait till I tell her how wrong she was."

"That's funny. I would have thought Sam would be happy to see you quit."

"Oh, she's always been secretly hostile and wanting me to fail."

That was a new awareness coming from Barbara.

"You always called her your best friend," I said.

"She is," Barbara said. "Best friend I have in the world. I don't know how I would have got through my attacks without her."

"But how can she be your best friend if she's hostile and wants you to fail? How can you have a best friend who is so destructive? Something's wrong there."

"She's always been that way, ever since I met her in the office where we both worked. My first job in television."

"Oh?" I said. "I never knew you two worked together."

"Sure. Don't you remember the story I told you about when I saw her in the Down Under Restaurant in Rockefeller Center having lunch with Ben?"

"Yeah," I said. "I remember."

"And I thought it was so funny because she didn't know Ben. And here she was cheating on Dale having a 'lunch' with Ben and they never knew I saw them. I kept it a secret because I didn't want to hurt Dale."

"Yeah, but wait a minute, if you met Samantha on your first job. . . . That would be the same time as when Ben was living with you. Wouldn't it?"

Barbara turned her head away. She was silent but something was happening inside her. I could hear countless wheels spinning around in her head. When you live close to a person you sense these times.

"Yes," I continued. "That's right around the time. Because you quit the job and then you got married. But there was always a gap in that story. I never could understand why you kicked Ben out who was such an ideal guy for you and married that creep you couldn't stand."

"I married him to please my parents."

"Yeah, I understand that. But there's a gap. How did Samantha get to be with Ben if she never met him?"

"Oh, I brought him up to the office to show him off. He was so beautiful. Imagine, an *artist*. And he sold his paintings, too! He was so much more exciting than the guy Sam was going to marry and I wanted to show him off. I thought he was the greatest thing since chopped liver. Sam thought so too."

"Oh?" I said. "What did she say? How did she react?"

"She didn't say anything. She didn't say a word. She *never* said anything! I was her best friend and she never told me a thing! That's why when I saw them, I—"

Barbara shut up immediately but she had gone too far.

"Ahhh," I said. "Ben was still your lover then. And he was out with your best friend, but it wasn't Dale you kept silent to protect, it was . . ."

A Niagara of curses poured over the breached dam of Barbara's memory.

"She took him, that bitch! She couldn't wait! The day after they met! I'll kill her! I'll fucking tear her big tits out! She was my best friend and she stole him! *My* lover! He was beautiful and he was *mine!*"

Barbara collapsed in tears. She sobbed and grieved over the loss and betrayal she had kept bottled up for so long. She was a long time crying. There was nothing I could do but hold her and comfort her.

"There, Babe," I said. "It'll be okay. You'll get over it."

Barbara raised her tear-stained face.

"All those years she never said a word! I followed her every day after that. I followed her the next day into a delicatessen on Sixth Avenue where she met him again. And they were kissing and holding hands. The next day! I stood up and *he* saw me. He didn't move. He didn't say anything to Sam. He just stared and looked at me. I asked her where she had been at lunch and you know what my *friend* said to me? 'Oh, I was out shopping. I was looking for a hat.' A hat my ass! They were out fucking. My lover! That prick! Making love with me weekends and then fucking her during the week!"

"So that's why you kicked Ben out," I said. "And that's why you married your Fort Lauderdale boyfriend whom you couldn't stand. You were on the rebound."

"My best friends. They're probably still laughing at me. I never want to see them again. If either one of them calls, I won't talk to them! Ever!"

"Babe," I began. "It happened twelve years ago. It's only because you've kept it bottled up for so long that it seems so terrible. But they're good people and they really love you. In time you'll get over it. What amazes me is that in all your years of analysis not one of your doctors has ever been able to help you uncover that."

"You're better than any doctor."

"No, you led me right to it. You obviously wanted to talk about it. I don't think about those people. Especially not in the last weeks. You brought it up and you led me directly to the source of your grief. I was only following you. You must have done this with your analysts."

"No. Twelve years of analysis by the best and they never made the sense you made just now. It's what you were saying in Venice. You're a genius. You accomplished in one afternoon what they couldn't do in twelve years."

"No, see?" I said. "You're doing it again."

"What?"

"Hooking me. You just said something very significant and I can't let the bait go by."

"What did I say?" she said, genuinely mystified.

"Twelve years."

"Yeah. So what? I've been seeing analysts for twelve years. So what?"

"It's a magic number," I said. "You also have been taking Valium for twelve years, right?"

"Well, sure. That's how long ago I had my first bad back attack."

"Before or after you knew that Samantha and Ben were cheating on you?"

"Right after I found out," she replied. "Huh! That's a funny coincidence, isn't it? My back had been fine after my disc operation in college. And then all of a sudden I got a really bad attack."

"Some coincidence," I said.

"And that was when I had my first Valium prescription. I took a lot of it because my back hurt so much."

Barbara sobbed softly as the memory struck her again.

"I loved them both so much. I wanted them both to be at our wedding. Samantha was going to be my maid of honor. But they would only have been laughing at me like they've been laughing all these years."

Tears streamed down Barbara's face as she broke down once more. She cried again and again over the long-ago loss of her lover and the treachery of her best friend as though it had happened yesterday.

Barbara had bouts of grief and anger about Sam and Ben for the next few days. This was only the beginning. Once the Valium was out of her system and these memories were released so easily, Barbara didn't seem able to hold back anymore. She felt sure there was lots more waiting to come out of her. I was more concerned that she get some exercise. She had been cooped up in the apartment for nearly a week. I kept trying to persuade her to come out with me and play some tennis, but she was still frightened at the thought of leaving the house and didn't want to go out for any reason. Finally on the following Sunday she reluctantly agreed to come out with me and try to play a set or two.

I had to make tennis reservations at the last minute to take advantage of Barbara's sullen acquiescence. The Wall Street courts were booked solid. I was able to get time in a new club that had opened up in the Armory on Lexington and Twenty-something Street. It hadn't been designed for tennis. The back courts were small and it was a bit claustrophobic, with dark green canvas to separate the courts. Barbara didn't like it the moment she walked in, but I insisted and she played grimly.

As she leaned back to serve a ball, her eyes widened in horror. The ball and racket fell from her hands as she stared at something above my head. I couldn't see anything in the old beams that disappeared into the darkness beyond the floodlights. Barbara screamed and waved her hands in front of her face as though warding something away. I ran to her and she collapsed in my arms.

"It's her!" Barbara said. "It's her!"

I followed her pointing finger. All I could see from this angle was a dusty regimental shield decorated with animals and intricate squiggles barely visible in the shadows of the rafters.

"It's my nightmare!" she said. "That's what comes to me in my nightmares! Get me out of here, please! Please take me home!"

As soon as I got Barbara home, we struggled to unravel her new tale. There were questions and answers for hours until familiar parts of her dream materialized. It was mainly about a woman whose face Barbara couldn't see but whose hair was long and wild. That's why the regimental crest had triggered her memory. Barbara called her nightmare companion Medusa with snakes for hair. She described how she was asleep in a tiny room and the Medusa appeared, silhouetted in a narrow doorway. Barbara tried to shake off the nightmare image, but she could no longer hold back the recurring dream which flowed out of her. In her dream, this Medusa tried to kiss her and then make love to her in the tiny room. In the middle of this love scene, Barbara had a sudden realization.

"It's Samantha!" she whispered. "Samantha is Medusa. The snakes are her long hair. She was in bed with me but I didn't like what she was doing. I didn't want her. It was right after I had broken up with Abe. The second Abe. And I was so upset I cried all weekend."

"Oh, that one," I said. "I remember him. You went to his place one night without calling and found him with another woman."

"Not only that, but on the way back to my apartment I tripped and that set off a killer back attack, too. I really took a nosedive. And Samantha, that cunt! She knew how upset I was. I had taken every Valium in the house for my back and Sam came to the house to take care of me. She brought me food and she massaged me. She came over when she finished work every day. But she wasn't helping me for myself. She wanted something else, too. That bitch! How could I have ever thought she was my best friend? She was probably still laughing at me about Ben. God, I hate that woman!"

"But the tiny room and the little door, what's that?"

"Of course the room was tiny," Barbara said simply, "we were on Dale's new boat and I was sleeping in a small bunk. Dale had just sold a big screenplay and bought a new boat. Sam hated it. She always wanted a beach house like our other friends, but Dale would never buy one for her. My back was just recovering and Samantha had invited me out for a long weekend. I thought it was to take care of me. I was so upset about losing Abe that I didn't have any fun. I cried the whole weekend. I was taking Valium by the handful and drinking and Dale always has the best dope. I wondered why Samantha kept pressuring me to try it. She wanted to get me stoned. How could I have been taken in by that awful woman? We all went to bed and I cried in my sleep. I heard the little door creak open and I saw her standing there, her long hair was wild, she had just gotten out of bed. Then she sat down on the little bunk and she began touching me and I didn't know whether I was asleep or awake. I was so stoned. And then when she tried to kiss me and I felt her breath and her lips and she tried to kiss me, but I didn't want it. And then I felt her fingers and I tried to say no, but I couldn't. I was too stoned. But I thought it! I didn't want her to do it, but I was too stoned to say no."

"So what you're telling me is that she did it. She made love to you."

"Well, yes."

"And she made you feel better?"

"I was too stoned to push her away. I didn't want that. You know I'm not a lesbian."

Oh, the old, "I was too drunk to know what I was doing" line. Barbara had received some warmth and love at a time when she needed it and she was too afraid of homosexuality to admit that it didn't feel so bad. I didn't think she was homosexual. There have been odd times when I've been with a man and it doesn't make me homosexual. I like women much better. That doesn't make me heterosexual, either. It doesn't make me anything. Those terms don't have the same significance to me as they obviously had to Barbara.

There was another possibility about this nightmare of hers. Barbara was in a very confused state during the weeks of withdrawal. Her dimly seen Medusa with the wild hair could very well have been the withdrawal therapist. Barbara was in another world when the therapist arrived. She had no idea I had called such a person to help her. This strange woman could have seemed to be a frightening female apparition suddenly appearing in her bedroom when Barbara began to have her first dim awareness of her surroundings as the withdrawal wore off. The therapist had been pretty chummy when I'd seen them in bed together. If relieving sexual tension was part of her therapy, in Barbara's semi-lucid state she could easily have confused her hazy image of the strange therapist with her old stoned memory of Samantha, since the two women would look alike in a darkened room. With all Barbara's new-found anger at Sam, Sam had become a handy repository for all her fears and rage. Barbara had been nearly unconscious in both situations and she would never be able to sort out those hazy drug dreams. It didn't matter. Barbara was getting rid of a lot of old ghosts and it was good they were gone.

"I feel safe with you," she said. "You know me so well and you always zero in exactly on what my problem is. I can't fool you the way

I always fooled my doctors. No analyst I ever had made sense like you do. You're the only doctor I'm ever going to have from now on."

"In dot case, Ms. Gordon," I said in my best Katzenjammer Kids Viennese, "I haf a zerious qvestion to ask you. Haf you ever schlept mit your analyst?"

"You know, almost every woman I know has done that, but I never did. Honestly."

"You vould like to try it vonce? All dot talk about zex has roused my analytical lust."

We did.

THIRTY

Nancy called early Monday morning because Evan, the executive producer, was worried. Barbara had told him she would only be out for a few days and she hadn't called in more than two weeks. Barbara wouldn't come to the phone.

I made excuses for her and thanked Nancy for the therapist before I hung up. I tried to persuade Barbara to call, but she was adamant. I followed her into the bedroom and dialled the phone.

"Who are you calling?" Barbara said.

"Evan."

"Don't you dare!"

"Oh, hi, Debbie? . . . Yeah . . . Barbara's still under the weather, but she'll be okay soon. Listen, she wants to talk to Evan. Is he there? . . . Sure."

I held the phone to Barbara's ear. She reddened with rage.

"No! You can't make me!"

I uncovered the mouthpiece. I could hear a teeny voice on the phone. Barbara's rage vanished in an instant. Her voice was weak, but almost normal.

"Evan, yes . . . " she began. "I'm still a little weak. I put in some long nights last month. I have lots of sick days saved up. . . . Oh, no. It's something I've had for a long time and I'm finally getting rid of it. I could come in now, but. . . . Oh, thanks, Evan. Yeah, I could use more rest. . . . Ha-ha! . . . Give my love to Arlene. Bye."

She handed me the phone.

"See?" I said. "You were fine. Nothing to be afraid of."

"Don't you *ever* do that again!" she snapped.

She was furious with me.

When I had forced her to go to the dentist, or play tennis, or speak to Evan on the phone, Barbara stared at me as though I was another person. I suppose I was, to her. Except for that one outburst on the road to Venice, I had never been stern with her before and she didn't understand it. She was not accustomed to taking orders from anyone.

A new relationship was evolving between us. I don't know when it started, but at some point Barbara had thrown aside her paperback guru in disgust and began to put me in that role. We eased naturally into the roles of doctor and patient without even being aware of it. Barbara had been accustomed to being an invalid for long periods of her life when loved ones would come and feed her, wash her, clothe her, and minister to her every need. She had done it so often, in all her relationships, that she had no shame in asking. It was automatic for her.

And I never shared this culture's custom of investing the medical profession with the reverence of a holy order. I was brought up with the assumption that the body healed itself and that's the way I have always lived. I rarely saw the inside of any kind of doctor's office. But that's my personal bias and I know it. I had scrupulously avoided any involvement with Barbara's illnesses before. I got involved now because her withdrawal seemed to me to be a giant step which she was taking purely out of love for me. Neither one of us wanted to stop her memories. I was proud to be able to help her accomplish this. For me to hear the woman I loved proclaim again and again that I was better than all her analysts was too seductive an ego trip for me. Prince Valium was ready and eager to rescue his fair maid from the clutches of evil.

Barbara wasn't able to sleep. Her nightmares were occurring more frequently and she tried to stay awake in order to avoid them. I tried to help her with hot milk, cocoa, and massage, but she wanted a sleeping pill. She was over the withdrawal for more than a week and she was sure it would be safe. She would need a prescription and she didn't want to call Doctor Alexander, so I thought of Mike, her gynecologist. I found his number and called him because Barbara was still apprehensive about speaking to anyone.

I had never met Mike, but Barbara had told me tales of how he had become a legendary gynecologist ministering to "the great and near-great" women of New York. He was also an ex-boyfriend of hers. He had written many prescriptions for Barbara and knew her tolerances. I told him exactly what had happened through the withdrawal, and he assumed as we did, that she was well past any critical period. He felt that a mild sleeping pill wouldn't hurt her now. She needed to rest and recover more than anything. He phoned in a prescription and I went out to pick them up. It was called Placidyl. Oh, the names they pick for these drugs!

The Placidyl didn't work too well. Barbara was only able to sleep for a few hours at a time. The first day she had to take them three times to catch up on her needed sleep. After that, they seemed to work better.

Although she could now sleep, Barbara's nightmares kept coming. She would carry the frightening but indistinct image from her drugged sleep into waking. Then we would talk and, with me helping as much as I could, Barbara would steadily spin her nightmare tale into reality and discover the human face in her dream.

There were no days or nights. We ate when we were hungry and we slept when we were too tired to go on. There was even more to the Samantha story. Locked inside Barbara was the reason why Sam couldn't make up her mind between Ben and Dale: she had become pregnant while fooling around and she didn't know which of them was the father. She left it up to the two men to decide who would have her. They, of course, didn't know she was pregnant until the slightly premature birth of her first child, a son who ended up looking a lot more like Ben than Dale. That's why Barbara always kept them apart.

Barbara swept me along further with her into the looking-glass world of her unconscious. In this secret world, everything was reversed. There were many friends whom she normally portrayed as loving her deeply who turned out to have been guilty of treachery in her eyes. None of them had done anything unusual. These were the normal personal clashes between friends. But Barbara had never dealt with even the slightest unhappiness before. Each painful moment had stayed locked up somewhere in her brain unexpressed. Over the years these petty betrayals had grown until they were of monumental size to her. She relived every unhappy experience again from start to finish. It was as though grief were a human function necessary to fully exorcise suffering and tragedy.

Barbara could stand to be alone if I only went down for the mail or to the pharmacy, but the hours necessary for my unemployment terrified her and she didn't want me to leave. Nancy was happy to come over and babysit with the excuse for Evan that she was doing research for Barbara's next show. Barbara immediately washed and changed and put her robe on. She still looked a bit haggard, but she pulled herself together. It had gotten late by the time Nancy arrived, so we greeted each other hurriedly as she passed me on her way to the bedroom. Barbara was sitting up in bed waiting for her. I heard Barbara regale her with an adventure story as I left the apartment.

"Oh, Nancy, wait till you hear," Barbara began. "The most marvelous things are happening. Anton is a genius. He is giving me this most incredible therapy. It's better than any doctor I ever had. Unbelievable things are coming out of me. . . . "

I closed the door on Barbara's excited narrative. I was exhausted but, I must say, somewhat proud.

In the space of two weeks Barbara poured out twelve years of accumulated grief. There were situations where Barbara had always portrayed herself as a victim, and it turned out now that she was often the guilty party. She experienced the new pain of guilt as though the event had happened yesterday.

Barbara had published a story in *Cosmo* about her long bittersweet love affair with a married man. I had read the story and she had told it often enough so I knew it very well. The way she always told it, she had waited five anguished years for him to leave his wife and marry her. Eventually he had turned Barbara down, choosing to stay with his wife and kids. Without her Valium, a totally different story emerged. Barbara described how he had really wanted to marry her but she turned him down. He came one night to Barbara's apartment for a showdown. He had told his wife he was leaving her forever and now it was up to Barbara to make a decision. He insisted that she marry him or break their affair. Barbara refused him.

She showed me where he had stood on the window ledge, threatening to jump if Barbara didn't marry him. He had left his wife and he had nowhere else to go. After Barbara's refusal, he relented about the suicide and, somewhat the worse for wear, went back to his wife. Barbara had the worst back attack of her life that night. Valium wasn't enough to dull that pain. She drank heavily and took sleeping pills by the handful, consciously courting suicide. The parallels between her married man's dilemma and my own were not lost on me.

As Barbara exorcised each daemon from her past, the nightmare did not come back. One day there was no nightmare when she awoke. And there was none the next day. We had reached the bottom, the beginning of her back attacks and the beginning of her Valium. We had voyaged through the sealed-up memories of her Valium years and now it was all over. Barbara was overjoyed. She didn't even mind my going out to get a bottle of champagne. We celebrated her triumph with champagne and love making and, that which had come to represent her freedom from anxiety, a walk outside.

It was around eleven at night when we decided to go. Barbara dressed in her brown velvet warm-up suit. She took my arm. For the first time in five weeks Barbara walked calmly out of the apartment with no fear. She walked happily beside me into a clear, crisp starry night on Central Park South. There were happy people all around us, horses trotting with hansom cabs, doormen whistling, and people coming from theaters and restaurants all laughing and with color in their cheeks. We walked along Fifth Avenue, past F.A.O. Schwartz, and looked in at Bendel's latest crazy windows. As we returned home we were surrounded by a formally dressed crowd laughing and chattering on their way back to their hotel. They, too, had chosen to walk on this bright, glittering night. The whole world seemed to be celebrating with us. It was something to celebrate. Our analytic marathon had worked. Barbara's anxiety was gone at last.

THIRTY ONE

We started coming back to life. Barbara was no longer afraid of being left home alone so I was able to get a lot of chores done. I walked over to Lincoln Center to pick up tickets for a new production of *The Threepenny Opera*. It had always been one of my favorite plays. This was my birthday present to me, and Barbara was excited about going to the theater again, even though the performance was a month away.

"You know," she said, "I haven't thought about the future in such a long time. It's almost as though the future didn't exist while I was withdrawing. But I can see it now and I like it. A life without Valium."

"A life without fear," I said.

She talked eagerly about our wedding, which would be only a few weeks from now. Barbara was thinking of having it down in Fort Lauderdale after all. It wasn't that she wanted so much to please her mother, but she still hadn't reconciled herself to her new conscious awareness of the story of Samantha and Ben. They had been Barbara's closest friends and now they were the last people she wanted to see at her wedding. I knew she'd eventually get over it, but she at that point still trembled with rage over their betrayal so many years previous.

I answered a call from a Doctor Charles Coblenz. He was in New York from the West Coast with some friends and wanted to see Barbara. Barbara ran to the phone and excitedly invited them all up to the apartment. I couldn't understand her sudden hospitality after four weeks of wanting no contact with anyone besides me. Barbara explained that he was a well-known psychologist and an expert on drug addiction. She wanted to tell him about her recent experience with Valium. I remembered his name then. He had been an expert witness in a trial involving drugs that had made headlines around the world.

Barbara and I tore through the house, cleaning everything in sight.

She ordered a huge assortment of liquor and wine and food for her first visitors since Nancy. The doctor arrived with a woman and another couple. He had a crew cut and thick glasses, turtleneck, and tweed jacket. Barbara regaled them with the terrible time she had had getting off the Valium and how it still seemed to be affecting her. She didn't leave out a single detail. His response was very different from what Barbara had expected.

"I love you dearly, Barbara," he said, "but you're so full of shit it's coming out of your ears. I know a lot about Valium. I've seen a lot of people withdraw from it. LaRoche is right. Valium is nothing. Withdrawal symptoms last three, five days, a week at the most and they're gone. If anything else is happening you must be suffering from something else or be hooked on some other drug with it."

"No, there's nothing. It's all a response to the Valium and the withdrawal. . . . ."

Barbara tried to convince him otherwise, but he was having none of it. The evening ended with Barbara very depressed but she transformed that into a new mission. She was determined to tell her story to help others whom she felt had been taken in by the deceptive advertising for this "innocent" drug. Valium was being ingested by people all over the world with no information at all about the possible consequences, consequences which Barbara now felt she alone knew all too well.

She talked a lot about writing a book based on this experience. We soon found there was a lot more in this subject of interest to both of us. This experience had a great deal of personal significance to me, too. We thought it would be a marvelous idea for both of us to write separate accounts of the experience without consulting each other and then compare them afterwards. What could be more logical and exciting for two writers?

"And we hold nothing back," Barbara said. "That would make it sensational."

"Sex, too?"

"Sex especially," she said.

"Would you mind if I wrote about love making with you? That could get pretty intimate."

"Mind? Me? The original First Amendment Freak? If I minded, I'd have to forfeit the politics of my entire life. But I don't mind at all. No one knows how to make love like you do. I owe it to the American woman to have you show the American man how it's done. I'll gladly sacrifice my privacy for that goal. It's the least I can do for the women of America. Of course it will sell a lot of books, too."

"We might even get them published together as a boxed set," I laughed, "tied with a yellow ribbon."

I helped Barbara get ready for her first all-day outing since the withdrawal. She dressed in her old maroon woolen shirt, jeans, her orange-yellow babushka and her Tretorn tennis shoes with the toes out. We were going to the beach house. It was time to open it up for the summer. There was also a big repair that would have to be taken care of before we could rent the house. Over the winter all the ceiling acoustical tiles had fallen down. In the seasonal change of hot dry air to damp cold, they had expanded and pulled out of their staples. On our first visit to the house after coming back from Europe we looked into a living room covered with broken white tiles scattered and piled from one end of the room to the other. I had intended to put in a suspended ceiling to allow for expansion, but I hadn't been able to get to it lately. It was only six weeks to Memorial Day and if we expected to rent the house for the summer the ceiling would have to be replaced.

The thought of being away from the apartment for a whole day made Barbara uneasy at first, but she soon relaxed into the familiar rhythm of the trip. It was Easter Sunday and we were full of thoughts about spring and rebirth. The house looked fine from the outside. We opened all the shutters. The long white tiles were still scattered where they had fallen. I started stacking them and separating the ones that were still good. It looked like only half of them would have to be replaced. Once I had cleared enough of them off the floor, I started to measure for the suspended ceiling hardware. Barbara got out her old cardboard box, her coffee can, and her trowel and went outside to plant dune grass.

I was high up on the ladder measuring the ceiling where it met the front windows when I caught sight of Barbara's bright yellow babushka. She was far below me on the dune with her box full of grass shoots beside her. I watched her tiny maroon back move steadily across the face of the dune as she planted her grass. It was a good sign that she was able to do that again. Work like that is health. Four and a half weeks of pain and torture and she had come through. And she had done it for me, to come to our marriage clean. I had to hand it to her. She was a stand-up lady after all. She'd be back to life soon, I thought, as I watched the slow rocking motion of her kneeling figure, digging and setting each shoot, inching her way along the new sand, *davening* to the gods of the grass and the dune and the sea and the sky.

THIRTY TWO

I leafed through the day's mail and glanced at the cover of the latest *New York* magazine. It headlined a feature story called "The Worst Drugs in America." Since we had some recent experience in that field, I opened it to see what they said about Valium. I never got that far because at the very top of the list, classed by their editor as one of the most seriously addictive drugs on the market, was a sleeping pill called Placidyl. I recognized the idiotic name immediately. I had innocently renewed the prescription and so far as I knew, Barbara was still taking it to help her sleep. I showed her the article.

Barbara was stunned when she read it.

"They won't let you get away from this garbage no matter what you do," she said. "I've gone through so much, I've worked so hard for so long and now I'm hooked on another filthy drug again. It's not fair!"

She threw the magazine across the room.

"That must be why I'm still terrified of leaving the apartment," she said. "You didn't say anything, but I know you're disappointed that I still can't leave the house."

"You went out once to the beach house and that was a good sign. I didn't want to push you. You need to rest and get your strength back, I know that."

"Don't try to make me feel good! I'm still scared to go out and you know it! It's no different from when I was taking Valium. This must be the reason I'm still scared. I'm dependent on another drug all over again. How could Mike *do* this to me?"

She flopped onto the couch and started to cry. I put an arm around her but she shrugged it off.

"It's nobody's fault," I said. "I'm sure Mike didn't know. He was only trying to help."

"I'm sick of this whole business! I hate that I have to ask you this, you've been so patient, but will you help me again? I've gone so far, I

255

can't stand the thought of being hooked again. Will you help me get all these drugs out of my system for good? Please?"

"Of course," I said. "We've been away from life so long, what's another week?"

Then I laughed.

"And we certainly have a lot of experience at this business."

Her withdrawal from the Placidyl was nothing compared to the torture of Valium. She knew how to take care of herself now, with long hot baths, cold towels to keep the fever down. Her only physical discomfort was a difficulty falling asleep for a few days. I stayed with her and massaged her and held her and she would drop right off. I was happy to help her. What was another few days? Even a week.

As soon as Barbara stabilized physically, that periodic buzzing in her head came back again, but this time it was stronger. She sat on the couch, staring into space as she tried to concentrate on the interior of her skull during one of these attacks.

"It's faster this time," she said. "It's another nightmare! And it's worse! I know it. I'm losing myself. I don't know who I am. I can't stop it."

And before I knew it we were off on another trip into the far reaches of Barbara's mind. Now it was through the years before the Valium. As before, these memories were a mirror image of her previous stories of innocence. When her friend, Bernice, ran off with the amorous Venetian gondolier, Barbara had immediately seduced the hotel manager and spent the rest of her time in Venice in his bed. Then, instead of going to Rome alone, Barbara said she had hitched a ride with a car full of guys and slept with them all.

Her childhood sexual memories tumbled out one after another. Barbara had often alluded to her experience with a child molester when she was around nine, but a different story emerged now. The molester, she now remembered, was a teenage hillbilly who had just been drafted in the army. Barbara remembered inviting his attentions. That little girl who was Barbara remembered liking him a lot. She liked the tentative feelings he aroused in her nine-year-old body and she met him often. The last time she had seen him, he was standing in the doorway of their house between two white helmeted MPs. The boy had been caught trying to sell books of ration stamps that belonged to Barbara's mother. They were worth a lot in those days. Barbara had stolen them from her mother and given them to the boy to entice him to come and see her again. The MPs had dragged the boy to their house to establish his guilt. While Barbara watched helplessly, he said he found the books on the street and Barbara's mother assumed they had fallen out of her purse. He never betrayed his child lover and Barbara's guilt at his arrest had always been mixed up with her sexual guilt and repression.

The childhood sexual themes carried over into our real life. I was rubbing Barbara's back the way I had done since I knew her. I straddled her legs to put both hands equally on her lower back to ease the stiffness. We had only our bathrobes on. Straddling her in that position, rubbing her back slowly and listening to stories of a sexually precocious nine-year-old I naturally got an erection which nestled neatly in her ass. The sexuality of her memory passed over into real life.

"Put it in there," she said in a low voice.

I worked around trying to find the right hole but she reached around and put it against her rectum.

"In there," she said.

This was new.

"Let me get something," I said. "It may hurt."

"No just like that. Now!"

I pushed gently, working it in. It's not easy, dry like that.

"Owowow!" she screamed.

"Are you all right?"

"Oh yes, more. Put it in all the way. Owww! Ohhh!"

"But it hurts you."

"Oh yes," she sighed, "but it makes me feel like a virgin for you. Every man I ever knew has wanted to fuck me there, but I never let them. You're the first. I promise you. I'm a virgin for you."

What a feeling. Don't mistake me. The vagina is infinitely more variable and much more satisfying. It wasn't the physical sensation, it was the head trips she was able to take me on. She had my undivided attention for the rest of her trip.

Barbara told me of her violent temper tantrums when she was little. She described how she used to scream and batter herself, pounding the floor with her arms and legs. Her mother was only able to control her by threatening her that she would go crazy and have to be sent away to the local funny farm called Chatahootchie. Mental hospitals always seemed to have funny names in those days. Her mother's horror stories of straitjackets, padded cells, and electric shock frightened her even now.

"Promise me, no matter what happens you'll never send me to such a place. No matter how bad I might get."

"What could happen to you?" I said.

"It happens all the time. Perfectly sane people get locked up by accident."

"Sane people don't get locked up in mental hospitals."

"You don't know. You remember the first movie you cut for me?"

"The old people," I said.

"I shot the footage just before I met you," Barbara's words came faster and faster now. "I had to go to the Bronx State Hospital to shoot that interview with the doctor. I was wandering through the halls alone, looking for her office. Just being in that place terrified me so much I had the first anxiety attack I can remember. I fainted dead away in the hall. I woke up in a ward room on a bed and this really nice young doctor was taking care of me. I felt okay when I woke up and tried to get out of the bed, but he wouldn't let me go. He wanted to know what ward I came from. He thought I was a patient! I told him I was a television producer making a movie at the hospital and the minute I said that I knew he didn't believe me. He was convinced I was crazy. When I realized that, I tried to run away but he held me down. He gave me a shot. He thought I was going to be violent."

"What happened?" I said. "You obviously got away."

"Only because Jill and Mario, my cameraman, got worried and started looking for me. They found me. The doctor still didn't want to let me go. It was the worst nightmare of my life. I honestly thought he would never let me out."

"But you see? You did get out."

"But it could have happened! I saw that R.D. Laing movie and I was so frightened I had to run out of the theater. It's like *The Snake Pit!*" she shuddered.

"Yeah, but there's another part of *The Snake Pit*," I said. "It's that handsome, gentle, caring doctor who does nothing but give you attention and makes you well again. I think it was Leo Genn wasn't it? Marvelous deep, soft voice. So understanding. I think under your fear it has a lot of attraction for you. It's a very seductive image."

"Seductive? Padded cells? Straitjackets? Do you know what they do with shock treatment? How can you call that seductive? Promise me, you'll never let them do that to me."

"I promise, of course I promise. Nothing's going to happen to you."

Barbara's memories came faster and faster. In a few days we rushed backwards in time to when she was a baby and then to the beginning of her awareness where there were only lights, colors, noises, and the clamor of something that could have been birth. I had no reason to doubt her. Who knows where memory begins? The brain exists at birth. It must function in the womb, even if crudely.

Would anyone believe this trip we had taken? That didn't matter. I had watched it all happen. We were face to face, mind to mind, and body to body through each experience. Barbara's elation and her thrill of discovery when she'd release herself from these ghosts was proof enough that we were on the right track of what ailed her. And we were on the right track. It just went to a place neither of us imagined.

THIRTY THREE

Barbara went into a kind of emotional limbo after that. She didn't want to leave the house to go for a walk yet. She didn't want to speak to Evan and Nancy about work. It was getting near to summer rental time and I still had the ceiling to put up, but she wasn't interested in the beach house, either. She just wanted to watch TV all day. I wasn't going to push her. I was sure she needed a lot of rest after what she had been through the past weeks.

I went out and resumed my life a little at a time, played a bit of practice tennis, went down to good old unemployment, and made a few work appointments. The last people I had worked for wanted a more detailed treatment of that series concept. I set the typewriter up in the living room and knocked out a revision for them. Having the typewriter in front of me, I sketched an outline of the experience Barbara and I had just been through. I wrote it as a screenplay, a diary of the two months' withdrawal period and the aftermath. It looked like an interesting project, but any extensive writing would have to wait until I had someplace to write. Either Barbara and I would move into a larger place soon after we married, or I would get my own place as I had dreamed, all of which seemed to hinge at the present moment on when Barbara would be fully rested and recovered.

Barbara's mood didn't change. One day she reluctantly agreed to go out for a walk in the park with me. She put on a skirt, for some reason. There were a lot of skirts gathering dust in her closets, but she hardly ever wore them. This one was a dark plaid pleated wool skirt, like part of a girls' school uniform, with a blouse and jacket and shoes to match. She was nervous, and I supported her out of the apartment with my arm around her waist.

It was a warm, sunny day . The streets were full of people going to lunch. After so long inside, Barbara had to squint in the unaccustomed bright sunlight. We walked to Sixth Avenue and crossed at the park entrance where the hansom cabs lined up waiting for customers. The horses were nodding in their canvas nosebags, eating their lunch. With the traffic behind us, Barbara felt surer of herself. She walked without my arm as we passed under the statue of José Marti, incongruously dressed in a business suit while riding his prancing bronze horse. I bought Barbara some Crackerjacks she wanted from a sidewalk cart. She steadily crunched them as we walked beneath the budding trees. She was doing all right. The lunchtime crowds made her nervous, so I led her to the high path behind the bird sanctuary. It was nearly deserted there. We could see the lake below us. Barbara began to hang back on my arm.

"I don't want to anymore," she said. "I want to go home."

I coaxed her further with my arm around her waist.

"Just a little while longer," I said. "We've only been out for a few minutes."

She wriggled out of my grasp and stood in front of me.

"I want to go home now!"

"Babe, you have to begin getting out of the house sometime. What's it all been for, if you can't take a walk outside?"

Then Barbara did something totally unexpected. She flung herself down on the ground and beat the pavement with her hands. I was so surprised, I just stared at her in amazement for a moment without saying anything.

"I'm not going to walk anymore," she said defiantly, "and you can't make me."

I didn't know what to think. I had never seen Barbara like this. With her pleated skirt spread around her she looked like a little kid having a tantrum, except that she was a rather tall woman in her thirties. People were looking at us. I tried to pull her up but she let her dead weight hang on my arm. I dragged her to her feet. Her knees wobbled, and she fell heavily in my arms. She grinned broadly, as though she had played a great joke on me, and it was suddenly all over. She seemed fine as we walked back.

"That was awful of me, wasn't it?" she said. "I don't know what happened."

I kissed her cheek. "You got out for a walk and that's the main thing."

"I'm sorry. Sometimes lately, I feel myself slipping away, like I'm . . . losing myself somehow and then I'm all right again."

262

After some of the things we had recently been through together, this didn't seem terribly significant. I thought that the walk might have been too strenuous for her. I might have pushed her too far. I thought it might be best to let her rest, as she wanted to, and take things at her own speed.

It happened again when I set dinner out for her. She had a similar brief tantrum and refused to eat. Then she jumped in my lap and laughed.

"I was bad, wasn't I?" she said. "I'm sorry. I was just teasing you. Don't be angry with me."

It had happened too fast and I was still confused. She kissed me and I reassured her I wasn't angry. She treated those bursts of childish hostility like a game, but I was unable to tell what was a game and what wasn't.

Sometime prior to this it had occurred to me that there was less liquor in the house than there should have been. We had always kept a large stock for last-minute entertaining and we had bought a lot more when Doctor Coblenz and his friends came up. I only drank vodka and Bitter Lemon these days, but I had the distinct feeling that those other bottles were steadily emptying.

In the light of Barbara's strange behavior, that suspicion came back to me with a sudden clarity. Barbara was awake for long periods during the withdrawal when I was sound asleep. I had been regularly leaving the house during the day for some time now. There was no reason not to trust her. The withdrawal was her own idea. I couldn't let her think I had lost confidence in her, so I took a pencil and marked every bottle with a tiny line on the label to indicate the level of booze in it.

I couldn't delay putting up the beach house ceiling any longer. When I insisted on leaving, Barbara began a long tearful story about how miserable she had been when she wasn't allowed to go to her grandfather's funeral. I hate to say it, but after all this time I was sick and tired of Barbara's tearful stories. I blew up at her.

"You should be getting out in the air, in the sun, with other people. You have to begin your life sometime. Otherwise what has it all been for?"

She sounded languid and sleepy when she replied, "I have to talk to you. There's more in my head. I know it."

"Fine. You'll tell me when I get back, or you'll come with me in the car, or you'll get another psychiatrist and pay him to listen, but I've had it."

"No, *you're* my doctor. You're better than all of them."

My ego didn't need this anymore. I was too tired and I needed to recharge. When she still refused to go, I picked up my tool box and left for the beach house.

I hired Herman the Hampton Handyman to help me attach the long metal strips to the naked rafters. After these were up, I could do the rest alone. Herman looked like a descendant of the *Bounty* mutineers. There was some common English ancestor who chose indentured servitude in the colonies instead of a stretch in Newgate Prison. Herman worked slowly but steadily and he didn't talk much. It was a pleasure to spend a whole day working in silence away from Barbara. I could think peacefully for the first time in a long while.

I felt bad about losing my temper with Barbara, but I knew she'd never get out of the house if I stayed with her all day long listening to her stories. It had been fine during the withdrawal and after, but she was well over that now. Except for a little insomnia after she went off the Placidyl, Barbara had had no withdrawal symptoms since the therapist left and that had been over six weeks ago. I could understand that she might need a lot of rest, but her reluctance to get back to living and those odd childish games she played lately bothered me. Something was wrong with her. When I got back from the beach house that night I checked the liquor bottles. A half bottle of scotch and a half bottle of Cinzano had disappeared. A lot of red wine was gone, too. At last I had a logical explanation for Barbara's strange behavior: she was drunk all day. It was only about eight o'clock. Barbara was sound asleep.

I confronted her the next morning as I made breakfast. She denied she had been drinking.

"No, of course not," she said. "Oh, maybe I had a glass of wine to help me sleep once, I can't remember."

She betrayed no suspicion or guilt at all that I could see. I took the scotch bottle out of the cupboard and showed her the marks I had made and the difference in the level of whiskey. Barbara's face turned beet red. She was humiliated at being caught in her lie.

"How *dare* you test me!" she yelled.

"There had to be some explanation for your bizarre behavior lately.

I thought these bottles were a lot lower than they should have been, so I marked them all. See?"

"You can't do this to me!!"

"Who do you think you're fooling?" I said. "You've been drinking it secretly when I'm gone, even washing the glasses and putting them away so's I won't notice. And then you lied to me just now. How could *you* do that to *me*?"

"I . . . I don't know," she sobbed. "I couldn't help myself. Don't be angry with me. Please."

"I'm not angry. I'm just getting terribly depressed. I thought you were so brave, but you've been pulling my leg all along while I trusted you. Is there anything else you've lied to me about?"

I hadn't expected an answer, but Barbara reached into her robe pocket, pulled out a crumpled, dirty handkerchief and handed it to me. There was something inside it. I opened the folds to reveal a large cache of little yellow Valium pills. There were some other capsules and pills, too, all mixed with tobacco shreds and dust balls. She must have sieved them from every pocket and purse in the house. There was a solid handful.

"Aw no!" I wailed. "Aw no, no, no, no, no!"

"Is there something wrong?" Barbara asked innocently.

The extent of her betrayal was too much for me to take in all at once. Not only was she drunk, she was taking Valium again and who knows what those other little capsules were. Eight weeks of torture and she was back exactly where she started. I was furious with myself and her at the same time.

"I give up," I said. "Take the fucking things. I don't care any more!"

I threw the pills at her and they scattered across the rug. Barbara dropped to her knees and frantically tried to retrieve them all. Something about the way she feverishly searched for them disgusted me. I grabbed some of the pills before she got to them.

"Here, you like these so much?" I said.

I held her head and tried to stuff them between her protesting lips.

"Here, eat them! Eat them all! They mean more to you than anything or anybody."

She tried to shake her head away but I managed to force some into her mouth. I half-carried her into the bathroom and turned on the light. I held her face by her chin and forced her to look at herself in the bright mirror. Her skin was pasty and wrinkled and tired.

"Look at yourself. You like your Valium and booze so much? This is what it does to you. You like that?"

She tried to shake her head away, but I held her fast.

"Don't run away from it. Eight weeks of work and it's all been a game to you. You've been lying to me all along. You never quit anything. As soon as you went off the Valium you went on the Placidyl and as soon as you went off that, you went right back on the Valium again, only with scotch chasers. It's all been a sick joke and I'm tired of being your straight man. You're a hard-core junkie. No, you're special. You're better than that. You're the Emmy-Award-Winning Queen of all the junkies."

I shoved her against the bathroom door and ran out of the apartment. I got no further than the elevator when a terrible thought hit me. Barbara had gobbled down pills and booze before when she was depressed. She was much less controlled this time. She could very well overdose. She'd do it for spite, if nothing else. I did love her. I cared. I couldn't risk it.

I rushed back to the apartment, pulled liquor bottles from the shelves, opened them, and upended them in the sink. I pulled the corks on the wine and dumped that, too. The sink was filled with chugging bottles. The mixed flavors of alcohol fumes were sickening. Barbara stood in the kitchen doorway, staring at me.

"What are you doing?" she asked timidly.

"I don't care what you do, Babe, but you're not dying on me. Not while I can help it."

"But I'm not drinking any of that."

"Fine. Then you won't miss it."

I went into the bathroom and searched the medicine cabinet. Barbara followed me and stood in the bathroom doorway. I found a bottle of that thirty-proof cough medicine and dumped it in the toilet.

"What do you want me to do so you'll like me again?" she asked.

"Whatever you want, Babe," I said. "It doesn't matter anymore."

"I'll quit!" she said. "I really will. I quit before. I'll really do it this time. I promise."

She reached into her robe pocket and emptied the handkerchief of pills into the toilet.

"See?" she said. "I really do want to. And there's more you don't know about. I'm going to throw that out, too."

She reached under her pillow and pulled out a fresh bottle of Placidyl which she showed me proudly. She must have gotten another prescription from Mike and had it delivered. The self deception of a true junkie! But I was beyond caring. I didn't say a word as Barbara dumped the Placidyl in the toilet and flushed all her drugs away.

"Is that what you want?" she asked.

"I couldn't care less," I replied as coldly as I could. "You do whatever you want."

"I want to quit the Valium."

"Fine. Quit. But don't bother me."

I went to the front door and was about to leave when Barbara stopped me.

"But you can't leave now." she said. "I threw them all away. You have to help me! Stay with me. Please!"

I had to get off this mad merry-go-round. I yanked the front door open and took a step to freedom when I saw the chain lock. I froze in my tracks. I remembered how she had told me her friend had had to break through to rescue her from her last sleeping pill binge. Barbara could order more pills any time she wanted while I was out. If she did take too many pills and chained the door, in her weakened condition the few minutes it would take to break through might make the difference between whether she lived or died. I grabbed the chain, thinking I could pull it off, but it wouldn't budge. I pulled at it again and again. My attempted clinical coolness disappeared. All my anger, frustration, and bone weariness with Barbara found expression at last as I focused it on that inanimate chain. Every atom of strength I had went into my hands as I twisted and pulled. I had visions of ripping it out of the door jamb. What a release! But *I* had installed it. And when I put them in, they stay. I was fighting against myself and I couldn't do much more than loosen a few screws. It held fast. Barbara stared wonderingly at me.

"I won't lock you out," she said. "Why are you doing that?"

"Don't you know?" I said. "Are you that far gone?"

I went into the bedroom and grabbed a screwdriver from the pile of tools that was still on the desk. I loosened the screws enough to take them out with my fingers.

"While I'm not here," I said, "I have no way of knowing what you're doing and I can't trust you anymore. You can call the liquor store, you can call the pharmacy, you can call the grocery store for beer, you can do whatever you want and there's no way I can stop you, but you're not going to die on me if I can help it."

"I'm not going to die," she said. "What a strange thing to say."

The last screws gone, I threw the chain across the living room and slammed the door behind me. I had to get out of that place. I ran through the lobby and burst out the front door to the sunlight. I plunged into the rush of the morning crowd. People chattered as they hurried by. The crowd's touches soothed me as I brushed through. I lost myself in the hurrying weave of the real world.

THIRTY FOUR

I walked for hours through the crowded city streets and I slowly came back to my senses. The knowledge that Barbara was drinking heavily again should have told me why she had no suspicion or guilt when I asked her about the marked bottles. At that moment she honestly didn't know she had been drinking. And when I got mad and held her face in the mirror, all she knew was that I was holding her and hurting her, and I was very mad at her, but she couldn't understand why.

I had been alone with Barbara for so long I had few benchmarks left for normal behavior, but I had to face the fact that for increasingly longer periods of time Barbara didn't know what she was doing. This is difficult to accept in a person you have lived with and loved. They have the same voice, the same way of talking, the same way of laughing and crying that you've always known. It's hard to not respond to those stimuli from someone you love, so it's impossible to tell where your loved one's reality begins and ends.

I decided that the best I could do for Barbara was to try to get her into one of those luxurious drying-out resort hospitals I pictured dotting the Connecticut countryside. They were staffed by psychiatrists who knew this addiction syndrome a hell of a lot better than I did and were familiar with all the games. I did not go to doctors and hospitals casually, but Barbara needed help and I could no longer give her what she needed.

I called Meyer, who lived in Connecticut, and explained the problem to him. He gave me the name of a well-known psychiatric hospital near him that specialized in drying out millionaire drunks and junkies. It sounded like just the place for Barbara. I called the hospital and told a woman admissions doctor the brief history. She said I could bring Barbara in for a checkup. A hit on the first nickel.

I had discussed my feelings about the hospital with Barbara earlier and she seemed resigned that it was the best way. She was quiet now as I helped her dress. She wasn't taking any clothes with her. We were only going up for a checkup, so I wasn't apprehensive. She walked calmly with me to the front door, but when I opened the door, she refused to step over the threshold. It was as though there was an invisible barrier she could not cross. I took her arm to help her over, but she resisted with an unexpected strength. I tried to carry her through. I wrapped my arms around her but she flung them off. I couldn't manage her.

"Babe, you have to come with me. I'm trying to help you but you have to cooperate."

"Where . . . ?" she said. "I'm losing myself again. Help me, please. I need help."

"I know that. That's what I'm doing. I can't get you to the hospital alone."

Barbara's eyes widened as though she heard that word for the first time.

"A hospital?"

"It's what we talked about. It's like a nice expensive hotel in the country, you'll see."

"No! It's just another name for Chatahootchie! Please! You promised you wouldn't send me away."

"Babe, it's not like that. Meyer gave me the name. You know Meyer. Meyer is a nice man. It's near where he lives. Meyer wouldn't want you to go to a bad place and neither would I. You know that."

"You're going to lock me up forever! You're trying to make me believe I'm crazy!"

"This is just a place to go to get rid of the drugs. It's got tennis courts and swimming pools. Nobody can make you stay. There will be very nice doctors who know how to take care of you."

"No! Don't send me away to a hospital! No!"

She ran into the bedroom and slammed the door. I didn't know what to do. I called the hospital again and had the first of what was to be a series of very frustrating contacts with the psychiatric business. I reached the same doctor again and told her the problem.

"This would not be a voluntary admission, then?"

"Well, that's the problem," I said. "I'm calling to see if you can arrange to pick her up."

"What is your relationship to the patient?" she asked coolly.

I knew what she was getting at the moment I heard those words.

"Ahhh, well, we live together."

"You're not married?" she said.

"No . . ."

"I'm sorry. You must be an immediate relative to commit someone."

"We've been living together for years," I said.

"We only recognize immediate family."

I could just see Al and Lilly. They didn't even know she was going to a psychiatrist.

"But this is an emergency," I said. "I can't handle her."

"Does she have a psychiatrist?" she asked.

"She used to but not right now."

"Her psychiatrist can recommend her, but he would have to examine her first and submit his evaluation. If he felt it was necessary, we could pick her up."

"But she won't see him."

"I'm sorry. Committing a person to a mental hospital against their will is not something you do lightly."

I understood that. But what could I possibly do? I went into the bedroom. Barbara was sitting on the edge of the bed, crying. She seemed to be herself again.

"I need help," she said.

"I know and I'm trying to help you. But I can't do anything without your cooperation. You need a doctor. You must go to see a psychiatrist."

"No! Never again. I never want to see him again."

"I mean another one. Would you see a different psychiatrist?"

She thought a long while.

"It's the only way," I said. "I can't handle this anymore."

"Well, only if he comes here, to me. I'm not leaving this house. Don't ask me again."

"But you will see a psychiatrist if I find one?'

"Yes, but I'm not going to any hospital. They're not going to lock me up and shock me. Promise me you won't let them."

"Don't worry," I said. "There's not going to be any shocks or locking you up or anything bad. Just a nice doctor."

"You promise you won't trick me?"

"I promise."

Tricking Barbara into a hospital was exactly what I had in mind. I didn't dare mention it for fear of setting her off again. We'd cross that bridge when the men in the white coats appeared at the door. What an ugly thought. What a betrayal she would feel. I could see the look in her eyes now. Would she ever forgive me? Many people would damn me for putting her in a hospital at this point, but just as many would damn me for *not* putting her in a hospital.

I had little experience with psychiatrists but I was sure that in an emergency like this I could easily find a doctor who would go along with Barbara's wishes. I had a surprise coming. Psychiatrists do not make house calls. No way. Never. After two dozen refusals, I dropped the qualification "good" from my standards of a doctor for Barbara. Any psychiatrist would do. I looked in the yellow pages and started with "A." By that evening I found a psychiatrist who seemed to understand her problem.

"Ah yes," he said, "classic agoraphobia. How long has she had this?"

"More than a year, but she was taking Valium and she stopped taking it and now she's terrified. She simply will not leave the house."

"I understand. It must be difficult for her."

"Then you'll come?" I said.

"We don't make house calls."

"But . . . I thought. . . . What am I going to do?"

"See how she is after a few days. Why don't you call me next week?"

"You'll come then?"

"I just said we'll see how she is. And if she is the same then, I would consider seeing her, yes."

"What if something happens in the meantime?"

"I'm sorry, there's nothing I can do. I'm going away for the weekend."

"Well, thank you. I will call you," I said.

Nobody was taking this as seriously as I was. I wondered what constituted an emergency in this business.

While I spoke to the doctor, Barbara had come out of the bedroom and listened to the end of the conversation. After I hung up, she began to slap her chest idly, and as she did this, she spoke in a faraway child's voice.

"Barbara is a bad girl," she said. "Barbara is such a bad girl. Barbara is a spoiled brat. Barbara is so bad she is going to be sent away to Chatahootchie!"

She continued this soft sing-song while she slapped her chest. I dropped my head in my hands. What now? I couldn't deal with this. I got up, walked around her and went into the bedroom. I sat at the desk, wondering what to do next. Barbara followed me and stood in front of me. She was still slapping herself. I looked away. She wasn't hurting herself, but I didn't know if I could cope with anything more.

"Barbara is a bad, bad girl," she continued in that faraway voice. "She's going to be locked in Chatahootchie and we'll never see her again."

I stood up and went back in the living room but she followed me, slapping herself as she walked.

"Barbara is a bad girl. . . . "

I couldn't stand her kidding around anymore.

"Will you stop it, Babe!" I yelled.

Barbara slapped her face as hard as she could.

"Stop that Barbara!" she shouted in the scolding voice of an adult. "See how angry you made that man? Bad girl!"

She slapped her face again. I took off my glasses and rubbed my eyes, partly from weariness and partly because I couldn't stand to watch her slap herself.

"Barbara . . . " I said softly, "Barbara, stop. Please."

"Barbara, stop that this *instant*," she said. "Ohhh, you're such a bad girl, we're going to have to send you to Chatahootchie!"

She slapped her face again and again until her cheeks reddened. I winced at the sight. She was acting as she had in those other childish episodes except it didn't go away this time. Barbara wasn't making a joke and laughing about it anymore. She hit herself harder and harder. I couldn't stand it. I held her arms but she kept trying to hit herself as though I wasn't there. I bear-hugged her, pinning her arms. I carried her into the bed and held her down with all my weight until she quieted. I massaged her and gently stroked her and she began to doze off. I let go of her arms. Her right arm jerked and quivered, but she didn't hit herself anymore. She started to talk in her sleep.

"Bad girl!" she murmured in that faraway voice. "Bad girl! Barbara is sooo bad, she's going to be locked in Chatahootchie and we'll never see Barbara again. . . . "

THIRTY FIVE

Barbara started hitting herself again the next night. Her robe opened and slid off her shoulders while she followed me around the living room. The robe fell to the floor and she stepped over it. She didn't seem to notice that she was naked as she steadily punched her chest and her arms with her fists. She was hitting bare flesh now and it felt painful to me. There were faint bruises on her arms and on the parts of her chest she could reach. I hadn't thought she was hurting herself with this, but I suppose the steady pounding brought up the bruises. I looked away. She walked in front of me.

"Look! Look!" she said. "I'm a bad girl and I have to be punished."

The little girl voice was gone. She sounded like Barbara now. My discomfort seemed to excite her further, so I tried to ignore her. I picked up a book and opened it on my lap. She covered the pages with her hands until I looked up at her. She hit herself some more.

"See? See?" she said.

When it got to be too much, I went into the bedroom and sat at the desk with the book in front of me. She followed me in and stood beside my chair. She attacked herself with greater fury.

"Look! Look! Look!" she said.

"Babe . . . please stop. You're going to hurt yourself."

"I hurt everybody, don't I?"

"No, Babe, don't say that."

"Don't say that! Don't say that!" she mimicked and punched herself with her fists. She started pounding her thighs now with a steady rhythm. She was getting light purple bruises on any spot she could reach. The sound of her fists on her bare flesh was getting to me. I couldn't ignore her any longer. I gripped both her wrists firmly. I stopped her for a moment, but she threw me off effortlessly and continued hitting herself. Her blows were harder and louder now. I grabbed her arm and twisted it behind her back. The pain made her stop. I released the pressure on her arm and she resumed hitting herself with her free hand. I twisted her arm again till it hurt her.

"I'm going to do this until you stop," I said.

She fought against it with a strength I didn't know she had, but eventually the pain in her twisted arm was too much for her and she quieted down.

I led her to the bed and made her lie down. I still held her arm behind her back, but with no pressure. It was late and Barbara had had only intermittent sleep since the liquor and all her pills were thrown out. I thought the steady erosion of the lack of sleep might be causing some of this strange new behavior of hers. I held her motionless on the bed.

"Now you're going to sleep," I said.

"I can't sleep. I won't."

"Then you're going to rest."

"I won't!"

"You will because I'll twist your arm until you do."

"You can't make me."

"Yes, I can. I'm still stronger than you. I can't let you do this to yourself. Now are you going to quiet down?"

She didn't answer. She nursed her arm where I had twisted it. A large purple bruise was forming.

"Here, let me look at that," I said.

"Get away from me!"

"Okay, okay. I won't touch you. I just want you to stay quiet and relaxed."

I hated to twist her arm like that, but I wasn't strong enough to restrain her any other way. It worked and it wasn't much worse than the way she was hitting herself now. It wouldn't do her any permanent damage, anyway. It was more important to control her over this weekend until I could get her into the hospital.

I opened the book again and tried to read while I watched over Barbara. I couldn't concentrate on it. I smoked some of her cigarettes. Foul things, but I needed some oral gratification. I had to stay calm and in control. I fidgeted with the tools on my desk. It seemed to make her nervous, but as long as I was in the bedroom watching over her, she didn't hit herself and she eventually fell asleep from exhaustion.

"Am I allowed to go to the bathroom?" she suddenly asked.

I had thought she was asleep. She was facing the wall.

"You don't have to ask me that," I said.

"You said I couldn't move."

"It was only when you were hitting yourself. Feel better now?"

"Can I go?"

"Of course you can go."

She got up slowly. She was looking bad. She hadn't eaten much of anything in the last days. I looked away from her to my book. She snarled as she walked around to the bathroom behind me. I didn't look up. She went to the toilet and then it sounded like she was slowly washing her face. Good sign. She hadn't bathed in many days. She walked out of the bathroom and stopped behind my chair. I kept my eyes on the book. Barbara didn't move from behind me. She snarled again.

"What is it, Babe," I said, looking up.

I turned to see Barbara's face distorted into a mask of atavistic rage. Her lips were drawn back baring all her teeth. Her neck muscles were stretched taut. Her cheeks were swollen. The extreme muscular distortion interfered with her breathing and she could only make guttural growls. She didn't relax that painful distortion. She began drawing her nails across her abdomen, leaving long scratches. I froze, trying to think. She pounded at herself really hard. Then she drew her nails across her arms and legs. She didn't seem to feel pain. I got up. I spread my arms and approached her cautiously. I didn't know what was going to happen. She stopped hitting herself and crouched slightly, alert to my every movement.

"Easy now. Come on, Babe."

I felt like a wild animal trainer as I got nearer.

"There you go, Babe. Easy . . . "

She flew at me and clawed the air inches from my face. I didn't move a muscle. Then she leaped back. She attacked and drew back again and again in the same manner. She never touched me, but she seemed to draw more energy from each feinting attack. When she saw I wasn't approaching her, she stretched erect and shrieked defiantly.

She scratched at herself again, scraping furrows of blood across her breasts. I could stand no more. I rushed her and grabbed her arm, twisting it as before, but this time she felt no pain. She had a strength I didn't believe. I pushed her down on the bed behind us. She pulled against her twisted arm until I thought she would rip the tendons out. She finally felt the pain and quieted down. I let her arm go loose. Her neck muscles and her stretched mouth relaxed slowly back to normal.

"Are you all right, now?" I said.

"I . . . I don't know who I am . . . anymore."

"Take it easy. I'm taking care of it. Just hang in there for another day and everything will be all right."

"Sleep. I want to sleep."

"Can you eat anything?"

"Sleep."

Barbara fell quickly asleep. There was no trace of what I had just seen in her sleeping face. Where had it come from? Where had it gone? Had that rage surfaced from the recent shock of finally having all drugs out of her system? Perhaps the calming effects of the tranquilizers and alcohol had kept this rage down before and now there was nothing to calm it.

Barbara was very quiet the next day. Her mother called and she spoke to her and to her father. She didn't show any signs of last night's explosion. But as the sun went down I began to get apprehensive. This new behavior of Barbara's seemed to always happen at night. Or did it really? Maybe it was just the ancient superstitions of night. Barbara was still quiet. She ate a little of the dinner I made. I hoped that might be a good sign. She went into the bedroom and read the paper while I did the dishes and cleaned up. The phone rang. It was Tina. She hadn't called Barbara or spoken to her since that day in Horace's office.

"Is Barbara all right?" she asked.

"Yeah, sure," I said.

I hesitated. I wasn't sure how to talk about Barbara's latest episodes or if I should.

"I mean, you know, she's still getting over her withdrawal."

"This long?" she said.

"There were some complications we hadn't expected."

"Serious?"

"She seems to be okay now," I said. "I think we've got it under control."

"The reason I called, I had this strange dream last night that something awful happened to Barbara. It was a nightmare. I'm not sure what it was, but I had a strong feeling that she was in trouble. I'm sometimes psychic, you know, especially about Barbara."

"Well, you were right this time. Something did happen last night."

"What?"

"I can't really explain," I said. "I'm not exactly sure."

"Is she all right?"

"She's fine now. She's been quiet all night and all today."

"Is there anything I can do?"

"I'm taking care of it. It'll be all right. Just a few days more."

"Can I speak to her?" she asked.

"Let me see if she's awake. She's not exactly stable at the moment so if she says anything strange, take it with a grain of salt."

I went to the bedroom and opened the door. Barbara was still awake reading the paper. She looked up at me.

"It's Tina. She wants to speak to you. Do you feel up to it?"

"Why shouldn't I?" she said.

Why shouldn't she? Except for her parents, Barbara had rarely spoken to another human being in two months was why.

"I thought you might be nervous after what you've been through," I said.

"What are you talking about?"

"We've almost got it now. Just another day or so and you'll be okay."

I hadn't dared utter the word "hospital" to Barbara again for fear of really setting her off. Particularly in the light of her present violent behavior, that would all have to be taken care of *sub rosa*.

"I still don't understand you," Barbara said.

"We've come this far, I just don't want you to blow it now with Tina, that's all."

Barbara took the phone in the bedroom and they talked for a long time. I stayed in the living room and made up the couch for sleeping. Tina's call did make me nervous. Since the withdrawal, when any of her friends wanted to speak to Barbara, she broke down and cried or refused to talk and handed the phone to me to make excuses. The soft murmur of a normal, quiet phone conversation made me very apprehensive.

When I went into the bathroom, Barbara looked up at me suspiciously and then said a hurried goodbye to Tina. When I came out of the bathroom she had turned out the light and seemed to be silently asleep. I went into the living room and took off my clothes and stretched out on the couch. When I thought Barbara was safely asleep, I turned out the living room light. She had gone through the whole day without incident. I quickly dozed off.

THIRTY SIX

I awoke later that night. The living room was lighted only by the soft glow of the night sky. The street sounds were muted by a steady rain that washed against the big window. I stared at the window, absorbing the gentle sensuality of the city at night and I wondered what had woken me so suddenly. I heard the soft whoosh of a dresser drawer opening and closing. Then I noticed the bright light under the bedroom door. Barbara was awake. I raised my head from the couch to see better. In the bright slit of light her shadow moved purposefully from one side of the bedroom to the other. I watched for a while, but she didn't stop. Her shadow kept moving back and forth. Something was up. Barbara hadn't done much of anything for the last few months. Nothing that required that much activity, that much "busyness." What did she have in store for me now?

I got up slowly. I never slept in pajamas and it was chilly so I put on the gigantic blue terrycloth robe I had practically been living in. I was so tired I decided not to go into the bedroom. I sat in a chair near the door and waited, hoping that whatever it was she was doing would tire her soon and she would go to bed. By this time I was afraid that would be a vain hope. Barbara switched off the bedroom light. The house was silent. I didn't hear a sound for a long time. Had Barbara gone to bed? Or was she standing behind the door listening for me? The bedroom door opened slowly. Barbara's dark silhouette peered into the dimly lit living room. The chair I sat in was out of her line of vision. She didn't move. The steady rain swished against the window. I suppose she saw the rumpled blankets on the couch and thought I was asleep because the door opened further and she stepped out. She was fully dressed in high-heeled shoes, a skirt, and a light sweater. She tiptoed into the living room, her eyes on the couch. Then she looked in my direction. She saw me and froze.

"Where are you going?" I said.

She didn't move. I stood up. She ran for the front door. I was closer. I caught her and held her fast.

"I'm just going out," she said.

She struggled to reach the door but I held onto her.

"What do you mean, 'going out'?" I said.

"Let me go!" she screamed. "Get your hands off me. I want to go out!"

"Fine, fine! I think that's a great idea. I've always thought that's a great idea. For two months I've been trying to get you to leave this house and suddenly you appear in the middle of the night, going out in the pouring rain with nothing but a sweater on? It doesn't make sense."

Then she did a totally unexpected thing. She snatched my glasses from my face, twisted the metal frame into a pretzel and threw them across the room. I was shocked. She bolted for the door and I grabbed her.

"Now just a fucking minute, lady!" I said.

She tried to shove me aside, but I managed to hold onto her. She kicked and struggled. For a moment I thought, the hell with it, let her go! But I couldn't let her wander the streets at night the way she had been acting lately. It was getting harder to hold onto her. She had that mysterious strength again. I grabbed her arm and twisted it and the pain quieted her as it had done before. I forced her back into the bedroom where I had a spare pair of glasses somewhere in a dresser drawer. Then I switched on the desk lamp. In that split second I let up the pressure, she struggled. I applied pressure to her arm again and sat her on the bed. It was obvious I couldn't hold her and look for my glasses at the same time. I took the sash from my robe and tied both her arms together behind her back.

"Take it easy now," I said. "I'll only be a minute."

I pulled out the dresser drawers one by one and groped around them as fast as I could while I spoke, "I'll let you go in a second, Babe. I just want to know what's going on, but I've got to find another pair of glasses."

I found a spare pair and quickly put them on. As I turned, Barbara leaped on me. She had freed her hands. Her face was distorted into that atavistic mask. I was so surprised that I did nothing as she slipped my spare glasses off and tossed them aside as easily as she had the others. I was helpless again, blind and confused and I couldn't understand what she was doing. I had only tied a loose knot to immobilize her for a moment, but after she freed herself she hadn't run for the door, she was attacking me instead. She pounded on my shoulder and back. I lifted my arms to shield myself from her blows, but I couldn't get away from her. She had me cornered against the wall and she shrieked as she hit me. I was scared to death. Time seemed to slow down and each image etched into my consciousness as acutely as a slow-motion shot. My bathrobe felt warm and wet. I reached under my arm and slid my hand over wet skin. I drew my hand back and it was covered with blood. I stared at it for a split second that seemed like forever. I could feel the carpet wet with blood under my feet. I realized that Barbara was stabbing me with something. I could feel it going deep, but with my adrenalin pumping, I felt no pain.

I tried to stop her, but with that unbelievable strength she had she tossed me easily to the floor and jumped on top of me, jabbing at me wherever she could. I tried to roll away, but I was tangled in the wet robe. She shrieked and went for my face. I stiff-armed her hand with both of mine but I was no match for her. She slowly bent both my arms and as her hand came closer, I saw the weapon clearly for the first time. It was a pair of needle-nosed pliers that had been with the tools on my desk. Barbara had opened the blue plastic-covered handle and gripped it like a dagger, its 3-inch spike pointed right at me. I couldn't hold her off anymore. I rolled under, deflecting her arm. She dug the spike into the carpet close to my head. I wriggled out of the robe but she jumped on me again and kept stabbing. The left side of my body was stiffening and going numb. I knew I wouldn't last much longer but Barbara didn't seem to tire. I had to do something. The sash of my robe was within reach. I grabbed it and caught her free left hand. I tied the sash around her left hand while she stabbed me with her right. She seemed oblivious to what I was doing. I threw myself on her. With my weight and the sash pulling her arm, she tumbled. I looped the sash around her right arm and yanked her two hands together behind her back. I tied her wrists as tightly as I could, pried the dagger from her clamped fingers, and tossed it out of her reach.

I stood up and then toppled against the dresser. I couldn't stand. The left side of my body was numb. I still had a little feeling in my left arm but that was going fast. I needed help right away. The sash was thick and strong, but I didn't know how long my knots would hold out. Barbara was still struggling and growling at me. She hadn't given up. I remembered Tina's call. She would be home and her husband Horace could help. Horace answered when I phoned.

"It's Barbara," I said. "I need help. I can't handle her anymore."

"It's late," he said. "What's the matter?"

"She's violent. Please Horace. I don't know how much longer I can last. I'm bleeding like a stuck pig!"

"I'll be right over."

I found my glasses in the corner. They were still intact. I put them on and hauled myself to my feet. I could see clearly for the first time. I was covered with blood and the pile of blue robe was now deep purple. But life is funny, you know? At that moment, all that was going through my head was what a dumb, fucking, cornball cliché I had said to Horace: "I'm bleeding like a stuck pig!" I considered myself something of a writer and I should never have let that pass. I was embarrassed. That's all I could say on the spur of the moment, a dumb, trite cliché? "I'm bleeding like a stuck pig!"? Standing naked in the middle of that carnage, all I could think was that I wanted to call Horace back before he left and rewrite that terrible dialogue.

I cleaned myself up with my one good hand and pulled on a pair of pants and shoes as best I could. Barbara was quiet now, waiting for their arrival, but I didn't dare untie her. My eye kept being drawn to the desk, at the pile of tools from which Barbara had grabbed her weapon. My matte knife with its razor sharp blade was in plain sight. It had been inches from the pliers. What luck she hadn't picked up the knife. The needle-nosed plier's spike had made deep wounds. I had lost a lot of blood, but the wounds were punctures and had mostly closed up by this time. If Barbara had grabbed that matte knife instead, the wounds would have been slashes and wouldn't have closed by themselves. I knew I would never have survived if she had used the matte knife. But was it merely luck? I kept wondering if something had been functioning inside Barbara to select the pliers instead of the knife. In her little girl world of playing tricks and games had she thought the one was harmless? Had she only wanted to scare me away? The answer would be sealed inside Barbara and lost to me forever.

"Thank God you're here," Barbara said when I let Horace and Tina into the bedroom. Tina ran to her and when she saw that Barbara was tied, she instinctively reached to free her.

"Careful," I said. "She's been pretty violent."

Tina hesitated, not knowing what to do.

"Don't listen to him!" Barbara said. "I'm perfectly all right. I won't hurt you, Tina. You're only here because I tricked him into calling you."

Some trick. Tina didn't know who to believe. Horace spoke quietly to her, "I think you'd better hold off for a moment. We must get the tempers cooled down first. Now what about you?" he said to me.

I turned so Horace could see my back. He took one look and hustled me into the bathroom, searched through the medicine cabinet and found a bottle of peroxide. While he cleaned the wounds and bandaged my back, I told him about Barbara's violent behavior of the past nights that culminated in the stabbing.

"You two shouldn't be together," he said.

"You're telling me? I still can't believe the strength she had. I need your help to get her to a hospital."

"Your wounds are deep. You have to get a tetanus shot as quickly as possible."

He finished and we stepped into the bedroom. Barbara started yelling.

"Don't let him near me! He's crazy! He was beating me!"

"Get her some milk, she's hyperventilating," Horace said.

Horace shooed me into the living room so Barbara wouldn't see me. Then he joined Tina in the bedroom. I called one psychiatric hospital after another, but none would take an emergency patient. In desperation, I woke up Nancy to see if she had any suggestions. I told her briefly what had happened to Barbara and of course she wanted to do whatever she could to help. She gave me some hospitals to call and asked me to pick her up when we went out with Barbara.

One of her suggestions for a hospital paid off. They would take an emergency patient, but only if Barbara had been violent. I assured them she had and they said to come right over. I told Horace I found a place and he went back to the bedroom to get Barbara ready. Then he discovered the snag that had frustrated me for so long. With one breath, Barbara wanted help and with another, she refused to leave the house to get it. I stayed out of it in the living room while Horace and Tina convinced her to go with them. Tina came in to me looking somewhat embarrassed. Horace stood in the doorway, glancing anxiously back at Barbara.

"We finally convinced her to go," Tina whispered, "but she won't ride with you. Is that all right?"

"Of course. I understand. That's why I called you. I wouldn't have been able to do this by myself. I'll take our car."

"You don't have to go," Tina said.

"I would hope that the doctor might want to know what happened," I said a little testily. "I'm the only one who was here. I'm the only one who knows. Barbara certainly has no idea."

"Sure, sure," Tina said.

"Let's all keep calm," Horace said. "We've got her to go, and that's all that's important."

I stayed in the living room while they untied Barbara and cleaned her up. She was no longer violent, but she couldn't coordinate her movements with her thoughts. Horace and Tina had to help her dress and put on her tennis shoes. It was still pouring out, so they put a raincoat and scarf on her. I put my raincoat on and followed a short distance behind them to the elevator. When the elevator door opened, the four of us crowded in. Barbara huddled as far away from me as possible. The night elevator man nodded at her.

"Good evening, Ms. Gordon," he said.

"Good evening, Arnold," she replied.

We picked up Nancy. My stiffened side made driving difficult at first, but it was possible to drive Bernie with one leg and one hand. We drove to the hospital in the pouring rain. I caught glimpses of Barbara in Horace's car. She was seated in between Horace and Tina in the front seat, waving her hands around whenever I saw her. When you live as closely as Barbara and I had, especially in the last two months, you get to know what that person will say even before they say it. I knew Barbara was telling her version of what we had been through. I guessed her story was not particularly flattering to me. It didn't matter. It was too bad it had to come this way, but she was finally getting help.

"What is your relationship to the patient?" the admitting nurse asked me. That again. It seemed there was absolutely no way I could get help for Barbara without being married to her. I had explained Barbara's drug withdrawal and the subsequent violence, but Barbara wouldn't sign herself in and since I wasn't a relative, I couldn't either. The nurse referred me to a city hospital as my only hope. We all piled in the cars and went to another hospital. This was the same, only different.

"What is your relationship to the patient?" the admitting nurse asked over a pile of forms.

"No, we aren't married, we live together," I said. "I know the whole routine, but she has no control over herself. I don't dare fall asleep tonight in the same house with this woman and I can't let her wander the streets by herself. What am I supposed to do?"

"I'm sorry. We can only take her in emergency if she is a threat to society. Are you willing to swear that she has committed a violent act toward someone you know of?"

"You want to see my back?" I said. "Sure, I'll swear. She has to get some kind of care as soon as possible."

The nurse pushed a form toward me. It asked for a detailed description of the violent act that led this patient to be committed to the hospital. As I filled it in, I began to think. This was a public record. There could be news stories, TV, and there goes Barbara's career. What I wrote now could affect the rest of her life.

"I don't think I should write this," I said. "I'd rather tell the doctor."

"As the person committing her, you must swear that she attempted to hurt someone. That's the only way we can take her in."

"There's no other way?"

"She can come in voluntarily and commit herself, but she can't do that until tomorrow morning."

Tomorrow morning looked a long way off. I tore up the form and put the pieces in my pocket. Horace was furious with me.

"I won't have that on a public record," I said. "That's a little more than a nervous breakdown, you know. It'll make a great news story."

"Yes, I thought of that, too. But what can we do?"

"We call more hospitals. If she signs herself in, she owns her own records. They're private. Her business. She'll be safe that way."

He threw up his hands in frustration. We were all getting tired.

"At least get yourself a tetanus shot while we're here," he said.

"I can't do that! Don't you see? If I get it here I'll have to say how I got it. Someone can put it together with her. I had shots years ago. A couple of extra hours won't hurt me, will they?"

"I suppose not," he said.

We stayed in the waiting room making calls to every hospital we could find but the answers were all the same. It wasn't worth making any more fruitless trips. Then Horace thought he knew of a place that might take her, but it was far out on Long Island. I didn't care about the trip. We piled into the two cars and drove out to Suffolk County. It was the same old story. They had room and Barbara could sign herself in, but only during business hours. We had driven so far and so much time had passed that it was just before sunrise. If we waited long enough it would be regular business hours. An admitting doctor would arrive at 7:00. We decided to wait until morning.

But when Barbara was told about this, she refused again to sign herself in. We all sat in the drab waiting room filled with folding chairs while Tina and Horace both tried to persuade her to cooperate. Horace pleaded with her. He would have to leave soon. He had appointments early in the morning. And Tina wouldn't be able to take care of her either. She had a life to live, too. Barbara held out until the dawn. It was like the Fantasia cartoon of *A Night on Bald Mountain*. The first light of the sun seemed to quiet her and she agreed to go in. Horace went back to New York. Tina sat with Barbara on folding chairs across the room. Barbara occasionally glowered at me. At 7:00 the doctor appeared. After another flurry of objections from Barbara, Tina shepherded her through the examinations and admission procedures. The admitting doctor interviewed me and I told her the entire story from Barbara's long addiction to Valium and alcohol, her first attempt at withdrawal which was tied to our upcoming marriage, the release of her repressed memories, her reversion to other drugs and alcohol, her second and then her third withdrawal from that mess of Valium, Placidyl, alcohol and who knows what else, which seemed to lead directly to her infantilism and her subsequent violence. The doctor asked a lot of questions and took notes. I let myself completely relax for the first time. Someone else was taking care of Barbara besides me and it felt good.

I drove Tina back to New York. We were both exhausted and we said very little to each other. The rest of the day went by in a blur of fatigue. Tina and I selected clothes and personal things Barbara would need. I went to the Writer's Guild and got all the medical insurance forms, then drove out again to the hospital to drop everything off. It was 3:00 in the afternoon by the time I parked the car in the garage and went home. I stopped at Roosevelt Hospital on the way. My Burberry trenchcoat notwithstanding, with my limp and haggard eyes and no shave, I blended in with the derelicts and the city's poorest.

"I need a tetanus shot," I said to the intern.

He and I were the only white people in the room. He drew a soiled green curtain around us for privacy.

"What happened to you?" he asked.

For an answer I stripped down and presented my backside to him. I could hear him draw in an impressed breath as he stripped off Horace's bandages.

"Wow! What made these wounds?" he asked.

"Oh, I. . . . Does it matter?"

"Well, in cases of violent assault like this, I have to put it in the records."

Those fucking forms. They are inescapable. I have to make an apology here. I have lived in New York City all my life. I was born in midtown Manhattan. I have worked and played 24 hours a day in the toughest parts of this town and in more than forty years I have never been mugged or even robbed in this city that I love. But I knew the best answer to satisfy this out-of-town, middle-class WASP med student and I gave it to him.

"It was late last night," I began, "I was walking on Central Park South when three kids leaped over the wall and mugged me. They were using some kind of pointed thing. I couldn't see clearly in the dark."

"Oh," he said simply.

He considered it an everyday occurrence. He happily filled out his form and gave me the shot. New York, I apologize.

THIRTY SEVEN

It was daylight when I finally woke up. The faint city noises sounded like afternoon. I had no idea how long I had slept. I had to take a piss something fierce, but now that my adrenalin was no longer pumping, I felt the pain of my left side for the first time. I couldn't move, it was so bad. My back ached deep in my bones. My left hand wouldn't function at all, but I had to pee. I inched carefully to the edge of the bed and pulled myself up. I couldn't put any weight on my left leg. I hobbled as best I could to the bathroom, but I was relieved that I hurt so bad. The pain was a good sign after the first paralyzed numbness. At least she hadn't severed a nerve.

For the next few days I did little more than lie in bed waiting for some movement to return to the aching left side of my body. When I wasn't asleep I drank steadily, sipping vodka. As I lay there on my back, half awake in the dim room, low moaning sounds began to issue involuntarily from my throat. The groans built into a loud keening which went on for hours until I shuddered into uncontrolled sobbing. There was a painful emptiness in my arms. My life had been totally focussed on caring for Barbara for nine weeks and she was suddenly gone. I felt like a part of me had died and my body was grieving for the loss. I had no control over it. Even when I could walk around a little, no sooner did I painfully ease myself into bed than a hollow wail would well up from deep inside me. I couldn't move until it had run its course. I had to lie there and howl steadily until I broke into deep sobbing. I always felt I had a controlled consciousness in my relationship with Barbara. I thought of myself as a cool and accomplished lover, but now I cried helplessly. I had never known how deeply I had come to love her.

It was a few days before I could move around well enough to clean up. My robe was still where I had wriggled out of it that night. It was a dark, stiff pile. I picked it up and pried it open. There was no sewing or cleaning that. I tossed it into the incinerator. There was nothing I could do about the stain on the carpet, either. The pair of pliers was nearby. It was covered with the brown rust of dried blood. My back ached as I picked it up and turned it over in my good hand. It scared me to look at it. I washed it off in the bathroom sink. As I opened and closed the blue plastic handles to clean it, it gradually changed from a weapon back into a pair of needle-nosed pliers. I dried it off and tossed it in with the other tools. The matte knife caught my eye again. I still wondered about that.

I found the first pair of glasses Barbara had snatched from my face and I tried to straighten the twisted metal frame. It was impossible to fix, but the lenses were okay. Since they're so thick, I always had to have unbreakable plastic ones. On my first trip outside I got a new frame for them.

I called the hospital often, but they told me Barbara didn't want to speak to me. I tried to find out who her doctor was, but since I wasn't a member of her family, they wouldn't tell me. I was sure that Barbara had little knowledge of what had happened. Her doctor would have to speak to me sometime soon. I wondered why he hadn't called yet. Then I realized that no one had called. The phone hadn't rung in more than a week. Even during the most insular times of Barbara's withdrawal some friend or relative always called. By now everyone must have known that Barbara was in the hospital, but no one called for news of her. I didn't understand.

I realized it was my birthday and that reminded me of those two tickets I had for *The Threepenny Opera*. Barbara was in the hospital and still not speaking to me, so I looked around for someone to go with. I thought one of our friends would want to cheer me up. I called everyone we knew. If they weren't in I left messages, but they never called back. When I reached someone they would say curtly that they didn't think we had anything to say to each other and they'd wait in silence until I stammered out a goodbye. I wasn't prepared for this cold reception. I called Nancy last of all. She wouldn't talk to me either. That hurt more than all the rest. I began to realize that Barbara must have told them how I appeared to her during her infantile and subsequently violent episodes. I had only a faint idea what she might have said, but no one would speak to me long enough for me to find out.

The wounds were healing. I could walk more easily. I could almost make a fist with my left hand. I relaxed under a pulsating shower feeling no pain for the first time in a week. The soap flipped out of my hands and I bent down to pick it up. ZINGGG!! My back locked in excruciating spasm. I froze, bent over double, not daring to move as the shower poured on my head. My back muscles had been weakened by the stabbing. With slow, careful movements I painfully shut off the shower and stepped out of the tub. I made my way back to bed and, even though it hurt to do it, I laughed out loud at this final irony. Barbara's back pain had haunted us for so long: it was only fitting that it get me in the end.

I stayed in bed with these various ills and I could only hobble around for short periods, so for ten days after Barbara went into the hospital I was physically unable to resume my life. I was sure I needed rest, but it was getting very lonely. Ten days and still no word from Barbara, or her doctors, or any of our friends. It was an eerie feeling. I had no idea what was going on. I didn't know what Barbara's condition was, whether she'd be in the hospital for another day, or a week, or a year, or what. The hospital would not give me information when I called because Barbara and I weren't married. It wasn't coincidental. Barbara had to be orchestrating this. But why? Sometimes silence is as loud as thunder if you listen to it. Of course you have to want to listen to it.

Memorial Day was at the end of that week, and rental agents had been calling about the beach house. Since I had no idea what Barbara's status was, I didn't know whether she would want to rent it or if she would want it for a haven if she might be getting out of the hospital soon. This was all dependent on information which Barbara had classified Top Secret, at least from me. With our shared love object as an excuse, I called Barbara. I had to say it was an emergency before she would come to the phone.

"Yes," she said.

"Hi, how are you?"

She didn't answer.

"Do you need anything?"

"No."

"How's the hospital working out?"

There was a long pause while I searched for more to say.

"Are you able to play tennis?"

"I don't have time for that."

"Well, your back is still going to be with you after this is all over, you know. While you have the time I think you ought to—"

"Everything is taken care of. Why did you call?"

"I've called a lot and you never speak to me."

"I'm too nervous."

"You're not too nervous to speak to everyone we know and now no one will talk to me. Why is that? What have you been saying to them?"

"Is this the emergency?"

I gave up.

"No," I said, "I called about the beach house."

"What's happened to it?" There was a note of panic.

"Nothing. I haven't been able to finish the ceiling yet and agents have been calling. I wanted to know what you planned to do this summer."

"I don't have time to think of that now. You take care of it. Is that all?"

"I don't know what's going on, Babe, but whatever it is, I want you to know that I love you."

There was a long silence and then she hung up without a word. She hadn't made even a polite reference to affection or love. Nothing. I was stunned. Our relationship seemed to have disappeared overnight without a trace.

I was totally isolated and I was getting desperate for some human contact. I still had those two expensive tickets to *The Threepenny Opera* and no one to go with. It had earlier popped into my head to call a girl I had run into at CBS while cutting Barbara's last film. She was a production assistant I had hired many times in the past. Her name was Judy. There was no romance between us, but we did have that familiar closeness of movie gypsy life. I liked her work and had recommended her for jobs, some of which she knew about and some of which she didn't. Even though we only met after stretches of months, sometimes years, between work and rarely socialized, Judy, with that funny gypsy intimacy, knew all about my life with Barbara and that we were going to be married. I had felt a little guilty thinking of her at the same time I was grieving for Barbara, so at first I decided against calling her. But by the time it was four o'clock in the afternoon of the performance, I said the hell with it and called. I reached her at CBS.

To my complete amazement, she accepted my invitation without a question and met me later at the theater.

Judy was somewhere in her mid-twenties. She was a sassy gamine with a short crop of wild dark hair, sort of like a boy's. She had olive skin and huge green eyes. She had always been attractive to me, but tonight she looked sensational. She was wearing a dark green pants suit with those elephant legs that short women wear, where the bell bottoms go all the way to the ground and cover their high platform shoes. And it wasn't just my sore eyes that she was a sight for. She knew what I liked about her and she had managed to run home and put herself together with care for me. I wondered why all through the play.

We went to a restaurant afterwards and the first thing she wanted to know was why I hadn't taken Barbara. I told her the story of the withdrawal, from start to finish, leaving nothing out. It took me nearly an hour. We sipped our espresso in silence for a long moment after I finished.

"I never knew a man could love a woman so much," she said softly.

She said it without thinking, but I bathed in her words for a long time before I replied. Those were the first kind words anyone had said to me in a month. For the last weeks of the withdrawal, all that came my way was Barbara's coldness, and her hateful looks, and then her ferocity, and now I had only the curt replies of all our friends when I tried to speak to them.

"Thank you," I said.

"What for?"

"You couldn't have said anything better to me right now. But there's something I want to know about you that I've been curious about ever since I called you to ask you out tonight. I never expected you to say yes and certainly not so quickly. How come?"

"I'm going into the hospital tomorrow," she said. "I'm having an operation. There's a chance it might be serious. I didn't tell anyone. Today was my last day on that film and I was getting real depressed. I had no one to talk to and then you called out of the blue. I didn't think. I needed to be with someone."

A roar of feelings welled up inside me. That enormous void I had felt when cut off from Barbara began to hurt again. I wanted to fill it by holding and comforting Judy. My response was completely instinctive and it was so strong that I had to hold my arms down with all my strength to keep from reaching out to Judy and enfolding her.

By the time I had taken her back to her apartment door, I couldn't control myself anymore. I held her and leaned to kiss her but she gently pushed me away.

"No," she said. "Nothing wrong. I'm not angry. But I don't want to sleep with you and I know if I kiss you . . . "

"I always knew you were smart. You take care now. Get a lot of sleep."

She stood in her doorway and we watched each other for a long moment while I waited for the elevator.

"It's all right," I said. "You can close the door. I won't take it as a rejection."

"Thanks," she said softly. "Goodnight. And thanks for calling me tonight. I needed it."

She waved a little wave and closed her door.

I woke the next day with a job to do. I found out the name of Judy's hospital and the approximate time she'd be out of the operating room. I went to her room while she was still hazy from the anesthetic. They had strapped her into the bed so she wouldn't move until the deep incisions healed. Plastic tubes ran in and out of her to full and empty bottles. I went over to her side. She looked so helpless and so hurt. I felt like my insides were falling out. She recognized me.

"Wha . . . wha' you doin' here?" she murmured.

"I thought I'd come by and see you. How are you feeling?"

"I ache like hell."

I reached down with my good right hand and started to gently massage her shoulders.

"How's that feel?" I said.

"Ohhh, be my guest."

I opened the hospital gown and touched her firm olive skin. I slowly worked out the tension in the muscles of her shoulders, her arms and her legs. She dozed off again. I couldn't stop massaging her. The caring that had been cut off so abruptly from Barbara now poured out of me to this young woman. Her skin felt good under my fingers. All those powerful feelings about Barbara that had surfaced in my grief now passed through my fingers to Judy's supple young body.

THIRTY EIGHT

I brought Judy flowers and books and I sat quietly with her for days massaging her sore muscles. I couldn't help responding to her body, but I wasn't thinking of romance or anything like that. This need to care was totally instinctive and I was quite conscious of the fact that it was for Barbara that I really wanted to be doing it. Except for that one cold phone call, I had no further contact with or information about Barbara. I let my frustrated caring instincts have free rein with Judy because it was plain to me now that my isolation from Barbara was not just an accident of neglect. I still didn't know why, but I was beginning to understand that Barbara must have put the word out to all and sundry that I was to have no contact with her whatsoever. It had been too easy for me to find and take care of Judy, but then she didn't mind being found. Barbara had had to erect a wall around herself so high that I could not surmount it no matter how hard I tried.

Judy healed rapidly and she was soon ready to leave the hospital. I was going to drive her home. She was still stitched up so she needed a lot of holding and carrying and supporting. On the day she was to leave, her mother showed up. She was obviously surprised at this strange new man holding and touching her daughter with complete familiarity. She had a hasty whispered conference about me with Judy which was answered by a loud, "Oh, mother, will you *fuck off*!!" which echoed through the hospital corridors. Judy had style. We drove to Judy's apartment and got her safely in bed. Then her mother and I went shopping for food. Now that we were alone, she gently grilled me. She wasn't your average middle-class mother. She was a movie gypsy, too, having kicked around the world as an international script girl. But mothers will be mothers. She wanted to know all about me and my movie life. I told her, leaving out Ms. Gordon, of course. We hit it off right away.

I drove Judy's mother home and then hurried downtown for another appointment. Al and Lilly had come up from Fort Lauderdale to visit Barbara in the hospital and they wanted to have lunch with me before they went back. They were still in shock, but they were very pleasant to me. They still assumed, as I did, that Barbara and I were going to be married. They kept shaking their heads, totally mystified about the whole thing. I tried to explain as much as I knew. When I mentioned her psychiatrists they were shocked, as I knew they would be. Barbara had always kept that a secret from them. I told them about Barbara's anxiety attacks and how terrified she had been to leave the apartment. I told them how bad it had been in the last year, how much Valium and booze Barbara used to take to get out the door, and how at the end it was so bad that she couldn't function enough to make her movies without Nancy and me to do a lot of the work for her. They didn't hear me. It was as though I was talking about another person, not their daughter. It was too much data all at once. They didn't understand. When I finished, Al kept repeating the same thing over and over.

"What I don't understand, An'n, is why you didn't take her to a hospital when she wanted to go? I just don't understand why you wouldn't do that for her."

"I did, Al. That's how she got to the hospital she's in now. I brought her there."

"She says you wouldn't take her to a hospital. I don't understand."

"It's not like she says, Al. She wasn't herself then. She doesn't remember."

"I understand that, but why didn't you take her to a hospital?"

I couldn't bring myself to tell him about Barbara's behavior during the last days. I didn't know what else to say to them except that I loved Barbara and that nothing had changed about our marriage as far as I was concerned. I was sure that everything would be back to normal soon. Lilly sat and stared straight ahead as I spoke, as though she might have received a hint on the women's wireless that told her something Al and I didn't know yet. When I said goodbye, they shook their heads again in stunned silence and wished me well. So I had heard one of Barbara's stories at last. And this was a story that was sure to arouse a sympathetic shudder from all her analys and friends.

I got a call from the hospital that Barbara's doctor wanted to see me. At last. I knew they would have to talk to me eventually. It was three weeks to the day that Barbara had been in and it was the first time I'd heard from anyone there. I drove out to the hospital and found the dormitory they called a "cottage." I looked through the front door into a sort of dayroom. There were no lights on. The room was darkly shadowed from the trees outside the windows. The walls were smudgy and the room was unkempt. Magazines were scattered on the chairs and tables. Board games in progress were set up, but no one was playing them. It looked like the bedroom of a sloppy teenager. I went in. I saw Barbara sitting on a couch reading a magazine. She was wearing an old pair of jeans, a top, and a scarf. She didn't look up until I had walked across the room and stood in front of her.

"Hi, Babe," I said. "How are you?"

She looked up at me but didn't answer. She wasn't happy or unhappy. There was absolutely no emotion in her eyes. It saddened me to see Barbara so lifeless. But I was here to help her in whatever way I could.

"Do you know where I'm supposed to go and see this Doctor Hoffmeyer?" I said.

She put down her magazine and got up without a word to me. She led me to an office. A man behind the desk looked up as she stood in the doorway. I assumed he was the doctor. He dressed conservatively in a dark suit with a vest. He was bald and wore glasses. He looked around Barbara and spoke to me with an accent I couldn't identify.

"Would you leave us alone for a moment, please?" he said.

I nodded and Barbara closed the door. I stood outside the door a long time while a heated conference went on inside. The best I could make out was that the doctor wanted Barbara to do something that she didn't want to do. I noticed for the first time that curious master-slave relationship between psychiatrists and patients. Barbara addressed him with his title and last name while he used her first name as though he were talking to a child or a maid. Finally there was silence and the doctor opened the door. We introduced ourselves.

The office was tiny and sparsely furnished. I noticed there was no squooshy leather chair here. I sat down and the doctor circled around his desk and sat opposite me. Barbara had retreated behind the doctor's chair and she gripped the back of it almost as though she were using it for a shield. I had waited for this moment for a long time. I was relieved to see the end of Barbara's isolation. This meeting was the beginning of healing. I didn't expect it to be easy, but we were at last coming together again. The doctor looked like an intelligent man. I waited for him to speak.

"*How dare you??*" he suddenly roared.

The tiny room shook with the sound of his voice and so did I. Of all the things I had imagined he would say, that definitely was not one of them. And I certainly hadn't pictured her doctor shouting at me. I thought he was going to be the essence of mature understanding. But here I was in front of Barbara's doctor at last. At such a time, in front of such a person, it behooved me to be cool.

"I beg your pardon," I said coolly.

"How dare you?" he repeated, a little lower this time.

"How dare I what?"

"How dare you do this to a person! Embark on such a reckless disregard for another person's life?"

"I don't understand you."

"A rank amateur attempting to engage in deep analysis!"

I looked up at Barbara but she betrayed no emotion. So that was another story I knew about. I didn't doubt for a moment that Barbara believed every word of it, but having been the other person on the scene, I knew there was a rather different interpretation of the two stories I had heard so far. I wondered how many other stories she had told and how bad she had painted me and, like a schmuck, I still wondered why. I formed my answer to the doctor as carefully as I could.

"I'm sorry. I really don't understand you. Barbara was taking large amounts of Valium and alcohol and she wanted to stop. She did stop. After a week of physical withdrawal symptoms everything was fine until two or three nights just before she came here. That's why I brought her here."

"That's still no reason to attempt deep analysis."

"What analysis?" I said. "I never set out to attempt anything. Barbara asked me questions and I gave her answers. I've done that all my life. Most people don't have a breakdown when you give them answers."

Barbara shifted her weight nervously. There was another chair near me, but she wouldn't leave the shelter of the doctor's chair.

"She wouldn't go to a doctor," I continued, "she wouldn't go to a hospital, she wouldn't even leave the house. I couldn't put her in a hospital against her will because we're not married. You should know all this better than I do."

"You're dealing in the mind here. You should have known better than to let it go so far."

"You just told me I'm a rank amateur. If Barbara's psychiatrist of five years didn't see this breakdown coming, how on earth could I?"

"I'm not a Freudian. I'm not interested in any of that. I'm a neuropsychopharmacologist."

His sesquipedalian rubric fairly danced on the tip of his tongue. I wondered how long it had taken him to memorize it, considering the way he rattled it off so fast and so surely without ever losing his way in its syllabic labyrinth. His tongue-twisting performance broke my train of thought completely. I had to think for a moment.

"Where was I?" I said. "Oh yes. . . . I think that what Barbara saw as 'deep analysis' started when we were in Europe. Her anxiety was worse than it ever had been. We were driving to Venice—"

"Do you know the meaning of the word, 'prolix'?" he interrupted.

My mind searched a mile a minute. Prolix, prolix . . . It was familiar, but I didn't know what it meant. I knew a little Latin, but "prolix"? What did the word "prolix" have to do with Barbara's condition?

"As a matter of fact, I don't know what it means," I said, "but doesn't it have something to do with—"

"'Prolix' means you talk too much," he said. "Get to the point. I'm a busy man. I only have ten minutes left. None of this interests me."

What was happening? I hadn't said anything yet. I had expected a mature, intelligent discussion. How could he treat Barbara without knowing what had happened to her? I was confused and not a little hurt.

"It will take me much more than ten minutes to tell you what happened," I said. "I came here because you called me. If nothing that I have to say interests you, why did you ask me here?"

"I only agreed to this meeting because Barbara found it impossible to speak to you. I think she is in stable enough condition to go home, but I will not let her leave as long as you are in the apartment. I want you to move out. It will only be temporary. I think that you and Barbara will be able to resume a normal life in a month or so."

So that was it. Barbara avoided my eyes and stared out the window.

"I'll do anything that will help," I said. "I only want Barbara to get well as soon as possible."

"Good," he said. "That's settled, then."

"Uhh . . . would I be able to see Barbara, just to visit her while we live apart? I mean to take a walk, have dinner, or something?"

"I think that's an excellent idea," he said. "And I'm sure this will only be for a month or two. Until her recovery is complete."

"I'll do it right away. I can get a small sublet for the summer easily. It's the end of the school semester and kids go back home."

"But . . . " Barbara spoke for the first time, "but I thought you'd be going out to the beach house. I thought you would go there and you . . . you would be writing while I'm . . . "

Her words trailed off.

"Babe," I said softly, "it's too far from the city. How will I work?"

"You don't have to work! You can write at the beach house just like you always wanted. You don't have to worry about money. I'll take care of you. I'll . . . "

She was near tears. It broke my heart to hear Barbara voice that old illusion that had bound both our insecurities for so long. Face to face with the reality of our separation, it had escaped from her battered memory and she grasped for it without thinking. But our threadbare fantasy was unraveling its last.

THIRTY NINE

I got an apartment the very next day. Two Julliard students were going home for the summer and they had a place to sublet that was just across from Lincoln Center. It had one bedroom, was furnished in clean Sally Army, and it was on the nineteenth floor. It had an unbroken view of the city looking down Broadway. My kind of place. Subletting was a little more expensive than the tenement I had visualized, but I needed to move fast. I paid them in advance for the three months and I moved right in.

I brought over my typewriter, the Nikon, the Braun coffee grinder, and all the plants. I was surprised at how many plants I had accumulated. The apartment looked a little bare without them, but I had no idea when Barbara would be getting out and besides, I didn't want to trust them to her "black thumb." I brought over the few clothes I would need for the summer and left everything else.

I bought a flush door at a lumber yard and made a couple of sawhorses. With the door on top of the sawhorses, I had an instant six-foot-eight desk in my new sublet. I bought a fresh ream of paper, set up my typewriter, and plugged it in. It was just like the writer's rat nest I had dreamed of before all this happened. I called Barbara to tell her I had moved out of the apartment.

"Thank God!" she said. "I can't wait to get out of here. I'm going stir crazy. Could you please come out and visit with me? I need to see a normal human being again."

I couldn't believe what I was hearing. She sounded like my Barbara again and she wanted to see me.

"Sure," I said. "I'd love to. When?"

"Tomorrow. As soon as you can. I've got to get out of this nut house. If you come and visit they'll let me go outside with you. I've got to get out of here."

When I met Barbara at the hospital, she seemed to have changed physically, too. She looked more alive than I had seen her since before the withdrawal. She wore clean slacks and a sweater and she had covered her hair with the familiar yellow-orange babushka.

"C'mon!" she said. "We don't have that much time. I want to eat outside. Feed me, please. Anything! You wouldn't believe the food they serve in here."

There seemed to be no reason for this sudden reversal in Barbara's attitude toward me, but I didn't want to look too closely. Her appearance fit right into my lingering dreams of our relationship and I went right along with her. She seemed to be completely relaxed as we walked through the grounds. Barbara whispered to me as we approached a group of women talking together.

"They're other patients here," she said. "If they look at you strangely, don't worry. I told them some pretty wild stories about you."

"Like what?"

"Oh, I'll tell you sometime," she whispered.

The women's conversation stopped and they stared wide-eyed at us as we passed. I signed Barbara out and we walked through the gate together. She stretched and ran and breathed the outside air deeply even though it was the same air that was on the other side of the chain link fence. She was happy to see Bernie again. She touched the dash and felt the seat around her as though she was rediscovering an old friend.

We drove into town and stopped at the first food place we saw. It was a pizzeria. We ordered a mushroom and sausage pizza. I was going to have a beer and Barbara asked me to order one for her, too.

"Is it all right for you to have beer?" I asked.

"Oh sure. I can do anything I want now."

I was apprehensive, but no one had told me anything to the contrary. I still knew nothing at all about her treatment so I took her word. She was going to leave the hospital soon. She would be on her own to do anything she wanted. I ordered beers for us both. We clinked frosty glasses in a toast and Barbara savored her first sip. The beer seemed to really open her up. She chatted and laughed as she hungrily devoured her pizza. Her behavior had changed so radically from the last time I had seen her that it was difficult to believe what was happening. But I soon understood why.

"Now that the thrill is gone," Barbara said, "nobody comes out to see me any more. I'm well enough to leave the grounds, but I haven't had a visitor in weeks."

"Not Nancy or Tina?"

"Nobody! I know Nancy doesn't have a car, but Tina . . . "

Barbara was so desperately lonely, she would even see me. She was being her old self again so I'd be sure to stay with her all day. She talked about things she knew would interest me.

"Doctor Hoffmeyer likes you," she said.

"Oh really?"

"He thinks you and I might have a good chance again if you go to see a psychiatrist."

"That's okay with me," I said. "I have no problem with that. I'll do anything to help."

"He said you were argumentative, but probably all right. He thinks I should marry you."

"What do you think?"

She shook her head.

"It's too early. I have to finish this therapy first."

"I understand. Will you be an outpatient here?"

"No. I'll have to find a doctor in New York, but it won't be that douchebag Alexander!"

"Do you know when you're getting out?" I asked.

"Monday."

"So soon? I didn't realize. What time should I pick you up?"

"I've already made plans. Tina's taking me home."

"Why don't I take you back? It's no problem."

"No. You don't have to," she said.

"But I want to. I want to do whatever I can to help you get better. I won't bother you, if that's what worries you. I'll take you home, help you unpack and leave."

"I . . . I can't."

"What do you mean? Of course you can."

"Tina wouldn't understand," she said.

"What's to understand? Just tell her you decided to have me do it."

"I can't do that. No. I can't do that."

The thought finally leaked into my slow brain.

"More wild stories?"

"Let's take a drive in Bernie," she said.

We drove around aimlessly for a while. There was nowhere else to go, and I soon parked outside the hospital fence. Barbara didn't want to go in until the last minute. We had nothing more to say to each other and our conversation petered out. I had my arm casually around Barbara and in this silent hiatus, I felt an odd sort of guilt, knowing that Judy had sat next to me in the car where Barbara was sitting now. I suddenly had an urge to kiss Barbara. She wasn't asking for it, but that thought of Judy sitting there made me want to prove something to myself about my feelings. And Barbara's surprisingly familiar, almost affectionate reception gave me the courage to overcome her lack of asking for that kiss. She knew me well enough to know what I was about to do. She didn't move as I leaned to kiss her. When my lips touched hers, I felt the soft skin of her mouth go dead. Her body was suddenly lifeless in my arms. I pulled slowly back from the kiss. Barbara stared at me with empty eyes. The happy mood of her trip outside had been put away somewhere. She quickly got out of the car and I followed her to the gate. I signed her in and we walked slowly back. Barbara stopped at the entrance to the "cottage" and as she was about to leave, I tried to kiss her goodbye on the cheek. She avoided me and nodded to that same group of women patients.

"I can't," she said. "They'd never understand."

"So, what do you care? You're going to leave on Monday. You'll never see these people again."

"I can't. I've got to go now. Thanks for coming. Goodbye."

Barbara turned and hurried down the hall, almost running from me. So she hadn't changed as much as I'd thought. Well, she'd been through a lot. Nothing was going to happen overnight. I had to walk past that group of women patients to get out of the place. As I approached, they drew back and stepped off the path, giving me a wide berth. They whispered to each other behind cupped hands as I passed. Their reaction was so exaggerated they were almost funny, but I wasn't laughing. I had the feeling Barbara's tales were going to follow me around for a long time.

I was sincere about doing anything I could to help Barbara. Seeing a psychiatrist seemed to have been put forth as a condition for us to get together again, and I also had great unresolved feelings of guilt about Barbara's breakdown. There was a real possibility that I might be hiding something from myself. I contacted one of the more intelligent doctors I had spoken to about Barbara. He had an available hour and I began talking twice a week. He was younger than me but he had the necessary complement of equipment: a full Freudian beard, a darkened room, and a leather couch. But while I was entertaining him and boring me with the story of my life, my present was getting confused faster than I could talk about my past.

Judy's apartment was only a few blocks away from my sublet. Odd coincidence, that. I went to see her every chance I could. She smoked some grass and offered it to me. I took a drag, mostly to be sociable. She held my arm as I led her outside for her first walk since the operation. It was a bright, sunny day. We walked along Broadway past Lincoln Center on the way to my new apartment. I liked that little place and I wanted to show it to her. I had my arm carefully circled around her waist. I couldn't touch her because she still had her stitches in her back. They were ready to come out and they bothered her a lot. I felt so grateful to this girl, this young woman. I had to tell her somehow.

"I'm not sure you know what you did for me," I said. "I mean, letting me take care of you. You saved my life. I don't think you know that."

"I know what I did," she said.

"No, I don't think you realize how much—"

"I know," she whispered softly.

When a woman says "I know" in a certain way, she knows. I understood for the first time that it had not been an accident. Maybe Judy had had a tough time breaking with a man once, or maybe she was even going through that now. I had been so wrapped up in myself I never thought to ask her and she never volunteered it.

"I don't know what will happen to us," I said, "but I want to tell you now, I owe you a big one. You have a due bill. I want you to know if you ever need help, if there's anything I can ever do for you, you can come to me any time and collect."

"Oh, don't be so melodramatic," she said.

"I mean it."

"I don't need anyone's help to live," she said. "I depend on myself."

"Admirable. I love it. Nurture it. But I'm older than you are and life is long. I want you to hear this and know it. A time may come when you need something. And if I can give it to you, I don't care if I haven't seen you in twenty years, just ask me. I owe you my fucking life, Judy."

Carefully holding her bandaged back so as not to touch her stitches, I kissed her on the mouth for the first time. She kissed back. I know a little about women, and at that moment I knew that if the inside of her mouth tasted as sweet as it did, the rest of her would taste like honey. My head spun and it wasn't from her dope.

FORTY

The day that Barbara was released from the hospital was the same day Judy was to have her stitches out. Any hurt or anger that I might have had at Barbara's rejection was eased by the pleasure of taking care of Judy, who happily accepted my help. Life seemed to be falling into a pattern. I spent the whole day with Judy. I drove her to her doctor's, stayed with her while her stitches were removed, and then drove her back home again. When I finally got back to my apartment, the phone was ringing. It was Barbara. She missed the plants and wanted them back.

"Okay," I said. "I'll do it right now, if you want."

"No! Not when I'm here."

"When would be a good time?"

"I'll be out tomorrow from one to three," she said. "I have to find a new doctor."

I took note that she didn't seem to have any trouble leaving the house now that I wasn't there.

"Would it be possible for us to get together sometime soon?" I said.

"I'm far from well."

"I thought your doctor seemed optimistic."

"He was a cretin. That's why I'm looking for another one."

"What are you planning to do about the beach house? I should have the ceiling finished soon."

"I can't think of unimportant things. Please don't pressure me. I've only been out of the hospital a few hours."

"Sure, Babe. I understand."

I took all the plants back the next day. I kept two of my favorites. One of them was a little grapefruit tree I had grown from a pit and the other was a miniature aralia with exquisite fan-shaped leaves the size of a fingernail. I didn't want to take a chance on Barbara's new horticultural interest fading before I moved back.

* * *

By a strange coincidence, Judy had rented a share in a summer group house right near Quogue and one week of her share was right after her stitches were out. By another strange coincidence, I was planning to drive out to Quogue to finish the beach house ceiling. By yet another strange coincidence, it happened to be the same week. I offered to drive Judy out and she took me up on it.

I stayed the first night at her place. We spent the night talking. We kissed and held each other, but she was skittish about making love. We were both coming from some hurt place. It wouldn't do to rush. She lay down in bed and I massaged her and stroked her as I had done for the past weeks. She soon dozed off and we slept innocently in bed together with bodies and hands touching.

Next morning I drove Judy to show her the beach house I had designed for Barbara. After spending the night together she was very relaxed with me. We kissed and touched easily and we very quickly found ourselves in bed. Barbara's bed. Judy knew it and I knew it and something about it being Barbara's bed was turning both of us on. Judy had had opportunities in other places, but something about this situation moved her to open up to me for the first time. I would have made love to Judy anywhere, but the memories of Barbara in that bed were very much alive and that made seeing Judy in her place even more exciting.

I couldn't wait to get to her. My heart was pounding as I took off her clothes. It felt good to have a woman in my hands to make love to again after so long. Judy had a tight little body that looked immature in a way, as though she had put off becoming a woman for many years. But a woman's smell rose from her. Her olive skin seemed to shine with health. I kissed her all over and touched every part of her. Judy was kind of removed, as though she was another person, observing herself. I had the distinct feeling that she thought she was doing it as a favor to me, a "mercy fuck" some women call it. I accepted her generous gift.

I went down on her. I had dreamed of this moment since the first time we kissed. Her lips were firm and full. I don't know where the ancestor came from who gave her that olive skin, but she tasted different from any woman I ever knew. Pungent, exotic, somehow. I couldn't get enough of her. She looked down dreamily at me.

"You really like women," she said with a note of genuine surprise. I looked up over the gentle rise of her belly.

310

"What a strange thing to say," I said. "What's not to like?"

"You don't understand. Men don't like women."

"Oh, Judy, no, no. Not all men."

"You don't know," she said.

I knew Judy had been apprehensive but I never guessed her past experience had been that bad. I gave her every pleasure I knew how to give. I had a mission, if only to show her that there was another kind of man. It was hard for her to respond. I could tell she hadn't had an orgasm in a long time; possibly she hadn't ever had one. When she finally let go she jerked and shuddered and cried out almost as though she were in pain. She didn't want me to go inside her, because of the recent operation, but she guided my cock between her legs from behind and squeezed it against her swollen wet lips. She did something with her hand that felt wonderful. Or maybe it felt so good because it was so long since I'd been in bed with a loving woman. I had masturbated a lot, but there had been no woman since the last time with Barbara, however long ago that was. I came, and months of anxiety went with it. We were both exhausted. I patted her shoulder softly.

"Sleep now," I said. "You need rest. We both do, I think."

"Okay, but I want you to tell me one thing."

She held out her closed hand to me, as though offering a gift. She opened her fingers to reveal a palmful of semen.

"What do I do with this?" she said.

We laughed until we both gasped for breath.

Judy went back to New York and I stayed at the beach house to finish the ceiling. It was approaching completion. One or two more days would do it. The phone rang. It was Barbara.

"What are you doing in my house?" she asked sharply.

I had instant guilt about Judy, but Barbara couldn't possibly know about that.

"I'm finishing the ceiling, as I said."

"I want you out of there!" she said.

"What? What's going on?"

"I want you out of my house!"

"Now wait a minute, Babe. Be practical. You'll never rent it without a ceiling."

"I just spoke to Herman. He's going to do the work. You don't have to."

"Well, I'm here now and there's not much more to—"

"*Get out of my house!!*" she yelled.

At that moment Herman came in the door. He nodded with a sad look that meant he knew he was coming in the middle of a family battle.

"Look, Babe . . . " I said.

She hung up. I stood there like a dummy for a moment and then hung up my phone.

"Oh, Barbara called me, uh, just now," Herman said.

"I know. I spoke to her."

"It wasn't my idea."

"I know, Herman."

I showed Herman what there was to do and he quickly ducked out, leaving me alone in the empty house. The ocean thundered just outside the windows. Barbara's call was a surprise to me. I thought the beach house was special. I didn't like the feelings I was getting, but then I had violated it's specialness too, and on the very same day. I opened the glass door and went out to the end of the deck. I jumped down to the dune and walked the perimeter of the snow fencing, checking the new sand that had collected over last winter. The dune was rebuilding fine. Another few years and it would be able to withstand anything the ocean could throw at it. I watered the dune grass Barbara had planted on her last visit. It looked healthy but it could always use water. I closed all the shutters on the ocean side, picked up my tools and walked down the long path to the car. I was very depressed as I drove back to New York.

I sat quietly for hours in my apartment, looking out the window down Broadway, absorbing the city with all my senses. The center of a city is the most soothing place I know, with its noises, its crowds of people, the constant movement and the occasional excited wail of a siren. It's stimulating too, like a mother's skin is both soothing and stimulating to a baby. I was born down there in a fifth-floor tenement without the insulation of a hospital's thick walls. The first noises I knew were garbage trucks, the call of street vendors, and the rumble of the Lexington Avenue subway that gently rocked our fifth floor as it went by underground. I belonged to this city and the city belonged to me, like a mother.

The sublet had no emotional association with any other person I knew. It was very private. I had nothing to do but think and this was an ideal place to do it. Barbara was out of the hospital now. She didn't want my help and there was nothing more I could do for her. That interlude was over—for me anyway. I was suspended in an island of time. My usual chain of freelance work had been broken and hadn't started up again yet. I had no job to go to, no other person to worry about, and enough money saved to keep me going so that I didn't have to worry about rushing out and getting a job. Open time like this was a rare luxury, and I let myself go with it. I immediately began to write as though it were the most natural occupation in the world for me.

I worked on that screenplay outline I had written about the withdrawal experience and added the later installments while they were fresh in my mind. It still looked like an extraordinary story, but it was somehow difficult to accept without knowing more about the unique personalities of Barbara and me. I wrote some exposition, but there was so much to tell that it got longer and longer and soon I knew it would never fit into the dramatic structure I had envisioned. I would have to allow it to develop and take me wherever it wanted to go. I had wanted to work this way all my life. It was the basis of my conscious fantasies about marriage to Barbara and I knew that no matter what happened with her, this was the way I was going to live and work from now on.

Barbara called.

"How are you feeling?" I said.

"Better. I have a doctor now. I'm starting a new therapy."

"Good, good. How is it?"

"I'm doing it. We'll see."

"Feeling well enough to meet for a lunch or a walk yet?"

"I packed all your things in boxes," she said. "They're down in the basement now."

"Could you say that again? I'm not sure I heard what you said."

"I said I have packed everything that you left behind here. It wasn't easy for me."

"But why? What happened to the temporary move and all that? I thought . . ."

"I can't stand to have your things around the house. It makes me too nervous."

"Well, when do you think that you might be well enough to have

313

me come back? Your doctor thought it would be a month or two. That's why I only got a sublet."

"It . . . it may take a little longer than I thought," she said.

"If it's going to take much longer, I'll have to start making plans. It's not that easy to get an apartment on a moment's notice. Can't you give me a guess?"

"I don't want to talk about it. Your things are all in the basement. That's all I can do. Goodbye."

They didn't lock the basement in that building. Any delivery boy was liable to go through there and steal something. I immediately got the car out of the garage and drove over. The boxes were still there. One by one I schlepped them up the stairs to the street and packed them in the car. There were cardboard boxes and shopping bags and clothing bags, books, papers, tools, clothing, everything that smelled of me. It was depressingly familiar. "It may take a little longer" my ass! This was the kiss-off. Barbara had ended our relationship and no fantasy I had would change that.

In a few short weeks, Barbara had gone from wanting to marry me and having our child, to stabbing me and then kicking me out. So much had happened so fast I was shell-shocked as I carried those boxes up out of the basement to the car. The images I still held of our love and our marriage and our creative work quickly evaporated. Barbara had been something of a mother to me, I suppose. She had completed the caring my own mother never did. Now I was being born, but without the merciful blind numbness of the infant at birth. The cord was finally cut while I was fully conscious. It hurt.

FORTY ONE

I piled all the boxes and bags against the walls of my small apartment. I could no longer hide from the knowledge that our separation was an integral part of Barbara's breakdown. It was almost the reason for it. The breakdown was another in her list of self-inflicted injuries. They went from her back, to her vertigo, to her anxiety, to her addiction, to her withdrawal, and finally to her breakdown. The breakdown had been imminent ever since that sunny February day more than a year ago when I called Barbara with what I thought was the good news of my divorce. From that day on, our ideal relationship was charged with unconscious terror for her. It was as though she feared she would perish if she married, and I suppose she would have. The single woman is no more when she becomes wife and mother. Even without a child, that's what marriage symbolizes.

Barbara told her friends, her parents, and me that I was the best man in the world and that she wanted to marry me and even have our child. By the time I brought home my divorce, she had boxed herself into an emotional corner from which she couldn't escape. She greeted the news of my divorce with Valium, alcohol, and anxiety. She kept her warring opposite desires stalemated this way for a whole year until I forced a confrontation with her. It was after that lunch at the Slate that she decided to withdraw, as a prelude to our marriage.

I saw her withdrawal as an act of love. It seemed an assertion of her independence which I respected and supported, but she gradually sought to give up all her independence and make me into her guru, father, analyst, and doctor all in one. Before I knew it, Barbara's withdrawal had changed into a rationale for the most dependent relationship I had ever known. It was as though there was a pliant, soft, dependent Barbara hiding coyly under her tough exterior and it only needed her love for me and the impending event of our marriage for that ever-present dependent princess to emerge and say, "Cawwy me, Daddy." She had trouble withdrawing all right, but it wasn't from simple drugs like Valium and alcohol. She had been trying to withdraw from her Prince Valium all along and that was much harder to do.

To my surprise, some of Barbara's oldest friends called and wanted to see me. Meyer asked me to come to dinner up in Connecticut and Lian and Ben invited me out to Sag Harbor. They had heard Barbara was out of the hospital, and apparently she wasn't returning Lian's calls. After all the time Lian felt she had spent taking care of Barbara, she was very hurt over this unexpected snub. Lian asked me to be sure and bring out any new girl friend I had, too. That shocked me. I had only just realized that my relationship with Barbara was over, but everyone else seemed to have known all along and had already chosen sides.

I told Ben and Lian of Barbara's revelations during the withdrawal and the fierce anger that had surfaced. She was apparently still angry. I didn't mention the confused paternity, but Lian sensed something. She was troubled. She cornered me alone and asked me flat out if there was more in Barbara's revelations that would explain why Ben and Dale were such bitter enemies. This wasn't the first time Lian had asked me about that situation, but it was the first time I knew the answer and I decided against telling her.

In the days to come, many of Barbara's old friends began to talk about her in a way that bothered me. Ben and Lian came down hard on her. They described Barbara as always having been emotionally sick and destructive. I got the same disturbing characterization from Meyer when I told him about the withdrawal experience and Barbara's unexpected violence. Then I bumped into Potter, Barbara's editor for many years, and he said the same kind of things, although he professed to love her very much. These were intelligent people who had known Barbara for a long time, but I couldn't accept what I was hearing. I found myself defending her against this kind of characterization. They didn't know Barbara as I had in her good times when all she wanted was for me to be happy. Maybe I was still in love with her.

Tina seemed to be the only person Barbara trusted now. I called and tried to explain to Tina all I was beginning to realize about Barbara's withdrawal and her breakdown and her violence. It was possible we still had a chance. Tina didn't say a word to me after she said hello. It was a strange feeling talking to a silent phone when you know there is someone on the other end. I suppose she still considered me a threat to Barbara. I exhausted my thoughts and my hopes and said Goodbye. I was very depressed.

My future had waited on Barbara's next move, and now that she had snipped those last strands of our relationship I was cut loose from every security I had and I began to quietly panic. It was like the last days of Pompeii and I reacted accordingly. Judy was all I had left and I suddenly had an overwhelming desire to mate with her, which made no sense at all. We had made love now and then, but I knew she didn't want any emotional involvement with me. In my panic, I began playing those mental numbers that only men play with themselves. I don't think there is a female equivalent for what I did next. I convinced myself that Judy was cool because she was testing me, that what she really wanted from me was an outburst of feelings, an unequivocal declaration of love. I knew it wasn't true, but by three vodkas past 10:00, I could persuade myself easily. I called her and in spite of her sleepy protestations, I told her I loved her madly, I wanted us to live together, and I wanted to have children with her. She begged me to stop talking that way. But she was a war baby, she didn't beg for long.

"*Get off my back!!*" she yelled and hung up.

I didn't blame her. She was only trying to protect herself. I was scared. I was looking for anything to hold onto and Judy certainly wasn't it. I don't know what I would have done if she had said yes.

I was alone and I had to face that fact.

Being alone was very new to me. Except for the army and a few weeks here and there, I had lived with a woman all my life. Not the same woman, of course, but I seemed to have gone from one home with a woman in it to another home with a woman in it for 25 years. This was the first place I had lived for any length of time without a woman. It was a strange realization. I no longer had to work for anyone but me. I had no wife, no children, no dependent "living together" mistress. I could do anything I wanted now. I could even go to Hollywood and pick up the career I wanted as I should have done years before. There was nothing to keep me in New York but memories and they didn't mean diddleyfuck. I decided to go to Los Angeles.

Once I made that decision, the days accelerated. There was a life in New York to wrap up but there wasn't much left of it. Before I left, I had decided to tell Lian the one missing piece of her puzzle, that the two men didn't know who the father was and it very well could have been Ben. If I didn't tell her, no one else would. She laughed when I told her as though it was nothing at all, but I suspect she felt more underneath.

Then I made my last visit to the psychiatrist to tell him I was leaving. He advised me to stay in New York. He didn't think I was emotionally ready to take such a step. He thought I should continue with him or, if I insisted on leaving, that at least I should agree to let him arrange for another analyst in Los Angeles. I don't believe these people. He was trying to foster a dependency in me when what I needed most of all was support for my independence. Sure, I still had some guilt about the tragic turn the withdrawal had taken. There were a thousand questions I would ask for years to come, but now I had to survive. A hundred fifty dollars a week would be a big deal to me out there in Hollywood. I would rather spend it on food and rent and gas while I tried to establish a new career. You don't survive by hiding in dark rooms with psychiatrists.

I wrote a letter to the two girls I sublet from telling them the apartment was empty and they could have it back any time. I had the car tuned. I knew I would need a car in Los Angeles so I had decided to take Bernie. The long easy drive would be relaxing. A sea change. Bernie had over 99,000 miles on his odometer, but those Ford V-8s are tough. I was sure he could make it. And what if he didn't? I didn't even need the few things I would take with me. If the car broke down I could ditch it all and continue with the money in my pocket and the clothes on my back. I was traveling light.

The boxes I had brought over from Central Park South were full of my past and I was leaving all that behind. I took everything out to the incinerator. The handle of the chute was warm and when I tilted it open a blast of hot air roared up the chimney. The fire was on. I went through all the boxes and threw everything down the incinerator. My whole life passed through my hands that afternoon, paper by paper, photograph by photograph. I stopped and stared a long time at the few pictures I still had of my daughters. They were babies in those shots. They would be young women in their twenties by now. I wondered if they looked like their mother or if they took after my family. I would probably never know. I hesitated a moment and then threw their pictures into the fire with the rest. I could afford no illusions. If I were to go on from here, I had to live as though there was no past. I burned everything. I burned all my books, too. Felt guilty about that. I might have found a home for them but I couldn't take the time. I couldn't risk changing my mind.

Early on a sunny July morning I emptied my bank account and got Bernie out of the garage. I bought a cooler and filled it with ice and dry Italian white wine for the drive, picked up my few clothes, my Nikon, and the Braun coffee grinder and tossed them all into the back seat with the few things I was taking with me. I put the two plants I had saved behind the tailgate of the station wagon where they would get some sun. Lastly, I nestled my typewriter carefully on the seat beside me. I didn't want to get that damaged. I was married to that typewriter now.

As I drove across the George Washington Bridge I felt a·pang leaving the city that had been home to me for so long. But I didn't need it any longer. That life was ending and a whole new life was waiting for me. It wasn't going to be easy, but I was alive, I was alone, I had a typewriter and all the time I wanted to spend on my work. For as long as I could remember, I had said that this was all I really wanted in life. As traumatic as it turned out, my relationship with Barbara provided the opportunity to start out fresh. It was time to back up what I had always said or shut up forever. As Mr. Yeats wrote, "In dreams begin responsibility."

The highway split three ways on the Jersey side. But instead of driving the southern route to Los Angeles, I headed west on Interstate 80. At the last minute I had decided to make a detour through Berkeley, California. It was the last place I knew where my daughters had lived. It was possible they were still in the area. I had a few extra bucks and I intended to hire an attorney to start a search for them. While I was there I would look around Berkeley for myself. It's a small town. I might even bump into them on the street. I wondered if I would recognize them after so many years.

* * *